PENANG
Postcard Collection
1899-1930s

Sponsored by
HSBC Bank Malaysia Berhad
HSBC
The world's local bank

Cover design by Cecilia Mak.

Published by Janus Print & Resources, Penang.

To order, contact

Janus Print & Resources
120 Armenian Street
10200 Penang, Malaysia
Tel: (604) 262 0123, 263 3985
Fax: (604) 263 3970
Email: januspenang@myjaring.net

Discounts are available for bulk orders,
schools and non-profit organisations.

Perpustakaan Negara Malaysia Cataloguing-in-Publication Data

Khoo, Salma Nasution

Penang Postcard Collection 1899-1930s / Khoo Salma Nasution
& Malcolm Wade.

ISBN 983-2885-00-0

1. Postcards – Collectors and collecting – Pulau Pinang.
I. Wade, Malcolm II. Title.
741.68309595113

3 ▸
A 43 – Clock Tower and Hongkong-Shanghai Bank, Beach Street, Penang.
Imprint: Nikko-Studio.

Front cover background: Map of Prince of Wales Island and Province Wellesley, by A.J. Thompson, 1839. *Reproduced by courtesy of the Penang Museum*.

PENANG

Postcard Collection

1899-1930s

Khoo Salma Nasution & Malcolm Wade

5 ▸

Caption: Panorama of Penang.

A rare double card of Penang.

Reverse, UNION POSTALE UNIVERSELLE, Straits Settlements (Établissements du Détroit) Post Card - Carte Postale

▾ 4

Caption: Rickshaw.

Imprint: Federal Rubber Stamp Co., Penang.

A rickshaw stops by a shop, the side walls of which are plastered with posters in English and Chinese, including an enticing announcement of the 'GRAND CIRCUS, WITH AN ENTIRE NEW COMPANY'. The Chinese notices advertise the movies, with 'daily show, night show, seven o'clock, eleven o'clock', 'No. 3 seat' and 'special discounts', 'cheapsale', 'six cents'. An itinerant woman hawker passes by the shop carrying her wares on a shoulder yoke. Another 'kandar' is left by the road side, while the vendor has rushed into the shop to buy some provisions.

Rickshaw.

Contents

INTRODUCTION

Greetings from Penang

In the early years of the twentieth century, Penang was prosperous and picturesque, attracting travellers, migrants and settlers from East and West. The F.M.S. Railway had just linked up with Prai, shortening the travel time between Penang and the rest of Malaya. As a centre for shipping, commerce, banking and insurance, Penang profited immensely from the tin and rubber boom in the hinterland.

After years of reclamation, Swettenham Pier was finally opened as a berth for deep sea vessels. The mercantile houses along the Weld Quay waterfront presented a new face to all those who approached by ship. Pride and prosperity also manifested itself in a better standard of architecture and public works. With increased revenue, the government built itself the magnifcent complex of Government Offices, as well as the handsome Municipal Offices and Supreme Court.

Penang made itself into a centre for regional trade. The populations of south Thailand, northern Sumatra and the northern Malay States looked to Penang for capital, communications, schools and shopping. With still no thoughts of nationalism, Penang was proud to be part of the British Empire, in the days when the sun never set on it.

We hear of the first photographers working in Penang in the 1860s – John Thompson, a celebrated photographer of the Far East; K. Feilberg who established a branch of the Singapore-based Sachtler & Co.; and a pioneering woman photographer Mrs. J.A. Moniot, wife of a pharmacist.[1]

Professional photographers mainly made their living by taking portraits. The technology then was highly unwieldy – expensive, heavy equipment and large, fragile glass negatives. All photographs had to be carefully premeditated, patiently set up and rather unspontaneously posed for!

The advent of picture postcards allowed photographers the opportunity of having their photographic studies of urban life, natural scenery and all sorts of subjects, published and admired. In an age before personal cameras were affordable, postcard pictures were by far the most widely circulated and consumed

[1] Falconer, 1987: 20, 24

◂ 6

Caption: No. 14 Weld Quay, Penang.
Imprint: P.L.I Da Silva, E.&O. Hotel.
Loading and unloading at the Weld Quay waterfront. Note the handsome buildings of the import-export houses, the granite embankment and the barges (tongkang), beached and immobile at low tide.

photographic images. These picture postcards give us realistic glimpses of life back then.

We behold the streets bustling with pedestrians, hawkers, rickshaws and animal conveyances, with only the occasional tram or motor vehicle in sight; the human-scale architecture, well-mannered walkways and civic spaces; the luscious environs of the Padang, the tree-lined boulevards and suburbs, as well as the rustic scenery of the hills and beaches. We marvel at the city shops, their signs and window displays, as well as the ventures in commerce, plantations and industry. Then there are the opening ceremonies, festivals and celebrations of Empire Day. We see the 'tuan' and 'mem', who fashioned their careers and adapted to lifestyles in the tropics, as well as the countless workers – builders, gardeners, road-sweepers - who made life comfortable, congenial and civilized.

We know that postcards were retailed on ships, at railway stations, in hotels, and at stationery shops. Perhaps like today, they were sold by Indian 'auto-shops' and promoted by tourist touts at the harbour, Snake Temple and Kek Lok Si.

The bulk of Penang postcards in this collection were mailed to Europe. Three groups of people, we imagine, bought postcards to mail back home. Travellers, who spent a few hours or days in Penang when their ships called, wrote home to impress their friends and family about the sights they saw. Officers, traders and prospectors heading out East and feeling the first pangs of homesickness sent postcards to their dear ones at home. Foreign residents based in Malaya, regularly used postcards to send news, good wishes and seasons' greetings.

Though postcards are characterised as ephemera, some were kept either for beauty or sentiment, and eventually came to be considered as 'collectibles'. Serious collectors and scholars of postcards are called 'deltiologists'.

Penang Glossary

Penang is a regional port and an international tourism destination. The second smallest of 13 states of Malaysia, the State of Penang (Negeri Pulau Pinang) consists of two parts, Penang Island (Pulau Pinang) and Province Wellesley (Seberang Perai). In popular usage, however, 'Penang' might refer to Penang state, Penang island, the Port of Penang or the city of George Town.

Penang Island or 'Pulau Pinang', which means 'betel-nut isle', is named after the *pinang* tree *(Areca catechu)* which was locally cultivated in pre-British times. Under British occupation (1876-1957), Penang island was officially named 'Prince of Wales Island' but popularly called 'Finang' or 'Penang'.

Province Wellesley is the old name for Seberang Perai. The main town, **Butterworth,** is located at Bagan Luar, to the north of **Prye River** (Sungai Prai), while Prye is located on the southern bank. Butterworth is sited directly across the **North Channel** from George Town.

George Town, the capital of Penang, is located on the northeast cape of Penang Island. The town developed from Fort Cornwallis and a few adjoining streets, and grew to the west and south. George Town (the correct spelling is two words) attained city status in 1957. The **Port of Penang** is located at the northeastern tip of George Town.

Penang Hill on Penang Island is the highest range in Penang, peaking at 2,722 feet or 830 m.

Brief History of Postcards

The postal stationery card was produced in 1869 in the Austro-Hungarian empire. Picture postcards appeared soon afterward in limited quantities in Europe, but the era of the picture postcard really began in 1898. The best quality cards were printed in Germany, the world leader in lithographic processes.

In the next decade, postcard collecting became the biggest collectible hobby the world had ever known, with hundreds of millions of postcards bought and mailed annually. Among the Penang locals, quite a few educated sons of affluent families began the hobby of postcard collecting, joining collectors' clubs and writing to their foreign pen-pals around the world. The German printing industry, as well as the hobby, collapsed with the outbreak of WW1 in 1914.

The first picture postcards of Penang were produced by 1899. Most of the Penang postcards can be categorized as 'view cards', that is, picture postcards showing popular views of Penang places. The first decade of the 20th century was the golden age of Penang picture postcards – many hand-coloured postcards date from this time. In the late 1920s and 1930s, we find postcards with a white border and caption at the bottom, as well as one-of-a-kind, 'real photo' cards. High quality real photos can reveal greater detail compared with commercially printed cards which appear as printing dots under the magnifying glass.

For researchers of old Penang or old Malaya, Malcolm Wade's postcard collection offers a rich repository of historical images of places and people. Some, not all, can be dated within a few years. Put together, they allow us to closely trace the evolution of a place, like certain parts of Weld Quay or the Magazine Road Junction.

In this book, some commentary has been provided for favourite subjects, like Swettenham Pier, the Fort Cornwallis, Penang Hill, certain streets and modes of transport. However, it was not possible to caption all the postcards with the same degree of consistency, as information on certain subjects is lacking. Scenes in rural areas were difficult to identify.

The images provide a great deal of visual information on things such as native boats, traditional signs, popular attire and dress, which are in themselves deserving areas of study. It is hoped that the publication of this book will further stimulate interest in Penang, and help to validate the historic port settlement of Penang as a cultural heritage site of world importance.

Khoo Salma Nasution

9 ▸

Caption: Penang. Dato Kramat Road.

Imprint: A. Kaulfuss, Penang. No 38.

Undivided back. Used to Amsterdam 17 June 1901.

The Magazine Police Station is on the left. Tram lines are clearly visible – they were used by steam trams, as electrical trams had yet to be introduced.

◂ 8

Caption: Penang Hills Railway. Entrance to Upper Station from Hill.

Real photo card, sepia finish.

View of the Upper Station nearing completion, circa 1922. Note the Governor's hill residence Bel Retiro on the skyline.

Picture Postcards of Penang

by Malcolm Wade & Khoo Salma Nasution

Photographers

August Kaulfuss is the greatest name in Penang cards. A profile of this German photographer appears in the voluminous work, 'Twentieth Century Impressions of British Malaya', which is itself a handsome record of Kaulfuss's photographic works:

> Mr. August Kaulfuss is the oldest established European photographer in Pinang, and has taken all the photographs of Pinang and district which are reproduced in this work. He was born at Rohnstock, Silesia, in 1861, and was educated there When he was fifteen he entered the photographic studio of Otto van Bosch, at Frankfort-on-Main, then the leading photographer of Southern Germany. He remained there two years, and afterwards followed his calling in various parts of Germany. He first came to Pinang in 1883, and has been in business as a photographer there since 1886. Mr. Kaulfuss has travelled extensively, having traversed on foot the whole of the Malay Peninsula, from Province Wellesley in the north to Johore in the south, at a time when there were few good roads and no railways. He explored the country behind the territory of Kedah, prospecting for minerals, and visited Bangkok. He is photographer to H.H. the Sultan of Kedah, and has taken a unique collection of photographs in the Malay Peninsula. He is a member of the Cricket, Turf, and Swimming Clubs, Engineers' Institute, and of the Masonic Lodge Royal Prince of Wales 1,555.
>
> *(Wright & Cartwright, 1908: 814)*

From another source, we find additional information about his photographic career:

> '(Kaulfuss) worked in the Frankfurt studio of the photographer Otto von Bosch c. 1876-78 and then in other studios in various parts of Germany, before serving in the German Navy for about two years. Arrived in Penang 1883 and around 1884 was assistant to the photographer J.M. Nauta; listed as a travelling photographer in 1886. In about 1888 he had a studio in partnership with Albert Schlump at 9 Farquhar Street, Penang, with a rubber stamp manufactory run by William Jones (also a photographer) at 9 Beach Street. From c. 1892 - c. 1908 the photographic studio was transferred to 27 Farquhar Street[2]. From around 1896 Kaulfuss was photographer by appointment to the Sultan of Kedah.
>
> *(Source: John Falconer, Curator of Photographs, Oriental and India Office Collections, The British Library)*

Through his art as a photographer and publisher, he captured and promoted images of Penang. In a few early montages, he tried to present exotic or romantic compositions, but for the most part, his postcards were realistic and depicted

[2] 'Ernest August Kaulfus, photographer, Farquhar Street', and 'Hans Von Katte, photographer, Farquhar Street' were both named in *The List of Qualified Jurors* (Straits Settlements Government Gazette, 23 December, 1904).

Advertisement, Straits Times Annual, 1906.

contemporary developments around the settlement, such as the port and shipping, new buildings and amenities, transport and municipal improvements.

During the early 1900s a few series of cards appeared under the Kaulfuss imprint, their main difference being format and imprint rather than subject. The Kaulfuss cards were not confined in subject to Penang, though these were by far the most numerous. Kuala Lumpur, Selangor, Perak all featured and even two of Malacca are recorded. The highest number of the coloured series which is found in this collection is 208 but not all are Penang. Kaulfuss appears to have returned to Europe before 1910, at a time when the coloured cards bearing his name were at their most popular.

Other photographers whose names may be found on Penang picture postcards are as follows:-

H. Bodom. There is one card inscribed H. Bodom, Penang. He was the proprietor of the Northam House Photographic Studio, 15 Northam Road, Penang ca. 1910-1920. It seems likely that many 'anonymous' cards may have been his work and that, in addition, he may have supplied pictures published under other 'imprints'.

C.J. Kleingrothe. This German photographer had a photostudio in Medan from about 1885. In 1891 he worked together with the photographer H. Stafhell, who liquidated his own studio in that year, and from 1901 on Kleingrothe continued on his own. He worked until about 1925, specializing in photographs of tropical agriculture, such as coffee and tobacco. Kleingrothe also produced a portfolio of photographs of Singapore and Malaya entitled 'Malay Peninsula', ca. 1907. Two postcards with his imprint are found in this collection, see page 290.

(Source: Marianne Fluitsma, Department of Historical Documentation, KITLV.)

M. S. Nakajima. A Japanese photographer based in Kuala Lumpur. A number of cards are to be found under the imprint of others, but with 'Photograph by Nakajima'.

Nikko Studio. A Japanese photographer K. Okaniwa, was the principal of 'Nikko' Photographic Studio at 7 Northam Road. He was considered 'the best photographer in Penang' in the 1920s, having been established here before 1907.

(MacMillan, 1923: 309)

Producers & Retailers

It is difficult to differentiate between producers and retailers of postcards, particularly in the early days. The following 'imprints' have been found on Penang picture postcards.

- Federal Rubber Stamp Co. 'Stationers, Booksellers, Newsagents, Printers, Bookbinders, Account-Book Makers, Brass-Seal and Rubber-Stamp Manufacturers and General Commission Agents'. With the head office in Kuala Lumpur, the company had branches in Ipoh, Penang (opened in 1913) and Singapore, and also controlled the railway station bookstalls. Cards with a wide variety of this imprint can be found.
- Pritchard & Co., Penang.
- T.N. Shaik Ismail.
- Straits Photo Coy., Penang.
- British Empire Series
- Raphael Tuck & Sons, London. See page 278.
- Tuck's super 'GLOSSO' published by Whiteaway Laidlaw, Penang.
- S.M. Manicum, Penang. See page 294.
- K.M. Mahmed Esoof, Penang.
- A.S. Mahomed Assan & Co., Penang.
- A.M.I. No. 56 Beach Street
- M.J., Penang, with the open scissors trademark.
- No. 35.A. Beach Street, Penang.
- Co-operative Agency S.S.
- T.C.B. Penang.
- Valentine and William, E.&O. Hotel, Penang.
- P.L.I. Da Silva, E.&O. Hotel, Penang.
- F.M.S.R., Crag Hotel, Penang Hills. (Photo by M.S. Nakajima)
- Malay States Development Agency, 111/113, Queen Victoria Street, E.C.
- Missions Etrangères de Paris, 128 rue de Bac.
- Methodist Publishing House, Singapore.
- The Penang Photo Store, 49 Leith Street, Penang. (This address was subsequently occupied by Chungking Photo.)

and possibly others including G.R. Lambert of Singapore and Max H. Hilckes of Singapore, though no Penang cards with their imprints have been discovered. 'Printed in Germany' postcards appear from about 1910 onwards.

▾ 11

Caption: Penang. Captn Ah Kevie House, Church Street.

No imprint. Undivided back.

The family temple and townhouse of Kapitan Chung Keng Kwee, Kapitan China of Perak and member of the Perak State Council. He was the leader of the Hai San secret society which fought with the Ghee Hin in the protracted Larut Wars of the late 19th century. The temple and townhouse, built in the 1890s, is lavishly embellished with exquisite terracotta sculptures, woodcarving, stone work, stencilled glass and decorative cast iron. Some of the decorative wooden panels were crafted by Chiw Shan Yau, see postcard 92a.

The bullock cart here appears to be transporting firewood, commonly used in cooking stoves.

(Source: Wong, 1963: 77-80)

12

Caption: Post Office, Penang

Imprint: Printed in Germany.

This postcard shows the Post Office building at Weld Quay. It was destroyed by Allied bombs at the end of WW2.

Postcard Postal Rates

by Malcolm Wade

The popularity of the postcard was increased when a picture was added to what had previously been a very useful but very functional means of communication. Early cards had undivided backs (UDB). Initially it was not permitted to write more than a brief greeting on the picture side, and nothing except the address on the reverse.

With the introduction of the 'divided back' ca. 1905 it was possible to write a message in addition to the address. However the message was costly and many card enthusiasts soon realised that if there was no message the card could be sent at the 'Printed Paper' rate so they deleted the word 'POSTCARD' and wrote in either 'Printed Paper', 'Printed Matter' or even 'Book Post'.

The Printed Paper rate was only really used during the days before 1910 when the novelty of the picture postcard led to fanatical collectors who sought to save money by its use. During this period the rate was 1c to all parts of the world!

Numerous card collectors' clubs were established and membership numbers are often found on cards used up to the early 1930s. Some of the messages found on these cards express in no uncertain terms the dissatisfaction of some members if they did not receive suitable cards. With the advent of regular air services in the 1930s, special airmail rates for postcards were introduced but being expensive were not frequently used. These rates and routes are of interest to postal historians and some are very difficult to find, but they are outside the scope of this book.

POSTAL RATES FOR POSTCARDS

	Straits and F.M.S.	Britain and Empire	Rest of the World
1.1.1899	1c	3c	3c
1.1.1918	2c	4c	4c
16.1.1922	2c	4c	8c
1.1.1926	2c	4c	6c
8.4.1940	4c	4c	6c
1.1.1941	4c	4c	8c

The Port of Penang

▲ 13
Caption: No. 5 – Penang. F.M.S. Pier & Offices
Imprint: T.C.B. Penang.

▲ 14a

Caption: No. 102 Penang Harbour.

Imprint: A. Kaulfuss, Penang.

All steamed and 'dressed' up for some occasion. The Union Jack and other British flags were displayed on buildings and ships on Empire Day, also called Victoria Day, celebrated on 24 May (Queen Victoria's birthday) each year.

The white steamer on the right could be the 'Sumatra'.

The ship in the background with the two funnels is the 'Kiatschou', 10911 tons, launched in 1900 for the Hamburg America Line Far East Service, renamed 'Princess' Alice for Norddeutscher Lloyd in 1904 and sailed on the Bremen-Suez Canal-Far East route until 1914. Sheltered in Cebu, Philippines, during WW1, seized by the U.S. government in 1917. Used by various American lines, scrapped in Japan in 1933.

(Source: Passenger Ship History Service)

▼ 14b

Caption: Penang. Harbour

No imprint. Undivided back.

▲ 14c

Caption: No. 106 Unloading cargo.

Imprint: A. Kaulfuss, Penang.

The small cargo ship is the 'UNITY TONSBERG'.

▲ 14d

Caption: Harbour, Penang

Imprint: S.M. Manicum, Penang.

Coastal ships in the port of Penang.

15a

Caption: B.I. Boat, Penang

Imprint: S.M. Manicum, Penang.

The 'M Meanatchy', 2111 tons, British India line. Built in 1881, used on the Singapore-Nagapatam service until broken up in 1911. The 'M' stands for Madura, the goddess.

(Source: Passenger Ship History Service)

'B.I.' is short for the British India Steam Navigation Company, also known as the B.I.S.N.. Its steamers started arriving in Penang in the late 19th century and mainly carried the trade between the Indian community in India and its counterpart community in the Straits Settlements. Their Penang agents were Islay Kerr & Co., Ltd.

The Port

The Port of Penang served as an entrêpot for northern Sumatra, southern Thailand and the northern Malay states. Throughout the 19th and early 20th centuries, Penang was also the first port of discharge for ships sailing from India and Europe to the Straits Settlements and the Far East, and the last port of call for returning ships. Army officers coming from or returning to India had to travel by the Peninsular & Oriental (P.&O.), under a contract by the Indian Government. Penang was the sole port of entry for all assisted Indian labour immigrants into Malaya, until 1903, when Port Swettenham and Singapore were also added as points of entry; the former only overtook Penang as the main labour port in the 1930s. On the other hand, Penang also represented the westernmost node of the overseas Chinese trading network, an entrêpot and distribution point for Chinese goods and labour.

15b

Caption: Penang HabouR

Real photo.

The white vessel with a three-coloured funnel is a Straits Steamship Company vessel, probably the 'Kinta'. In the foreground is the 'Borneo' of the P.&O., 4573 tons, built in 1895, used on the Calcutta-Malaya service, sold to Kishimoto KK, Osaka in 1914 and renamed 'Harima Maru', scrapped in 1927.

(Source: Passenger Ship History Service)

15c

Caption: No. 204 Penang Harbour.

Imprint: A. Kaulfuss, Penang.

The Railway Jetty, the Penang Foundry (on which site was subsequently built the Railway Station) and the minaret of the Acheen Street Mosque can be seen in this picture.

The single funnel black ship is P.&O.'s 'Ceylon' built in 1894, 4094 tons, operated in the Far East 1894-1913, then sold to the Japanese and renamed 'Yamato Maru'. Sold to the French in 1916 and renamed 'Depute Pierre Goujon'. Sunk by a submarine in the Bay of Biscay.

(Source: Passenger Ship History Service)

16a ▸

Caption: No. 69. Penang wharf and Harbour

Imprint: A. Kaulfuss, Penang.

Swettenham Pier, a deep water wharf, under construction (1889-1904). The foreground is a sandy beach – the lighter basins have not yet been constructed. The bridge appears to have collapsed in the centre!

The two ships docking at the pier appear to be from Norddeutscher Lloyd. The left one is 'Darmstadt' of 1891, 5012 tons, and the right one is 'Oldenburg' of 1890, 5006 tons. Both sailed to Australia 1892-1906, and were scrapped in 1923.

(Source: Passenger Ship History Service)

◂ 16b

Caption: Clock Tower, Penang.

Imprint: No. 35.A. Beach Street, Penang.

A most unusual view of the entrance to Swettenham Pier, showing the goods sheds and the Queen Victoria Diamond Jubilee Memorial Clock Tower.

▾ 16c

Caption: F.M.S. goods shade, Penang.

Imprint: S.M. Manicum, Penang.

The completion of the Swettenham Pier development was paid for by the F.M.S..

16d ▸

Handwritten caption: 'Penang'

The goods sheds at Swettenham Pier, built 1904-7.

◂ 17a

Caption: No. 99 Penang Harbour.

Imprint: A. Kaulfuss, Penang.

As the original wharves at Swettenham Pier were still very cramped, work started again in 1908 to undertake extensions to 1,200 feet together with the construction of two lighter basins. Note the bullock carts at the right bottom corner.

17b ▸

Caption: No. 84. Harbour Penang

Imprint: A. Kaulfuss, Penang.

Loading and unloading at the lighter basin.

◂ 17c

Caption: Harbour, Penang

Printed in Germany.

Tongkangs and sampans are moored in the lighter basin at Swettenham Pier. The ship on the right, marked with an 'X', is the 'Elephanta' of British India, 5,128 tons, which sailed Madras-Rangoon-Singapore (1911-1939). The ship on the left looks like the 'Pekin' of P.&O., broken up in 1911.

(Source: Passenger Ship History Service)

18a ▸

Caption: No. 109 Sweattenham Pier.

Imprint: A. Kaulfuss, Penang.

The principal passenger steamers usually tie up alongside the Swettenham Pier, a property of the Penang Harbour Board.

▴ 18b

Caption: No. 67. The wharf Penang.

No imprint. Undivided back.

This postcard bears the date 21.4.05 and a handwritten message, 'This is the New Pier. When I was living close to it I often used to walk down at 7 in the morning.'

Port Facilities

The natural harbour of Penang consists of a three-mile stretch of water between the city of George Town on the island of Penang and Butterworth and Prai on the mainland. As the initial trade was of an entrêpot character, 'there has always been a tradition of free port facilities, which remains in Penang in the form of inalienable free rights along the shallow Georgetown frontage, now known as Weld Quay.' With the advent of modern ocean ships, a demand arose for deep water wharves on the island. Swettenham Pier, a project undertaken by the Straits Settlements government, was fully developed by 1909. The Federated Malay States (F.M.S.) Railway also constructed similar facilities at Prai on the mainland, mainly for handling Malaya's regular imports and exports. The three elements of the port of Penang 'had grown up independently and in bitter competition'. As a result, the port was less subject to charges of monopoly than Singapore.

(Allen, 1951: 18-19)

18c ▸

Caption: Shipping Tobacco by Norddeutscher Lloyd. Penang

Printed in Germany.

Penang was an entrêpot for tobacco grown in the Sumatran plantations.

In the early 20th century, the Norddeutscher Lloyd with its headquarters in Bremen, Germany, was the second largest steamship company in the world. The Penang agent was Behn, Meyer & Co.. Both ships in this photo are Norddeustscher Lloyd's: left, 'Derfflinger' 9060 tons, launched 9 Nov 1907, scrapped in Bremerhaven in 1932; right, probably the 'Bulow' in the background, 9028 tons, 1906-1940.

(Source: Passenger Ship History Service)

◂ 19a

Caption: Swettenham Peir, Penang

The postcard is dated 1935.

The Straits Steamship Company boat (with three-coloured funnel) named 'Malaya', registered in Singapore, was formerly a Norddeutscher Lloyd ship 'Vulcan', bought in 1922.

(Source: Passenger Ship History Service)

Eastern Smelting Company Railway

The trucks with the initials 'E.S.C. 15' belong to the Eastern Smelting Company. A 1.7 mile railway operated between the Eastern Smelting Company at Dato' Kramat Road and Swettenham Pier, bringing tin ingots to the harbour and returning with stores and tin ore for the smelting works. From Swettenham Pier, electric trains ran the tramway line on the public roadway, with about 150 yards of private track laid in the smelting works itself. Within Swettenham Pier, the trucks were pulled by a diesel locomotive on the Penang Harbour Board's own railway.

◂ 19b

Caption: Tin-slabs, Swettenham Pier, Penang

Imprint: Federal Rubber Stamp Co.

Tin ingots stacked up and ready for loading by Tamil coolies. Each coolie carried one slab at a time on his shoulder.

Tin, mined in Perak, was smelted in Penang and exported from Penang.

◂ 19c

Caption: Norddeutscher Lloyd loading Tobacco, Penang.

Printed in Germany

The ship on the left is 'Lutzow', 8,818 tons, Norddeutscher Lloyd, launched 1908, scrapped in Germany in 1933.

(Source: Passenger Ship History Service)

The Lighter Fleet

In the early days, junks and tongkang carried much of the entrêpot and even ocean-going trade. However, with the advent of modern steamships, the tongkang were largely used for providing lighterage services to larger ships, but continued to operate mainly from Weld Quay.

> This Quay has never been suitable for craft other than lighters; ships of all sizes used to anchor in the Roads and discharge into lighters and for the most part coasters still do.
>
> *(Allen, 1951: 18-19)*

Not including the Harbour Board's fleet of lighters, the junks, tongkangs and cargo boats registered in Penang altogether represented a tonnage of 32,750 tons, of which about one half to two thirds at any one time was available for use in the harbour. Since the 1930s, the port began to face congestion, but little was done due to differing priorities of the European shipping industry on the one hand, and that of the local entrepreneurs on the other.

> The functioning of Weld Quay depends on the existence of an adequate lighter fleet. This is principally Indian owned and manned, and the ships are for the most part not confined to the harbour, but operate on the neighbouring coast as trade offers. .... While there have been in normal times sufficient lighters not to delay ships, the congestion at Weld Quay, when, during low tide, almost all lighters were beached and immobile, has always been highly uneconomic and has added materially to the cost of lighterage services.
>
> *(Allen, 1951: 25-26)*

The decline of the port culminated with Penang's loss of free port status around 1969. Lighterage services are now practically irrelevant in an age of modern container shipping. Only a few cargo ships and Burmese barges remind us of the bustling scene that Weld Quay once was.

▼ 20a

Caption: Swettenham Pier, Penang

Printed in Germany.

Lighters or tongkang along Weld Quay. Several types of cranes can be seen operating on Swettenham Pier in the background.

▲ 20b

Caption: Native Junks in Harbour, Penang

Imprint: M.J., Penang.

Large tongkang moored at Weld Quay.

◂ 21a

Caption: No. 14. Landing, Penang.

No imprint. Undivided back.

Boatmen in small sampans and stevedores in launches bring passengers and luggage to shore at Victoria Pier.

Crowding the pier are a Chinese man in a bowler hat (right) and Tamil coolies in chequered cloth (kain pelikat).

Sampan

'(The Chinese) have boats of all sizes built on the model of the well known Chinese junk. The smallest are used for carrying passengers and are called shoe boats; and are propelled by one man who stands facing the prow of the boat; the oars are suspended with a loop on a strong peg at the side of the boat: when under sail and the oars are not used they are let go, when they swing to the side of the boat and do not impede her way.'

(Vaughan, 1879: 10)

▴ 21c

Caption: Victoria Pier, Penang

Printed in Germany.

A good example of a sampan being rowed in the foreground; near the steps of the Victoria Jetty is a larger Chinese boat for carrying goods.

▴ 21b

Caption: No. 14. Landing Pier, Penang

Imprint: A. Kaulfuss, Penang.

▴ 21d

Caption: Penang. Shipping

Imprint: Co-operative Agency, S.S.

Guan Lee Hin Steamship Company operated launches, such as the one on the left, to and from Victoria Pier.

22a

Caption: Victoria Pier, Penang.

Printed in Germany.

The 'Zieten' of Norddeutscher Lloyd, 8,066 tons, 1902-1917 berthing in the Penang harbour.

(Source: Passenger Ship History Service)

The small white boat moored alongside the steamer looks like a water boat which supplies vessels with fresh water. The agents of the Pinang Water Boat Company were Messrs. W. Mansfield & Co..

(Wright & Cartwright, 1908: 177)

22b

Caption: No. 155 Business Sea Front, Penang

Printed in England.

'It is impossible to imagine how many boats, barges, canoes and dugouts (perahoe, tongkang, djongkong dan sagoer) are found on the shores. Dozens of vessels, big and small. The masts look like branches in a forest, which have lost their leaves'.

(Isma'il, 1924: 48)

22c

Caption: Victoria Peir, Penang

Hundreds of boats in those days. Note the Penang Harbour Board Waterboats in the foreground.

22d

Caption: 9. Victoria Pier, Penang, S.S..

Imprint: Tuck's photogravure.

◂ 23a

Caption: The Pier of Penang. Published by Nikko-Studio.

A compressed view showing the Victoria Jetty, boats, Weld Quay, the F.M.S. Railway clock tower and the hills in the background!

▴ 23b

Caption: No17 Landing Place, Penang

Imprint: P.L.I. Da Silva, E.&O. Hotel.

Victoria Pier

The construction of Victoria Pier was commenced in 1885 and completed in 1888. Victoria Pier, at the end of Downing Street, was a public jetty used by stevedores and small boats. When ocean steamers anchored in the Roads, the shipping companies provided a free launch service to and from the shore. The launches usually arrived at and departed from the Victoria Jetty. Travellers would be met by hotel runners and porters.

▴ 23c

No imprint.

The harbour of Penang was marked by an intricate division of labour. In the 20th century, international shipping lines were locally represented by European shipping agents. These shipping agents in turn subcontracted the ship-chandling and stevedoring operations to Tamil Muslim companies. Ship-chandlers provisioned the large ocean-going ships with supplies. Stevedoring companies provided loading and unloading services by contracting boatmen and labourers for the job. The stevedoring companies did not own lighters, but commissioned manned lighters from another group of businessmen, the lighter owners. The lighter owners in turn paid haulage rates to the boatmen. There were other small groups associated with the servicing of the ships and lighters. At the bottom of the hierarchy were the manual workers, the waterfront workers, the dock workers and the porters.

23d ▸

Caption: Victoria Pier, Penang

24a

Caption: Penang. Harbour View from the Post-Office.

No imprint. Undivided back.

An early view of Weld Quay from the Post Office building, before the Jetty Sheds have been built. At the landward end of the Victoria Jetty (left front) is the hackney carriage stand. Further down is the Boustead Pier (in front of Boustead building) and the Church Street Ghaut Wharf.

Views of Weld Quay

24b

Caption: Weld Quay, Penang

Printed in Germany.

Coastal barges docked alongside Weld Quay. Note the very clear tramlines and vehicle tracks along the road.

▲ 25a

Caption: Harbour, Penang.

Imprint: Federal Rubber Stamp. Co.

The landward end of the Church Street Ghaut Wharf (left), and the jinricksha stand next to it. The sign on the building (right) reads 'F.G. Taylor & Co. Ltd.'; the latter were general merchants with a large share in Penang's cotton piece-goods trade. The firm was managed by Lim Keong Lay, who became well known as a Municipal Commissioner of George Town.

(MacMillan, 1923: 297)

25b ▸

Imprint: Federal Rubber Stamp Co.

A later photograph of Victoria Pier, at the end of Downing Street. The view of Weld Quay is obscured by the Jetty Sheds on either side of Victoria Pier.

26a ▸

Caption: Weld quay, Penang.

Imprint: S.M. Manicum, Penang.

The buff-coloured Boustead building is gaily decorated with festoons, bunting and palm fronds, probably in celebration of Victoria Day celebrations on 24 May.

The waterfront buildings are still standing today.

Weld Quay Waterfront

Weld Quay was named after Sir Frederick Aloysius Weld, Governor of the Straits Settlements (1880-1887), during whose term the quay was created through land reclamation (1883-1889).

In the first decade of the twentieth century, the most prominent ensemble along the Weld Quay waterfront were the premises of Penang's largest mercantile offices, all general importers of cotton, piece-goods, hardware, beer and spirits and many manufactured items, as well as exporters of raw products such as tin, rubber, copra and sugar. These firms also held the agencies for shipping lines and insurance companies and acted as representatives for plantation companies.

Positioned on long lots stretching from Beach Street to Weld Quay, these import-export houses had their shipping offices facing the waterfront and granite stone-paved alleyways passing through the buildings to the godowns at the back. The Tamil name for the stretch of Weld Quay from Swettenham Pier to China Street was *Kitengi Teru,* (The Street of Company Godowns).

◂ 26b

Caption: Behn Meyer & Co. Ltd., Penang.

Imprint: S.M. Manicum, Penang. No. 37.

Although wound up at the outbreak of WW1, Behn Meyer re-established itself in Malaya in the 1920s. However, its old premises had been taken over by the East Asiatic Company Limited.

◂ 27a

Caption: Weld Quay, Penang.

Imprint: K.M. Mahmed Esoof.

Coastal barges docked alongside the granite embankment of Weld Quay. Compared with postcard 26a, this is a later postcard – the balcony on the Boustead building was tacked on afterwards.

◂ 26b

Caption: Penang, Buildings on the Beach.

Undivided back. This postcard is from a very early series, distinguished by a number in the upper left margin.

Victoria Pier is in the background. The photo was taken before 1903, as the Post Office Wing has not yet been constructed.

◂ 26c

Caption: Penang. T.N. Shaik Ismail. No. 6.

Undivided back. Used 1902.

Handwritten caption: 'Mail Offices'.

The words 'MAIL OFFICE' can be seen on the far building. In the foreground is the landward side of the Church Street Ghaut Wharf, see postcard 24a.

◂ 28a

Caption: No. 66. Scene on Weld Quay, Penang

Imprint: A. Kaulfuss, Penang.

Tongkang and sampan moored at Weld Quay. Note the scores of workers unloading the boats.

▴ 28b

Caption: No. 66. Scene on Weld Quay. Penang.

No imprint. Undivided back.

Merchant Houses

Boustead & Co.'s offices and godowns at No. 1 Weld Quay were built on reclaimed ground and first occupied in 1893. The firm's chief export was the 'Boustead' brand of tin ingots, produced in their own refinery. It is the only firm in the whole row to maintain its premises on Weld Quay to the present day.

Schmidt, Kuestermann & Co., No. 2 Weld Quay, one of the oldest import-export firms in Penang, was a branch of the Singapore house of Rautenberg Schmidt & Co. started by entrepreneurs from Hamburg. The firm acted as agents for Kaiser Brewery of Messrs. Beck & Co., Bremen, and Austrian Lloyd's Steam Navigation Company, with Swiss and German partner firms. During WW1, Schmidt, Kuestermann & Co. was taken over by the custodian of public property, while the firm Sturzenegger & Co. took over the premises.

Messrs. Behn, Meyer & Co., Ltd., at No. 3 Weld Quay, also founded by entrepreneurs from Hamburg, was one of the first German firms to make a bid for a share of the growing trade in Asia. The Penang branch of the Singapore office was established in 1890, by taking over the tin smelting business of Messrs. Friedrichs & Co..

Shiffman, Heer & Co. at No. 4 Weld Quay, was established in 1891 by former chief assistants in the firm of Messrs. Friedrichs & Co. Amongst other things, the firm was known as the sole importers of the well-known 'Straits Dollar' safes.

Behr & Co., at No. 5 Weld Quay were the Penang branch of the 'Behr Brothers', London. Like many other German firms in British territories, Behr & Co. faced difficulties during WW1.

(Wright & Cartwright, 1908: 785, 801, 803; Gale, 1987: 59-60, 80)

▴ 28c

Caption: Penang. Weld Quay

Imprint: Co-operative Agency S.S.

Post-1906 since the overhead wires for the electric trams have been installed. The construction rubble to the left indicates that the wharf is being extended to widen the road.

29a

Caption: No. 39. Weld Quai, Penang

Imprint: A. Kaulfuss, Penang.

Goods unloaded at Weld Quay. Rice stalks (jerami) were used in packaging perishables, or breakables such as crockery.

29b

Caption: Weld Quay, Penang.

Imprint: S.M. Manicum, Penang.

This view makes Penang look like the Venice of the East.

29c

Caption: Nr. 4. Weld Quay. Penang.

Reverse: Top left, 'W.N.E.' Lower left, 'Printed in Germany' has been obliterated and above it is printed 'Sold by S.K. Md. Yusoff & Co.'

29d

Caption: Weld Quay, Penang

No imprint.

29e

Caption: Commercial Offices, Penang

Imprint: Co-operative Agency S.S..

30a ▸

Caption: Harbour, Penang

Printed in Germany.

Possibly the early appearance of Church Street Pier.

The two funnelled ship in the background is British India's 'Bangala', built 1902, sold to Osaka Shosen KK in 1924 and renamed 'Taizan Maru', sunk in 1943.

(Source: Passenger Ship History Service).

Church Street Pier

The Church Street Ghaut Wharf, built 1897-8 appears to have been constructed as a lighter basin. A 'ghaut' usually refers to a path of descent leading down to the river or sea, the name arising from the time when Beach Street was a beach. After lighter basins had been created at Swettenham Pier, the Church Street Ghaut Wharf was replaced by the Church Street Pier.

Also called the Ferry Pier, the Church Street Pier catered to ferries which conveyed automobiles across the channel. This ferry service was originally provided by the Eastern Shipping Company but this was taken over in 1924 by the Penang Harbour Board. According to the *Penang Information Guide 1939*,

> 'Motorists on the mainland can reach Penang by the Harbour Board Passenger and Car Ferry Steamers running from Bagan Luar (Mitchell Pier) on the mainland to the Church Street Ghaut Jetty on Weld Quay, Penang. The Piers have special landing stages to enable easy handling of cars at all states of the tide.
>
> *(Thorpe, 1939: 7)*

▾ 30b

Caption: Penang Harbour, Penang. Photo. by M.S. Nakajima

Imprint: F.M.S.R. Crag Hotel, Penang Hill.

The Penang Hill Railway was constructed (1920-23) and actually operated by the F.M.S. Railways before it was handed to the colonial government on 1st January 1924. During the same period, the F.M.S.R. also ran the Crag Hotel and published postcards with this imprint.

◂ 30c

Caption: Penang Harbour.

Imprint: Federal Rubber Stamp Co.

Sepia postcard of Weld Quay.

▲ 31a

Caption: Penang

The Church Street Pier.

▲ 31b

Caption: Penang Harbour

Imprint: Federal Rubber Stamp Co.

A double-decker ferry steamer docking at the Church Street Pier.

◂ 31c

Caption : No. 171 Church Street Pier, Penang

A 1930s view of Church Street Pier, when the pier had been upgraded to cater to car ferry steamers.

◂ 31d

Caption: 2939 Weld Quay, Penang.

Real Photo.

The goods apparently included wooden latticed screens that were used above the windows in many prewar buildings. Handcarts were used to deliver the goods to the wholesalers' warehouses.

The white ship in the background is the 'Klang', 1450 tons, Straits Steamship Company.

(Source: Passenger Ship History Service)

32a

Caption: No. 70. Chinese junks discharging Cargo

Imprint: A. Kaulfuss, Penang.

The stand-alone building on the left is Paterson, Simons & Co..

The cargo in the front sampan could be the curry cooking pots sold in the 'Native Tamil Bazaar Shops' near Chowrasta Market, postcard 105b.

Paterson, Simons & Co.

The branch of Messrs. Paterson, Simons & Co. of Singapore commenced business at Penang in 1902. The firm handled diversified trade as importers, exporters and general merchants, with a special branch devoted to tin and coal.

The building was put up by Phuah Hin Leong under Khie Heng Bee Company and then rented out. The signboard for 'Khie Heng Bee' can still be seen above the gateway to the granite-paved alleyway leading to the godowns at the back.

(Wright & Cartwright, 1908: 796)

32b

Caption: No. 70 Chinese junks. Penang harbour.

Imprint: A. Kaulfuss, Penang.

32c

Caption: No. 70. Chinese jinks. Penang harbour.

No imprint. Undivided back.

32d

Caption: Copyright Photo No. 17. Weld Quay, Penang

Published by The Penang Photo Store, 49 Leith Street, Penang.

Sampans docking at high tide at Weld Quay, between Paterson, Simons & Co. (right) and F.M.S. Railway Pier. Cargo is being transferred from bullock cart to sampan.

▲ 33a

Caption: No. 136 Clock Tower, F.M.S. Railways, Penang

Not only was the Railway Station itself a popular subject of picture postcards, but being the tallest edifice on the horizon, it created a marvellous focal point for vistas and panoramas.

These pictures show the Wisma Yeap Chor Ee (left), the F.M.S. Railway Station, a warehouse, Paterson Simons & Co. and the Borneo Company Ltd. (right).

33b ▸

Caption: No. 104 A Penang Harbour with Sailing Sampans.

The harbour between the Church Street Pier and the Railway Pier was sometimes called the 'sampan harbour', as this was the place where smaller sampans used to dock and unload, as in postcard 32a.

34a

Caption: Landing Goods at Weld Quay, Penang

Imprint: M.J., Penang.

The railway building viewed from the north.

34b

Caption: China Street Ghaut, Penang

Printed in Germany.

The jetty entrance has signs for 'Federated Malay States Railways' (centre), 'Passenger Entrance' (left) and 'Goods Entrance' (right).

34c

Caption: (A8) F.M.S. Rail way Station, Penang. Photo by Nikko-Studio.

The silhouette of a steam-roller can be seen (right). The site opposite the Railway Station is under construction.

34d

Caption: Chaina St. Penang.

Real photo card.

◂ 35a

Caption: 366 – Federated Malay States. Railway Buildings, Penang.

Imprint: Federal Rubber Stamp Co.

The words 'F.M.S.R. 1907' can be seen on the central pediment.

▴ 35b

Caption: F.M.S. Railway Buildings, Penang

Printed in Germany.

The newly built railway building. It was formerly the site of the 'Penang Foundry.'

The F.M.S. Railway Station

From the moment it was built, the F.M.S. Railway Station with a clock tower and pier became a prominent landmark for the port of Penang. The 'Penang Station' was widely known as 'the only station in the world without a rail':

> This is a Railway Station without platforms or trains, the actual northern terminus of the Railway track being at Prai, connection with Penang being maintained by a ferry service owned by the Railways. The ground floor of the building consists of the usual booking offices and waiting hall and a spacious restaurant, bar, etc. The two upper storeys consist of offices which are leased to the public.
>
> Plans were originally prepared for the building in 1902, but building operations were not commenced until 1905. The foundations consisting of bakau piles gave considerable trouble but were eventually made satisfactory, and the building completed and opened to traffic in 1908. The building, with its lofty clock tower, is a conspicuous landmark from the harbour.
>
> *(Fifty Years of Railways in Malaya, 1935: 71)*

◂ 35c

Caption: 186 Station Hotel, Penang, S.S. Pub. by M.S. Nakajima

The Railway Buildings at one time had a 'Station Hotel', but this was later converted to offices. According to the *Penang Information Guide 1939*, the railway restaurant was a 'first class Restaurant with Bar and Grill Room'.

(Thorpe, 1939: 13)

36a ▸

Caption: F.M.S. Railway Penang

The section of harbour between the Railway Jetty and the Church Street Pier was mainly used for mooring small sampans.

▾ 36b

Caption: No. 164 F.M.S. Railway Pier, Penang

F.M.S. Railway Jetty

The railway ferry service from Prai was inaugurated in 1899, and the railway jetty was constructed in 1901 for the use of ferry steamers. About 644 feet in length, it was the longest jetty along Weld Quay:

> At the landward end it is carried on brick piers for a distance of 114 feet from the quay wall. This portion being 45 feet wide originally accommodated the station master's and booking offices (subsquently relocated to the new F.M.S. Railway Buildings in 1907) ... The jetty then narrows to 16 feet for a length of 500 feet with a Tee head 96 feet by 30 feet at the seaward end. This portion is on screw piles with a timber deck and corrugated iron roof.
>
> *(Fifty Years of Railways in Malaya, 1935: 53)*

▴ 36c

Caption: Penang Harbour

Imprint: Pritchard & Co. London.

A Railway Ferry Steamer docking at the Railway Pier.

▴ 36d

Caption: F.M.S. Railway Penang

Southern Harbour

▲ 37a

Caption: Penang. Harbour

No imprint. Undivided back.

▲ 37b

Caption: No. 115 Penang Habour (South).

Imprint: A. Kaulfuss, Penang.

◀ 37c

Caption: Harbour, Penang

Imprint: S.M. Manicum, Penang.

A picturesque view with the clan jetties and the hills in the background.

▲ 37d

Caption: No. 65. Chinese harbour Penang.

Imprint: A. Kaulfuss, Penang.

'A. Kaulfuss, Penang' is also stamped at the bottom left corner, photo side.

◀ 37e

Caption: No. 65. Chinese Harbour, Penang

Imprint: A. Kaulfuss, Penang.

38a ▸

Caption: Swettenham Wharf, Penang.

From the F.M.S. Railway Station clock tower, looking northeast towards Weld Quay and Swettenham Pier. The roof in the foreground is the Paterson, Simons & Co. building.

▴ 38b

Caption: General View of George Town, Penang

From the F.M.S. Railway Station clock tower, looking west down China Street Ghaut, catching a glimpse of the Georgetown Dispensary (built 1923) on the right. Rising from the rooftops are the corner building with the domed turret along Beach Street and the four-storey Eu Yang Sang medical hall at the corner of Pitt Street and Chulia Street. The Neoclassical building (right) was the first building of the Chinese Town Hall on Pitt Street, and next to it, the three-sectioned roof of the Opium & Spirit Farm Offices (subsequently the STAR Publications building).

39a

Caption: 65-V Church Stee Pier. Penang

From the F.M.S. Railway Station clock tower, looking eastward. Though captioned 'Church Street Pier', it actually shows the F.M.S. Railway Pier.

The two Chinese characters read 'Ping Chen', meaning 'Penang'. Probably the same Chinese photographer or publisher as postcard 64b.

Rooftop Views of George Town

39b

Caption: Beach of Penang

From the F.M.S. Railway Station, looking southward. A few fishermen's piers and 'clan jetties', with fewer houses on them compared to today. The prominent advertisement of Milkmaid Milk probably steered many a local mother away from breast-feeding.

40a

Caption: Chinese Bamboo Pier in the Sea, Penang

Imprint: M.J., Penang.

The waterfront settlements along Weld Quay were developed by Hokkien (Fujian) Chinese labourers involved in port activities as well as the coastal barter trade. At first the jetties were mainly used for berthing the sampans, while the place was a wood yard littered with planks and firewood. The jetties then came to be monopolised by groups of the same surname. The next development was a communal house occupied by male labourers. When these bachelors started families, they erected rooms, and then houses, along the jetty.

(Chan, 2002: 8)

Clan Jetties

40b

Caption: Southern Port. Penang.

A later view of the clan jetties. Note the long line of clothes being hung out to dry.

40c

Imprint: Federal Rubber Stamp Co.

Notwithstanding the handwritten note 'Malay fishing village', this photo probably shows the clan jetties at Weld Quay. Many of the jetty dwellers are boatmen; their sampans are berthed alongside the jetty.

Government Offices & Beach Street

▲ 41
Caption: Beach Street, Penang
Imprint: S.M. Manicum, Penang.

42a

Caption: Penang. A. Kaulfuss, Penang. No. 24.

Undivided back.

Very early view, before the clock tower was built (1902).

Some very large trees can be seen around the Government Office. The Post Office wing has yet to be built (1901-1903).

42b

Caption: Penang, Penang from the Sea.

Undivided back. This card is from a very early series distinguished by a number in the upper left margin.

The photograph was taken after the clock tower had been built (1902) but before the Post Office wing had been completed (1903). Two very large trees can be seen near the clock tower.

42c

Caption: No. 97 Penang from North.

Imprint: A. Kaulfuss, Penang.

A nice combination of steam and sail in this unusual view of the harbour, from the north, showing the point of the cape of George Town. On the right, the flagstaff is prominently visible; next to it, the Government Offices, the Queen Victoria Memorial Clock Tower and the Fort Cornwallis. The island on the left is Pulau Jerejak.

An important item carried by steamship was the mail – the P.&O. and British India companies ran a weekly mail service from Penang to Europe, while the Norddeutscher Lloyd and the Messageries Maritimes ran a fortnightly service.

(Wright & Cartwright, 1908: 325)

42d

Caption: Harbour, Penang

Printed in Germany.

In the foreground, the 'Teesta', 6296 tons, British India line, 1903-1927. The one behind could be the 'Okhla', 5288 tons, British India, 1895-1917.

(Source: Passenger Ship History Service)

43a

Caption: No. 73. Penang from the Seaside.

Imprint: A. Kaulfuss, Penang.

The Post Office wing (1903) and Swettenham Fier (1904) have been built.

43b

Caption: No. 73 Penang wharf.

No imprint. The same view as the one above, but different hand-tinting.

43c

Caption: No. 72. Government offices and clock tower, Penang.

Imprint: A. Kaulfuss, Penang.

Dated 12 December 1906. Same signature and date as postcard 43d.

43d

Caption: No. 73 Penang wharf.

Imprint: A. Kaulfuss, Penang.

Dated 12 December 1906. Same signature and date as postcard 43c.

43e

Caption: Government Offices and Clock Tower, Penang

Printed in Germany.

This view was probably taken from the flagstaff at Fort Cornwallis.

Note the construction activity to the left.

▲ 44a

Caption: Government Tor clock & Building Penang.

44b ▶

Caption: No. 4. Govt. Building & Clock Tower, Penang

Imprint: P.L.I Da Silva, E.&O. Hotel. Artist signed.

Government Offices

Penang's administrative complex, located at the tip of the cape, looked quite impressive from the harbour. Upon landing, travellers would be driven around:

> ... a great block of buff-coloured Government buildings ... from Weld Quay into King Edward Place and Beach Street, and thence round into Downing Street. They comprise the General Post Office, the Government Telegraph Office and the Government Telephone Exchange; the Governor's Office, for the use of his Excellency when visiting Pinang; the Resident Councillor's Office, the Audit Office, the Public Works Department, the Land Office, the Marine Department, including the Harbour Master's Office and the Office of the Solicitor-General.

The block facing King Edward Place was the first to be built (1884-9), then the Land Office wing was added (1890-91), followed by the Post Office wing (1901-1903). The Land Office wing was again extended (1907), and this block is the only one surviving today. During the last months of the Japanese Occupation, Allied bombing destroyed the Government Offices and, together with them, the bulk of British and Japanese government records on Penang.

(Wright & Cartwright, 1908: 315, 730)

▲ 44c

Caption: No 168 King Edward's Place, Penang

Used 1939, but probably a much earlier image. A street sign for 'KING EDWARD PLACE' is visible. On the right are what appear to be large diameter drums of electrical power cable.

▲ 44d

Used 1923. Two Thornycroft buses, introduced in the early 1920s, can be seen.

◂ 45a

Caption: 1. Government Buildings, Penang, S.S.

Imprint: Tuck's. Artist signed.

◂ 45b

Caption: Penang, Government Offiece Weed Quay.

No imprint. Undivided back.

Wonderful view of handcarts and no tramlines. Could have been taken before the first lines were laid along Weld Quay for the horse tram in 1898.

▴ 45c

Caption: Penang. T.N. Shaik Ismail No. 7.

Undivided back.

Used 1904 but stamp removed.

◂ 45d

Caption: Jetty Sheds & Govt: Offices, Penang.

Compared to the photo above, the tramline has been laid, the Post Office wing and new Jetty Sheds have also been built (both 1901-3). The government goods sheds were leased out to landing and shipping agents.

(Wright & Cartwright, 1908: 315)

46a ▸

Caption: Penang. Harbour of Government Office.

One of a group sent by Tye Kheat Kwong of 50 Gladstone Road, Penang, to Canada in 1910; he was probably the son of Tye Kee Yoon, see postcard 126a.

A fleet of tongkang lined up in front of the Government wharf. Compared with postcards 46b and 46c, there is no side door and no 'POST OFFICE' sign here. See postcard 122c.

46b ▸

Caption: Penang. A. Kaulfuss, Penang. No. 10.

Used 1902. The view, at low tide, was taken from Victoria Jetty (left). The pavilion-like building is not recorded on the 1893 map.

46c ▸

Caption: Tongkargs discharging cargees, Penang.

Another view from Victoria Jetty. Note the scaffolding and painting of the parapet and gable.

Post Office

In 1906, the Straits Settlements Department of Posts, Telegraphs and Telephones was responsible for the mails, postal orders, postal telegraphs, telephones and the post office savings bank. A total of 190 staff were employed in Penang, headed by the Postmaster-General's Assistant and two Superintendents. The number of letters, postcards and parcels received in Penang was 3,743,917.

(Wright & Cartwright, 1908: 325-326)

▲ 47a

Caption: Government Post Office, Penang

Imprint: M.J., Penang.

The card is used in 1910.

The Post Office wing along Weld Quay, built 1901-1903. The entrance to Victoria Pier is on the right. This photograph clearly shows poles for electric trams, introduced in 1906.

◀ 47b

Caption: Government Building, Penang

Imprint: M.J., Penang.

A view of the Post Office wing from Downing Street, looking into the quadrangle.

48a ▸

Caption: Penang. Lightstreet

Although taken from the junction with Light Street, this picture really shows the entrance to Beach Street. The old Chinese Protectorate Building is on the left, with a verandah supported by wooden posts, set back around 1905. The light-coloured double-storey building on the left was the old Chartered Bank premises, see postcard 53.

48b ▸

Caption: Penang. Entrance to Beach Street.

Almost the same view as postcard 48a.

▾ 48b reverse

'UNION POSTALE UNIVERSELLE, Straits Settlements (Établissements du Détroit)' (red ink). The postcard addressed to Paris was only paid at 2c but untaxed.

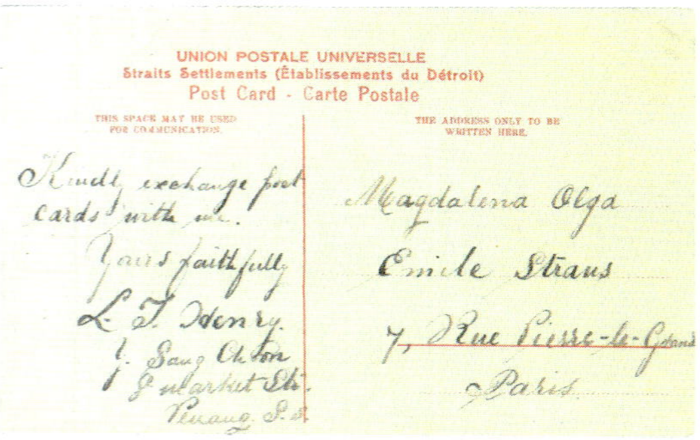
UNION POSTALE UNIVERSELLE
Straits Settlements (Établissements du Détroit)
Post Card - Carte Postale

THIS SPACE MAY BE USED FOR COMMUNICATION.

Kindly exchange post cards with me.
Yours faithfully
L. T. Henry.

THE ADDRESS ONLY TO BE WRITTEN HERE.

Magdalena Olga
Emile Straus
7, Rue Pierre-le-Grand
Paris

48c ▸

Caption: Beach St Penang

The Government Offices have been extended with the Land Office wing (left).

The building on the right, at the junction of Light Street and Beach Street, was the 'Police Office', the administrative block of the Central Police Station, built in 1889-1890. In the *Penang Information Guide 1939*, it was called the 'Registration of Aliens' Office; it is now the Immigration Office.

(Thorpe, 1939: 19)

◂ 49a

Caption: The Town Glub, Penang

Imprint: Tuck's 'sepia' series. Artist signed.

The Exchange Office was built (1901-1902) at the junction of Downing Street and Weld Quay. The premises were shared by the Penang Chamber of Commerce, the Penang Turf Club, and the Town Club. The Town Club, formed in December 1901 by Robert Yeats of Boustead, was 'largely resorted to by business men for tiffin and commercial talk'. The Penang Chamber of Commerce, formed in 1885, had the privilege of nominating the only Penang unofficial member of the Legislative Council.

(Wright & Cartwright, 1908: 730, 742-744)

Downing Street

◂ 49b

Caption: Downing Street, Penang.

Printed in Germany.

Used to the United Kingdom in 1913.

This was the government building housing the Education Department and the Treasury Office. A Sikh policeman in turban is standing guard.

49c ▸

Caption: Government Building, Penang

Imprint: S.M. Manicum, Penang.

On the southern side of the government quadrangle is the Chinese Protectorate (left) along Downing Street. Arriving junks were required to report to the Chinese Protectorate, established in the late 1870s to check on the excesses of the Chinese coolie trade. The Cantonese called it 'mau wa kun' (asking questions house), where female immigrants from China were examined under the Women and Girls Protection Ordinance. Behind it was the Indian Immigration Depot.

(Lo, 1900: 223; Vaughan, 1879: 7)

▲ 50a

Caption: Hong & S'hai Bank Buildings, Penang

Imprint: Co-operative Agency S.S.

A view of Beach Street, showing the Hongkong & Shanghai Bank building and the Netherlands Trading Society further down.

The extension to the Land Office wing of the Government Offices would later be built on the empty site in the foreground.

Bank Architecture

In 1905-1906, the architect Henry Alfred Neubronner was responsible for the 'erection (including the supervision and engineering of the foundations) of the Hongkong & Shanghai Bank in Penang.' The new bank architecture set the fashion in Penang for domed turrets, emulated by the Straits Chinese in their palatial residences. Next to the Hongkong & Shanghai was the Netherlands Trading Society building, also designed by Neubronner one year earlier.

50b ▶

Caption: Hongkong Bank

A view of Downing Street, with the Hongkong & Shanghai Bank (left). Note the private jinrickshas parked in the verandahway of the Chinese Protectorate building (right).

The Hongkong & Shanghai Banking Corporation

The Penang branch of The Hongkong & Shanghai Banking Corporation was established in 1884. It was one of the three British exchange banks that provided currency and credit for the internal and external trade of the country. The notes issued by the bank were recognised as part of the regular currency of the Straits Settlements and the Federated Malay States.

The Hongkong & Shanghai Banking Corporation Limited first opened for business in Hong Kong on 3 March 1865 and a month later in Shanghai, on 3 April 1865, then rapidly established a network of agents and branches around the world. The Penang branch was opened 19 years later. By the early 20th century, the bank's international reputation had grown tremendously. It was a banker for the British government's accounts in China, Japan and Singapore, and also served as banker to many Asian governments, including Hong Kong.

In Malaysia, the Hongkong & Shanghai Banking Corporation was instrumental in the development of the rubber and tin industries in the beginning of the 20th century. Today, it is known as the HSBC Bank Malaysia Berhad.

▲ 51a

Caption: Hong Kong Shanghai Bank, Penang.

Imprint: S.M. Manicum, Penang.

◀ 51b

Caption: No. 140 Downing Street, Showing Bank Buildings, Penang

Real photo card, sepia finish.

A trolley-bus passing in front of the Hongkong & Shanghai Bank building (left). The Standard Chartered Bank, designed by Stark & McNeill in 1925 and built shortly afterward, is seen at the end of Downing Street. On the right, where the Chinese Protectorate Building used to stand, the land is vacant.

▲52

Caption: Beach St Penang

Real photo card.

Two sections of Beach Street – the old narrow section north of Church Street Ghaut has yet to be widened, while the new buildings, right foreground, has allowed a substantial set back for road-widening.

On the front left is a building dated 1886 (still extant), with legible signboards, from front to back (Chinese character names in small letters, Romanized names in capitals):

'Nanyang ICE WORKS'

Sanhai BROTHERS COY. ... FACTORY'

'HOONG KEE & CO.' which offers 'LIPTONS' and 'MILK STOUT'

'LOCK & CO'

Kongsoon House, newly built in 1914, at the corner of Beach Street and Church Street, is already visible.

On the right, 'GROSVENOR MOTORS', and above that, the street sign 'CHURCH STREET GHAUT'.

The new building on the right became well-known as the premises of Sandilands Buttery & Co., Ltd..

Beach Street

The northern section of Beach Street is known as the financial and commercial centre of George Town. In 1908, it was observed that of the fifty odd public roads and streets within municipal limits,

> 'The majority are badly laid out, and, strange to say, the greatest offender in this respect is Beach Street, the very "hub" of local trade and commerce. It stands at right angles to Downing Street, and is long, narrow, irregular, and ungainly – some parts, especially in what is known as the Chinese quarter, being extremely narrow and altogether ill-suited for the requirements of the go-ahead business community. In years gone by, before the present development of Pinang was ever dreamt of, Beach Street, as its name naturally implies, was not a street but a sea-shore; and as, by the evolution of Nature, the sea receded and the land was reclaimed, first one row of shops and houses and then another arose in rapid succession, but without any apparent idea of symmetry on the part of the builders. The natural effect of this haphazard arrangement is seen in the Beach Street of the present day.
>
> *(Wright & Cartwright, 1908: 730)*

In the early 20th century, parts of Beach Street were progressively widened and rebuilt. While much of the irregularity remains, Beach Street is distinguished by a number of outstanding banks and mercantile buildings designed by well-known architects.

Pritchard & Co.

Established in the 1880s, Messrs. Pritchard & Co., Penang, started out as a small tailoring and outfitting store, but soon grew into 'universal providers':

> With the advance of Pinang and the opening up of the Federated Malay States and the Siamese territories, the undertaking grew rapidly, and department after department was added. First came the general department, containing harness, saddlery, bicycles, stationery, plated ware and other goods; and this was followed by a provision department; a china, glass, and hardware department; and a drapery, dress-making, millinery, and outfitting department.
>
> *(Wright & Cartwright, 1908: 806-810).*

Pritchard & Co. had its own double-storey building but also occupied a section of Logan's Buildings across the street. Around 1900, Pritchard hired an English cabinet-maker and steadily grew into the biggest furniture-maker in northern Malaya:

> The firm here turns out its own shop fittings and all kinds of household furniture to any design desired. .... The sales in this department demonstrate that few people in Penang nowadays trouble to get furniture from England.'
>
> *(Feldwick, 1917: 847)*

Not surprisingly, a large share of the antiques still found in Penang today originated from Pritchard & Co..

▲ 53

Caption: Penang. Beach Street.

No imprint. Undivided back.

Used 1905 but a much earlier image. A similar view is found in photomontage postcard 287a.

On the left, front to back,

Parre's Tiffin Room (on which site the Netherlands Trading Society building was built in 1905) – this was also the likely location of William Jones' rubber stamp manufacturing, in which A. Kaulfuss worked in the 1890s.

The earlier premises of the Chartered Bank, marked by a penciled 'X'.

'PRITCHARD & CO.', the double-storey detached building next to the Chartered Bank.

On the right, front to back,

'PRITCHARD & CO.' at one corner of the three-storey Logan's Buildings. Note the row of rickshaws lined up in front of it.

The Whiteaway, Laidlaw & Co. building is under construction and the scaffolding can be seen.

Logan's Buildings

Logan's Buildings on Beach Street occupies an entire block between Union Street and Bishop Street. Originally a grand three-storey building with cast iron balconies, it was reduced to two storeys in response to a dangerous building notice. The alteration plan was submitted in 1932 by Lim Soo Loon for the Chung Keng Kwee estate.

In 1907, Logan's buildings housed the accountants Messrs. Kennedy & Co.. The principal was James Young Kennedy, who once served as President of the Municipality, and ran *The Pinang Gazette* for a number of years from this building.

In the early 20th century, Logan's Buildings were the address of the following companies: Hug & Co., German commission agents and importers of European textiles, with a branch in Medan; Graham & Co., chemists and druggists; Cunningham, Clark & Co., which started out as importers of musical instruments and general merchants and became auctioneers and general brokers. The courtyard was used for public auctions.

(Wright & Cartwright, 1908: 781, 785, 800-801, 810, 814, 828)

▲ 54

Caption: Beach St., Penang

A Ford model 'T' that doesn't know where it's going.

On the left, Logan's Building with the signs:

'ESTD. 1910, INDIAN HAIR DRESSING SALOON, COME INSIDE'

'PRINTING DEPARTMENT IN CHINA STREET' below 'G.H. KIAT & CO. LTD.', booksellers, stationers, printers, newsdealers and general merchants with headquarters in Singapore.

(MacMillan, 1923: 268)

'COLUMBIA GRAFONOLAS' (phonographs) at the corner.

The Chartered Bank is under construction (circa 1925). The three-storey building beyond that used to be the Marine Police Station.

On the right, front to back:

'PRITCHARD & CO.'

'EASTERN EXTENSION TELEGRAPH COMPANY'.

55a

Caption: Logan Building, Penang.

Imprint: S.M. Manicum, Penang.

The signs on the premises in Beach Street include:

'ROBINSON PIANO CO. LTD.',

'RESTAURANT',

'DISPENSARY'

'JAPANESE HAIR-DRESSING SALOON'.

Robinson Piano, with its headquarters in Hongkong, was the principal firm supplying and repairing musical instruments in Penang since the early 20th century.

(MacMillan, 1923: 306)

55b

Caption: Beach Street, Penang

Imprint: K.M. Mahmed Esoof.

The street is decorated with flags, bunting and palm fronds, possibly for Victoria Day (Empire Day). The signs on the right: 'ROBINSON PIANOS CO.' and 'GEORGE TOWN DISPENSARY'.

On the left is the festooned building of the Netherlands Trading Society.

The Georgetown Dispensary, established in 1889, was a regular supplier of imported drugs and chemicals to dispensaries and hospitals. The firm also specialized in optical appliances and photographic materials.

(Wright & Cartwright, 1908: 812)

55c

Caption: Beach St. Penang.

The Penang branch of the Netherlands Trading Society (left, with tower) was established in 1888. It was subsequently renamed the ABN-AMRO Bank.

(Wright & Cartwright, 1908: 149)

◂ 56

Caption: Junction of Bishop Street, Penang

Imprint: M.J., Penang.

A beautiful picture of the shopfront of 'WHITEAWAY, LAIDLAW & CO.', 'OUTFITTERS' at the corner of Beach Street and Bishop Street, with 'EASTERN EXTENSION TELEGRAPH CO.' on the upper floor. On the side of Logan's Buildings across Bishop Street, is a sign for 'CHEMISTS – THE DISPENSARY – OPTICIANS', which opened in 1910. See postcards 57b and 57c.

This 'jerry-built' Beach Street block had just opened for business in 1904 when a fire razed the new Pinang Gazette newspaper office at the corner of Church Street and spread northward to Bishop Street. It was quickly rebuilt and revived as one of Penang's premier commercial addresses by 1907.

(Hamilton, 1925: 2)

The European Stores as Postcard Publishers

In the early 20th century, Pritchard's and Whiteaway's, Penang's two leading European emporiums, competed with each other to provide the latest fashions, furnishings and fittings. Both stores also published picture postcards of Penang.

Pritchard & Co. published postcards with early photographic views of Penang, featuring individual photographs or photomontage, notably during the era of the 'undivided back'.

Whiteaway, Laidlaw's postcards were produced on commission by the royal printers, Raphael Tuck & Sons, featuring artists' oils and photogravures.

Whiteaway, Laidlaw & Co.

A famous Calcutta firm, Whiteaway, Laidlaw & Co. Ltd. established a department store chain, with 'branches in almost every Eastern city'. The Singapore branch opened in 1900 and the Penang branch in 1903. By 1914, the department store moved to its own double-storey building at Bishop Street, adding a third storey after the end of WW1.

> 'Only high-class European trade is done, and the firm's clientele is composed principally of resident and touring Europeans and the better class of Malays and Chinese. In addition to being drapers and general outfitters, the firm has boot and shoe and crockery departments, and deals in every kind of household necessary.'
>
> *(Wright & Cartwright, 1908: 689, 812)*

The Whiteaway, Laidlaw & Co. block, along Beach Street also housed the following companies – the Nederlandsch-Indische Escompto-Maatschappij (Netherlands-Indian Discount Bank) which had its head office in Batavia; Alfred Stuhlman & Co., established in Penang in 1903 as an import-export house with trade to Sumatra; and the Penang branch of Riley, Hargreaves & Co., engineers for bridge building, the installation of electrical lifts, the construction of iron godowns, and the supply of machinery for rubber factories and rice mills. Another firm which moved into this block was Allen Dennys & Co., well-known landing, shipping and forwarding agents.

(Wright & Cartwright, 1908: 146, 800-801, 806)

57a

Caption: Beach Street, Penang.

Imprint: No. 35.A. Beach Street, Penang.

The premises of the publisher or distributor of postcards with the imprint 'No. 35.A. Beach Street, Penang' probably appear in this photograph. Signs can be seen for 'TONG JOO & CO., GENERAL STOREKEEPERS & COMMISSION AGENTS', advertising 'LIPTON'S', and 'GEORGETOWN DISPENSARY' which occupied 37A Beach Street.

The vertical Chinese signboard reads 'Tai Tong Kongsi, importers of leather and textiles from Europe and America, wholesalers'.

57b

Caption: Bombay Shop, Penang.

Imprint: S.M. Manicum, Penang.

The shop window for No. 8 Beach Street, see postcard 57c below. It advertises, 'TOLLARAM DHOLIAMALL & CO.. BOMBAY MERCHANTS – INDIAN, CHINESE AND JAPANESE GOODS. JEWELLERY & SUNDRY GOODS.'

Note the railings which were meant to prevent people from falling into the open monsoon drains.

57c

Caption: 2963 Beach Street, Penang.

A later photograph of 'B.H.T. DOULATRAM & CO. BOMBAY MERCHANTS', occupying the former premises of Whiteaway, Laidlaw, at No. 8 Beach Street. B.H.T. Doulatram & Co. were Sindhi textile merchants.

▲ 58a

Caption: Beach Street, Penang.

The Straits Echo, an English daily paper published by the Criterion Press, was founded by the Lim Kongsi headman Lim Hua Chiam in 1883, and flourished under his son Lim Seng Hooi. *The Straits Echo* was launched in 1903, engaging the Hong Kong-trained Chesney Duncan as editor. One of its managers, Ung Bok Hoey, was a Queen's scholar from the Penang Free School, and later co-founder of the World Chinese Students' Federation in Penang in 1905. For some years, the Criterion Press also published the Chinese daily *Pinang Sin Poe*, and the Malay weekly *Chahyah Pulau Pinang*.

A sign on the left reads 'CHIN HIN COY, PENANG'. On the right, a street sign hangs at the entrance of 'CHE EM LANE', while a Chinese signboard on the three-storey buildings reads 'Khie Heng Bee Kong Si'. See postcard 249a.

◀ 58b

Caption: Beach Street, Penang.

The three-storey building on the left, past Market Street, is Koe Guan Company at No. 63 Beach Street, belonging to the Khaw family of Ranong, Southern Thailand. The prominent three-storey building at the corner of Market Street and Beach Street, has a corner turret emulating that of the Hongkong and Shanghai Bank up the street.

58c ▶

Caption: Beach Street, Penang. Photo by Nikko-Studio.

▲ 59a

Caption: No. 17. Penang, Beach Street.

Imprint: A. Kaulfuss, Penang.

Tiang Lee & Co. (front left) at 53 Beach Street. Established in 1896, it had 'The distinction of being one of the first Chinese firms in Pinang to open direct business with merchants and manufacturers in Europe and America and to conduct their business on Western lines.'

(Wright & Cartwright, 1908: 824, 926)

A granite alleyway runs between No. 51 and No. 53 Beach Street, leading to godowns along Victoria Street.

On the right, the street sign for 'CHE EM LANE'.

▼ 59b

Caption: Nr. 22. Beach Street, Penang.

Imprint: W.N.E. sold by S.K. Md. Yusoff.

The three houses 55, 57, 59 Beach Street have been rebuilt, replacing those seen in postcard 59a. The new houses are distinguished by an ornate façade with roof entablature, in vogue around 1910.

The street sign for 'CHE EM LANE' can be seen on the right. Two vertical Chinese signboards hanging side by side read, 'Kong Ban Heng importers of goods from Europe' and 'Sundry Shop'.

◂ 60a

Real photo.

Street arch along Beach Street at the junction with Chulia Street, with Chinese characters that read, 'Kang A-khau Kay Independence Day Commemoration' referring to the Independence of the Republic of China on the 'Double Tenth' (10th October 1911). *Kang A-Khau Kay*, meaning 'harbour entrance street', is the Hokkien Chinese name for the section of Beach Street between China Street and Chulia Street. A number of street arches placed closely together, interspersed with bunting of the Kuomintang flag, indicate the scale of the celebration in the Chinese wholesaler's quarter along lower Beach Street.

The first shop on the right is 'Chin Chuan Press' while the corner three-storey building just next to it belongs to Badjenid & Sons, established by Sheikh Mohamed Badjenid from Hadhramaut, South Yemen, in 1917 to sell spices from India, cloth from Indonesia and velvet from Persia. Today, it is a well-known supplier of perfumes and canvas.

Street Arches

Two street arches along lower Beach Street show how the Penang Chinese community commemorated China's Independence Day and the British King's coronation with equal pageantry.

274c ▸

Caption: Beach St. Arch Png.

An arch commemorating the Silver Jubilee of King George V. The Chinese characters on the arch read, 'Celebrating the Silver Jubilee of the British King, 1910-1935' (centre), 'Toan Lo' (right) 'Sin Kay' (left). The arch was put up by the Chinese business community from the section of Beach Street known as *Toan Lo-Sin Kay* ('Tengku Syed Hussain Street') – between Armenian Street and Acheen Street. Refer to postcard 212.

Tengku Syed Hussain was the founder of the Acheen Street Mosque in 1808, and the roof of his trading office, the four-storey Gedung Aceh, can be glimpsed further down the street (on the right), at the junction with Acheen Street.

The southern end of Beach Street was dominated by Chinese wholesalers. Note that the majority of signs are in Chinese characters only. The signs on the right side of the street, from front to back:

'Sin Tong Ya Co.'

'Tai Seng Pawn(shop)'

'Chinese Medical Hall'

'Lee Chan Ho Chinese ... Wholesale'

'Printing Co.'

'Lee Eng Thye Chinese Medicine'

(Lo, 1900: 200)

The Padang, Courts & Schools

▲ 61
Caption: Supreme Court, Penang.
Imprint: S.M. Manicum, Penang.

62a ▸

Caption: Penang. The Clock Tower.
Pritchard & Co, Penang. No. 36

Artist signed.

A marvellous picture showing a crowd gathering around the clock tower close to six o'clock in the evening. The large Union Jack being flown from the tower appears to be superimposed.

The crowd could have been celebrating the inauguration of the clock tower, the annual Victoria Day (Empire Day), or some other official function. Queen Victoria's birthday, on 24 May, was celebrated with patriotic gatherings, special ceremonies in schools, the display of flags, the wearing of badges, the singing of songs and the exchange of British greetings.

The Straits Chinese fondly suggest that the clock chimes to the following rhyme: *I am Chen Eok, I gave this clock, tick-tock, tick-tock.*

▴ 62b

Handwritten caption on reverse: 'Clock Tower'

Imprint: Real Photo Copyright
The Federal Rubber Stamp Co.,
Booksellers etc S.S. & F.M.S.

Queen Victoria's Diamond Jubilee Memorial Clock Tower

> 'The clock tower was presented to the town in 1897 by Cheah Chen Eok, J.P., one of Pinang's Chinese millionaires, as a permanent memorial of the late Queen Victoria's Diamond Jubilee. It is sixty feet in height – a foot for each of the sixty years of her Majesty's reign up to 1897 – and cost the donor some thirty-five thousand dollars.'
>
> *(Wright & Carwright, 1908: 732)*

The contract was only signed in 1900 and Queen Victoria had passed away by the time the clock tower was finally completed in 1902, but the Straits Chinese were still loyal to her memory for many years afterward. The clock tower started leaning slightly after the bombing over King Edward Place during WW2.

(The City Council, 1966: 47)

63a

Caption: No. 41. Clocktower. Penang.

Imprint: A. Kaulfuss, Penang.

The young trees here are fully grown in postcard 63b.

63b

Caption: Clock Tower, Penang

Imprint: Co-operative Agency S.S. No. 16.

Rush hour at the top of Beach Street.

63b reverse

An example of a collector sending a card to France at the 'printed matter' rate of 1c. His name and address are stamped.

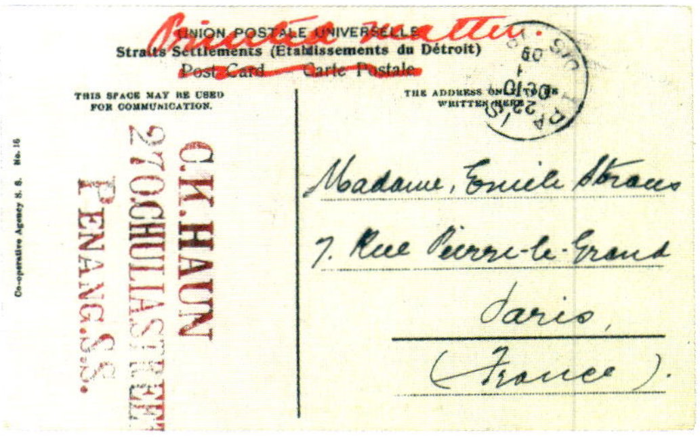

63c

Caption: Govt Office Penang

The Land Office block has been extended to Downing Street.

The sign reads 'The Far Eastern Extension Australasia & China / TELEGRAPH COY Ltd.'. The company's cables were first connected with Penang and Singapore from India in 1871. With the amalgamation of several earlier telegraph companies, the Eastern Extension Company had a monopoly of the cablegraphic business between the Straits Settlements and the rest of the world by 1907.

(Wright & Cartwright, 1908: 327)

64a ▸

This is one of a series of cards produced during the Japanese Occupation, which are rather rare. This pre-war photograph shows the Queen Victoria Memorial Clock Tower and the Government Offices, Penang. In the foreground is a policeman's shelter.

◂ 64a reverse

The handwritten caption 'A Market Centre Singapore' found on the reverse is misleading. The Japanese characters printed on the left edge reads 'Inspected by the Syonan Military' while that on the right edge simply reads 'Postcard'.

At the close of the Japanese Occupation, the Government Offices were bombed and largely destroyed by American B-29s.

(Kratoska, 2002: 13)

▴ 64b

Caption: 395. Clock. Tower. Penang

This postcard shows the 'GENTLEMEN' side of the public 'LAVATORY' built in 1927!

The Chinese characters read 'Ping Chen' or 'Penang'. Probably the same Chinese photographer or publisher as postcard 39a.

▴ 64c

Caption: No. 138 Clock Tower, King Edward Place, Penang

65a

Caption: Clock Tower, Penang

Imprint: M.J., Penang.

Note the building next to the Fort Cornwallis.

65a reverse

An example of a collector sending a card to Belgium at the 'printed matter' rate of 1c. He was apparently a member of a collectors' club; the membership number is written below his neatly stamped name and address.

65b

Caption: No. 77. The Fort and Government Offices, Penang

View of the eastern face of the fort, with a bridge across the moat. The moat or 'ditch' was 27 feet wide and 5 feet deep. It was fed from the sea and well stocked with large fish. Due to reports of malaria among the police quartered at Fort Cornwallis, the moat was filled up in 1919, 'spoiling appearances for the sake of health'.

(Wright & Cartwright, 1908: 938; The City Council, 1966: 68)

65c

Caption: No. 53. The Clock-Tower and Fort, Penang

Imprint: A. Kaulfuss, Penang.

66a ▸

Caption: The Fort, Penang

View of the northern face of the fort. The embrasures average 19° feet thick.

▾ 66b

Caption: Fort, Penang

Printed in Germany.

Fort Cornwallis

Soon after 'taking possession' of the island in 1786, Francis Light erected a fort of nibong palm at the tip of the cape. With the first batch of convict labour despatched from India, Light had the fort rebuilt in brick, without approval from Bengal. In the official records relating to the settlement, the last document bearing the signature of Capt. Francis Light is dated Fort Cornwallis, January 25, 1794.

Upon Light's death, his successor, MacDonald, complained that the fort had been built by a 'jobbing Chinaman' at a cost of about 57,000 Dollars, and superintended by Lieutenants Raban and Gerard. In 1795, MacDonald's superiors ordered the work to be suspended.

Fort Cornwallis, named after the Governor-General of Bengal, was by no means adequate. Colonel Wellesley, later to become the Duke of Wellington, remarked in 1797 that, 'As the town and fort stand now, it is impossible to defend them.'

▾ 66c

Caption: Penang. The Fort.
Pritchard & Co., Penang. No. 37.

Artist signed.

A view of the south-east corner of Fort Cornwallis, from the corner of Light Street and Fort Road.

Governor Farquhar in 1804-5 ordered extensive works on the fort, but the additions were structurally unsound. The fort was substantially rebuilt in 1808-10 during Norman Macalister's term as Governor. During this period the Malacca Fort was being demolished, and William Farquhar arranged for the shipment, from Malacca to Penang, of 'large quantities of bricks, tiles and iron-stone saved from the ruins of the fort and public buildings' in January 1808. It is thus probable that Fort Cornwallis and the embankments were partly rebuilt with the materials of the Malacca Fort.

The first recorded service which took place in the fort's chapel was the marriage of Francis Light's widow,

◂ 67a

Caption: Fort, Penang

View of eastern face of the Fort, from Fort Road.

Martina Rozells, to John Timmers in 1799. The chapel was the building in the south-west corner of the Fort. In 1814, a proper powder magazine was constructed within the north-west angle of the Fort.

The garrison of Fort Cornwallis consisted of a handful of Europeans, who resided within the fort, and Sepoys, who dwelt in attap huts next to the Fort. The adjacent Padang or field, demarcated the garrison from civilian areas, and was used for military practice. In 1811, barracks were built to house a company of European artillery, but this was subsequently converted to a jail. In 1820, the Penang Council reported that granite stones were being laid at Fort Point to stop the encroachment of the sea.

In 1805, when Penang was elevated to a Presidency, there were plans to rebuild a fort further inland, but it would have involved demolishing the existing fort and half the commercial town. Around 1908, there was again a proposal to remove the fort, 'by order of the Straits Government, to make more room near Swettenham Wharf for the claims of commerce...'

> In the early days of Pinang the Fort occupied a prominent position in the affairs of the town .... When the military rule of Pinang was superseded by a civil administration and, subsequently, when the British regiment was withdrawn from the island, the Fort lost much of its importance, and at the present day is used only as a signal station for the shipping of the port, as quarters for European and Sikh police, and as a Drill Hall for the local volunteer corps.
>
> *(Wright & Cartwright, 1908: 732)*

Fortunately, Fort Cornwallis is still with us today, though most of the officers' quarters and other ancillary buildings within the Fort have been done away with.

(Harrison, 1985: 64; Iyer, 1957: 16-23; Harfield, 1987: 4)

▴ 67b

Caption: Flag Staff, Penang. Photo by Nikko-Studio.

The ramp next to Fort Pier (Kedah Pier) is used here for unloading cargo, possibly firewood.

68a ▸

Caption: Clock Tower, Penang.

Imprint: No. 35.A. Beach Street, Penang.

This photo shows the old harbour light. The clock tower and the dome of the Hongkong and Shanghai Bank can be seen in the distance.

Two rickshaws and two gharries are parked along the Esplanade. This picture has been taken from the Fort Pier (Kedah Pier).

◂ 68b

Caption: The Fort, Penang

Printed in Germany.

This card shows the old harbour light.

▾ 68b reverse

The card is paid at the correct rate to Brussels.

68c ▸

Caption: Fort Road, Penang.

The Swettenham Pier goods shed can be seen on the left.

▾ 68c reverse

An example of a card sent to France in 1909 at the 'printed matter' rate of 1c.

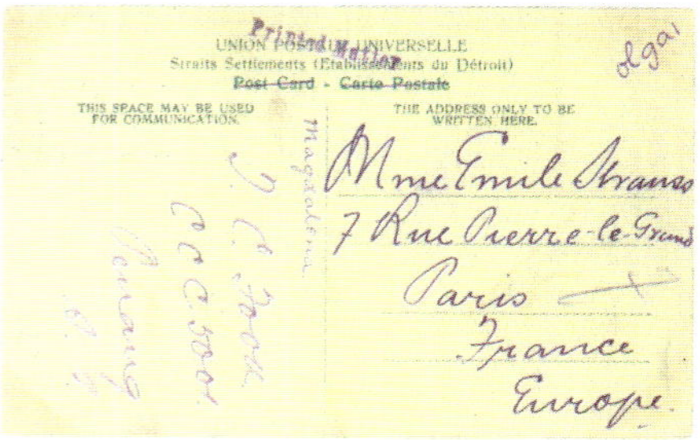

▲ 69a

Caption: Penang

To the left is Fort Pier (Kedah Pier).

The proposal to demolish Fort Cornwallis in 1908 was scrapped. Instead, improvements were made for the functioning of the pier, such as the addition of the new harbour light and the single-storey Harbour Master's Office.

▲ 69b

Caption: Flag Staff, Penang

Imprint: M.J., Penang.

The flagstaff at the north-eastern point of the fort was used to communicate with the flagstaff at Bel Retiro on Penang Hill to announce the arrival of mail ships or important visitors.

▲ 69c

Caption: Esplande Road, Penang

Imprint: K.M. Mahmed Esoof.

▲ 69d

Caption: Esplande Road, Penang.

Imprint: K.M. Mahmed Esoof.

▲ 69e

Caption: 361 – New Harbour Light, Penang.

Imprint: Federal Rubber Stamp Co.

The old harbour light was replaced with a taller new one in the early 20th century.

▲ 70a

Caption: Penang. Flagstaff by Moonlight.

Used 1910.

The moat of Fort Cornwallis added to the recreational value of the site. The old harbour light is still in use here.

Note the long Manchu-style 'tails' of the Chinese boys leaning against the railings. Before the Chinese Revolution of 1911, it was compulsory for all Chinese male subjects to shave the fronts of their heads and keep long queues.

▲ 70b

Caption: No. 137 The Esplanade, Showing Bandstand. Penang

Park benches were placed along the Esplanade for the convenience of strollers. Note the double-storey building between the bandstand and the Fort Cornwallis.

Padang, Esplanade & Bandstand

The Padang served as a parade ground as well as a field for football, cricket and other sports. The Esplanade has always been a popular area for evening strolls.

From 1890 to 1954, the Town Hall maintained a Town Band made up of Filipino musicians. The 'Manila Band' held open air performances from the bandstands at the Esplanade, Dato Kramat Gardens and the Penang Botanic Gardens.

> At the south side of the athletic ground is a bandstand, where a Filipino band plays for an hour or so on Mondays, Wednesdays, and Fridays, besides on special occasions. The ordinary "band night" sees the Esplanade thronged with rickshas and carriages, while the southern portion of the recreational ground is for the nonce transformed into a public park in which Europeans, Eurasians, and Asiatics alike stroll to and fro listening to the music.
>
> *(Wright & Cartwright, 1908: 741; The City Council, 1966: 37)*

▲ 71a

Caption: Esplanade, Penang.

Imprint: K.M. Mahmed Esoof.

Lawn tennis in progress, with green netting in place. Note the municipal bandstand in the middle and the Cricket Pavilion of the Penang Recreation Club (right).

71b ▶

Caption: Penang. Cricket Pavilion.

Imprint: Co-operative Agency S.S.

Such was the social segregation in colonial times that the Europeans and Eurasians had separate cricket pavilions. This cricket pavilion, on the Fort side of the Padang, catered to the Eurasian community's Penang Recreation Club.

◀ 71c

Caption: Penang, The Esplanade.

Undivided back. This card is from a very early series distinguished by a number in the upper left margin.

This photo is pre-1902, since the Municipal Offices have yet to be built. The Town Hall and old cricket pavilion can be seen. Next to the bandstand, a cannon points seaward.

▲ 72a

Caption: Memory of Benet Vermont C.M.G. M.L.C., Esplanade, Penang

Imprint: M.J., Penang.

▲ 72a reverse

Another 'destination gem', Penang 1912 to RABAUL which was then in German New Guinea.

72b ▶

Caption: Esplanade, Penang

Imprint: M.J., Penang.

Another view of Ben Vermont's Monument at the Padang.

Ben Vermont's Monument

J.M.B. Vermont was the manager and part proprietor of the sugar plantation at Batu Kawan Estate, Province Wellesley. He was regarded as the 'grand old man' of Penang during the sugar boom days of the 1880s and 1890s.

The new Cricket Club is in the course of construction, dating the photograph to 1908. It is possible that the construction workers from this site are among those posing around the monument or sprawled out on the grass in the background.

(S. Durai Raja-Singam, 1939: 73)

▲ 73a

Caption: Cricket Club, Penang.

An atmospheric view of the Padang, with Ben Vermont's Monument on the left, the new Cricket Club in the middle and the Municipal Offices on the right.

◀ 73b

Caption: Esplanade, Penang.

Imprint: S.M. Manicum, Penang.

Smartly dressed Indian Muslims or Jawi Peranakan strolling around the Padang.

▲ 74a

Caption: No. 107 Penang Cricket Club

Imprint: A. Kaulfuss, Penang.

This postcard shows a picture of the 'Pinang Cricket Club, at the Cricket Club Pavilion on the Occasion of the Annual Match, Straits Settlements v. Federated Malay States, August 1907'. The white tent on the right is the women's pavilion. The architect H.A. Neubronner is tentatively identified as seated bottom row, fourth from left.

(Wright & Cartwright, 1908: 734, 751)

74b ▶

Caption: Cricket Club, Penang

Imprint: M.J., Penang.

The New Cricket Club was built in the fashionable Edwardian style of the time. Distinctive features are the multi-gabled roof and short tower. The gables are striped in a 'mock Tudor' fashion.

75a

Caption: No. 75 Sports in Penang

Imprint: A. Kaulfuss, Penang.

While cricket was an exclusive 'English' sport, it certainly attracted a large crowd of 'native' spectators. Possibly the same event as in postcard 74a.

Penang Cricket Club

The pride of the Padang was the Penang Cricket Club. Around 1907, the government leased the Esplanade site to the Penang Cricket Club for 30 years, and the old one-storey pavilion was replaced by a new double-storey pavilion in 1908. The Penang Cricket Club later changed its name to the Penang Sports Club.

The 'New Cricket Pavilion for the Penang Cricket Club' was designed by the architect H.A Neubronner, himself an outstanding cricket player and all-round sportsman. Since 1899, he played both cricket and football for Penang in all the interstate and inter-settlement matches, captaining on two occasions. As part of his candidate's statement to the Royal Institute of British Architects, Neubronner submitted a postcard photo of the new cricket pavilion.

(Wright & Cartwright. 1908: 734, 751; Candidate's Separate Statement, submitted to RIBA by H.A. Neubronner, 18th March 1911.)

75b

Caption: No. 75. Sports in Penang.

Imprint: A. Kaulfuss, Penang.

75b reverse

Example of a divided back card, 'Printed by A. Kaulfuss, Penang'. 'Printed in Germany' appears in the stamp box.

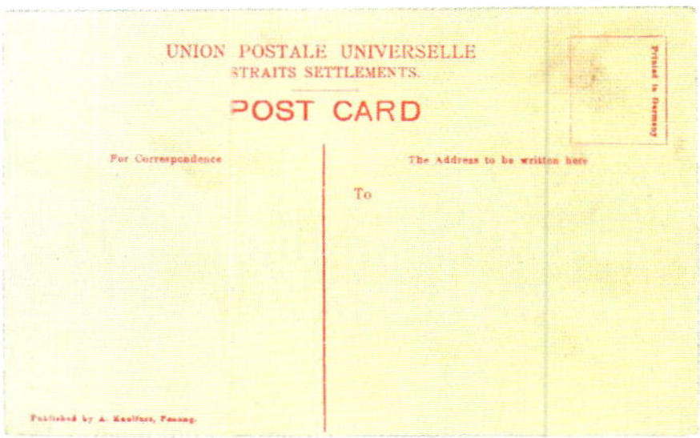

75c

Caption: 368 – Penang Cricket Club, Penang

Imprint: Federal Rubber Stamp Co.

Perforated left edge indicates that the postcard originated from a postcard booklet.

76a

Caption: Penang, The Town Hall.

Undivided back. This card is from a very early series distinguished by a number in the upper left margin.

The Town Hall before the extensions in 1906.

76b

Caption: Town Hall, Penang.

Imprint: Federal Rubber Stamp Co.

The Town Hall

The Town Hall, built in 1880, was the premier venue for the town's social events, balls and dramatic performances. The old Hokkien Chinese name for it was 'Ang Mo Kong Kuan' or European Club. In 1890, the entrance hall was enlarged and four more rooms were added.

> Used by the Municipal clerks in the daytime, these were to be supper rooms when a Ball was held. The stage was improved at the same time. Nor was this all, for a Town Band was formed, partly by subscription and partly at the Commissioner's expense. A grand piano was ordered but did not arrive until 1892.
>
> *(The City Council, 1966: p. 31)*

76c

Handwritten caption on reverse: 'Town Hall'

Imprint: Real Photo Copyright The Federal Rubber Stamp Co., Booksellers etc S.S. & F.M.S.

◂ 77a

Caption: 345 – Town Hall, Penang.

Imprint: Federal Rubber Stamp Co.

The Town Hall, after the 1906 extensions.

With the completion of the Municipal Offices in 1903, the administration moved out of the Town Hall and the opportunity was taken to renovate it yet again. The covered balcony was added over the original portico and the side wings were extended. Retrofitted with electric lights and fans, the Town Hall reopened in 1906 with an amateur concert.

▴ 77b

Caption: The Straits Urchins. Penang.
Imprint: S.M. Manicum, Penang. No. 81.

Twenty boys posing in front of the Municipal Fountain. The Edinburgh House (left) and the Town Hall (right) can be seen in the background.

Municipal Fountain, Light Street

The fountain bears an inscription, 'Presented to the public of Penang by Koh Seang Tat, Esq., J.P., 1883'. Koh Seang Tat, a Municipal Commissioner, provided hospitality to the Duke of Edinburgh in 1869, and his house at Light Street was subsequently called 'Edinburgh House', while the road next to it was named 'Duke Street' to commemorate the Duke's visit.

(Wong, 1963: 16)

78a ▸

Caption: No. 78, The Esplanade, Penang

Imprint: A. Kaulfuss, Penang.

This postcard shows the Fort Cornwallis, the old Cricket Club and the Municipal Offices.

▴ 78b

Caption: No. 78. The Esplanade, Penang

Imprint: A. Kaulfuss, Penang.

◂ 78c

Handwritten caption on reverse: 'Esplanade Penang'

Imprint: Real Photo Copyright The Federal Rubber Stamp Co., Booksellers etc S.S. & F.M.S.

◂ 78d

Caption: Penang. T.N. Shaik Ismail No. 31.

Handwritten caption: 'Municipal Offices, Cricket Club'

The Town Hall, the old Cricket Club, the newly completed Municipal Offices and the bandstand, all in one photograph.

▾ 78d reverse

Correctly paid to India at the Empire rate, the card is of particular interest since it was passed from Government House, to which it was addressed, to the Viceroy's Camp P.O. on 2 JA 06.

◂ 79a

Caption: Penang. Municipal Building.

Used 1910.

Municipal Offices

The Municipal Offices were built just twenty years after the construction of the Town Hall. Toward the end of the 19th century, there was a great increase in the taxes and assessments collected, resulting from the rapid expansion of George Town as the export centre for agricultural produce from Province Wellesley and tin from Perak. The Municipal Council needed a new office:

> The decision to build such a headquarters was taken in 1900, the plans being approved in May and the main contract, with Mr. Lee Ah Cheang, signed in September for $75,400. The total cost, including ironwork from Europe, would amount to $100,000 and the work was to be finished by September 1902.
>
> *(The City Council, 1966: 47)*

▴ 79b

Caption: Penang, No. 27 – Municipal Buildings and Cricket Club Pavilion and Ground

British Empire Series. Artist signed, 'Hood'.

◂ 79c

Handwritten caption on reverse: 'Municipal Office Penang'

Imprint: Real Photo Copyright The Federal Rubber Stamp Co., Booksellers etc S.S. & F.M.S.

80a ▸

Caption: Ben Vermont's Monument, Penang

Printed in Germany.

The sign on the left reads 'BROOKE BOND'S TEA', that on the right reads 'LIGHT STREET'.

The building on the left was the home of Foo Tye Sin, one of the Chinese leaders of the late 19th century, and a partner of Koh Seang Tat in the firm Tye Sin Tat & Co. Around 1900, it was the meeting place of a group of Chinese footballers who played at the Padang, before they formed the Chinese Recreation Club (postcard 133a) in the early 1900s.

80b ▴

Caption: No. 180 Penang Chamber of Commerce, Light Street, Penang.

Real photo, 1930s series.

The building has the date 1928 above the sign 'CHINESE CHAMBER OF COMMERCE'. When this picture was taken, the ground floor was already a 'BATA' shoe shop. The first BATA store in Malaya opened in Singapore in 1930, and a branch in Penang was probably opened shortly afterward.

On the left is the Chinese gate of the Foo Tye Sin Mansion at No. 1 Light Street (now a bank).

80c ▸

Caption: Light Street Arch, Penang.

Imprint: S.M. Manicum, Penang. No 111.

The Chinese words read 'Welcoming the arrival of the Duke' – referring to the visit of Prince Arthur, Duke of Connaught, to Penang in February 1906. Temporary arches were put up by the community to commemorate significant occasions and celebrate the arrival of important dignitaries. Although captioned 'Light Street Arch', this arch was really located on Farquhar Street, for the International Hotel can be seen on the left and the E.&O. Hotel can be seen at the end of the street.

◂ 81a

Caption: No. 58. Light Street, Penang.

Imprint: A. Kaulfuss, Penang.

The sign on the building in the centre is 'CENTRAL HOTEL'. The same travellers' palm can also be seen in postcard 81c.

▴ 81b

Caption: Penang. Light Street.
A. Kaulfuss, Penang. No. 58.

Undivided back.

◂ 81c

Real photo. Nicely dated April 1923 but unused.

A view down Esplanade Road and Union Street, and the junction with Light Street. Union Street used to cut an L-shape between Light Street and Beach Street, behind the police block.

The road sign above the bullock cart says 'LIGHT STREET'. In the distance is the sign for 'PRITCHARD & CO., CHINA AND GLASS MERCHANTS', advertising the firm's premises at Union Street: 'The building is a fine, imposing one of reinforced concrete and used solely as a glass, china, and furniture store.'

(Feldwick, 1917: 847)

◂ 81d

Caption: Light Street, Penang

Printed in Germany.

Used 1910.

The poster on the wall advertises 'FERNANDEL'S BURLESQUE and VARIETY COMPANY – THE ROARING SUCCESS OF LONDON, PARIS AND NEW YORK', performing at the 'TOWN HALL'.

82a ▸

Caption: (A15) Light Street, Penang. Photo by Nikko-Studio, Penang.

A large crowd can be seen gathering in the compound of the Police Courts.

▾ 82b

Caption: Police Courts, Penang.

Printed in Germany.

Note the full grown trees on both sides of the street.

Police Courts

The Police Courts, also called the Magistrates' Courts and Recorders' Courts, were located on Light Street across the road from Fort Cornwallis. They occupied public buildings dating from the early 19th century, designed to look like 'temples of justice' with classical porticos and colonnaded verandahs. They are currently used for the State Assembly. In Hokkien Chinese dialect, Light Street was called 'Po Le Khau' (literally, police mouth), meaning, the 'entrance to the Police Courts'.

(Lo, 1900: 212)

82c ▸

Caption: The Supreme Court. Penang

Imprint: Tuck's 'sepia' series.

The Supreme Court building occupies a traffic island bounded by Light Street, Pitt Street and Farquhar Street. Logan's Monument is positioned prominently in front of the Supreme Court.

83a

Caption: Soupreme Court, Penang

Imprint: M.J., Penang.

The south-facing wing (right) used to house the Penang Library.

Logan's Monument

James Richardson Logan devoted his life to justice and knowledge. He ran the *Journal of the Indian Archipelago and Eastern Asia*, also called 'Logan's Journals', in 27 volumes. He took over the *Pinang Gazette*, and was apparently responsible for persuading the P.&O. liners to call at Penang.

As an advocate, he was admired for defending a non-European against the East India Company itself; eventually, he became a favourite lawyer among the wealthy Straits Chinese and Indian Muslims. He died in 1869 and a monument was erected to his memory: 'He was an erudite and skilful lawyer, an eminent scientific ethnologist and he has founded a literature for these settlements.'

(Thomson, 1881: 75-81)

The Supreme Court

The Supreme Court building, of neo-classical design, was built (1901-05) at Farquhar Street, on the same site as the first Court House dating from 1809.

> The present edifice is a very handsome one, with a statue of Justice gracefully occupying the topmost niche of the main portico roof. There are two divisions of the Court proper, so that two judges can hear cases at the same time, and between the two divisions is the bar library and bar-room for the convenience of the legal profession. A session of Assize is held quarterly, when the presiding judge, wearing a scarlet robe, is preceded by a native Court official in uniform bearing a sword.
>
> *(Wright & Cartwright, 1908: 733)*

The Penang Library occupied the southern wing of the Supreme Court building. The library received an annual grant from the Government and was considered 'one of the cheapest circulating libraries in the East'. In 1923, it was mentioned that the Penang Public Library, 'with its 25,000 volumes, many of great rarity and value, is the largest in Malaya'.

(MacMillan, 1923: 286)

83b

Caption: Supreme Court, Penang No 50.

84a ▸

Caption: Penang Free School, Penang.

Imprint: Printed in Germany.

Used to the United Kingdom in 1913.

Here the Penang Free School building can be seen almost in its entirety. In the foreground is Logan's Monument, erected in tribute to a man who stood for justice and knowledge. It was once a prominent focal point for the courthouse and the surrounding schools.

84b ▸

Caption: Penang. The Free School. Pritchard & Co., Penang. No. 1.

Undivided back.

The first half of the Penang Free School building, near the St. George's Church, was erected in 1896.

▴ 84c

Handwritten caption on reverse: 'Penang Free School'

Imprint: Real Photo Copyright
The Federal Rubber Stamp Co., Booksellers etc S.S. & F.M.S.

▴ 84d

Caption: No. 233 Penang Free School, Green Lane, Penang 1930s series.

The present school building in Green Lane was built in 1927.

◂ 85a

Caption: Free School, Penang

Imprint: One of a group of postcards sent to Canada in 1910 by Tye Kheat Kwong. Sent at a printed paper rate of 1c.

The Penang Free School now houses the Penang State Museum.

Penang Free School

The school was founded in 1816 by Reverend R.S. Hutchings, Colonial Chaplin, who was also behind the founding of the Anglican Church. The first premises were at the corner of Love Lane and Stewart Lane. In 1821, the school shifted to the Church Square in Farquhar Street, occupying a group of small single-storey buildings.

The Penang Free School was established in the tradition of a British public school. The new schoolhouse was erected in two stages – the half near St. George's Church in 1896, and the other half in 1906 – unified by a central portico. In 1927, the Free School moved to much larger premises in Green Lane, leaving its building to be occupied by the Hutchings School. During the Second World War, half of the school building was bombed. The half that was built later survived.

St. George's Girls' School

The school was started by Mrs. Biggs, wife of the Colonial Chaplain of the St. George's Church. Classes were held on the verandah of the chaplain's residence, 'The Manse' which faced the North Beach, near Farquhar Street and Leith Street Ghaut. It was officially opened in 1885, after a year of classes. In 1888, a bungalow was constructed next to The Manse, to serve as the school building. The government took over the school in 1909 and called it the Government Girls' School. The school was handed back to the Anglican Church around 1920, and thereafter continued to be called the St. George's Girls' School.

▴ 85b

Caption: St. George's Girl School, Penang

Imprint: M.J., Penang.

◂ 85c

Caption: St. George's Girl School Home, Penang

Imprint: M.J., Penang.

The sign on the front of the building reads 'ST. GEORGE'S GIRLS' HOME'. It was located along Farquhar Street.

86a

Caption: Brothers' School, Penang

Printed in Germany.

The two views of St. Xavier's Institution were taken from almost the same angle.

St. Xavier's Institution

The St. Xavier's Institution was founded by the LaSallean Brothers in 1852. A double-storey building was erected on Farquhar Street by Father Favre, who had built the church of St. Francis Xavier in Malacca. Under Brother James Byrne as Director, a third storey was added in 1901. The Moorish-style facade was modified in later years due to problems in maintaining the elaborate ornamentation, bits and pieces of which kept falling off.

Japanese bombing at the start of WW2 badly damaged the chapel, but the Japanese were still able to use it as their naval barracks. After further destruction by Allied bombing at the close of the war, the building had to be pulled down. Due to post-war shortage of building materials, parts of the rubble were used by a teacher Mr. Yeoh Seng Chan and his friends to build the single-storey shops at Market Street.

(Brown, 1997: 32-33, 100-101)

Convent Light Street

The Convent Light Street, the oldest girls' school in Malaysia, was founded in 1852 by a small group of sisters from the Holy Infant Jesus order from Antwerp, Belgium. In 1859, they acquired 'Government House' together with the 7 acre site on which it stood. This was formerly Francis Light's property, called the 'Well Estate'.

The school was built in stages, wing by wing. Apart from the girls' school, the sisters also ran an orphanage and a boarding house. The Chapel was built in 1930; the design has Art Nouveau and Gothic elements, with French stained glass windows. Many old photographs and French postcards of Convent scenes have survived.

86b

Caption: Penang, St. Xavier's Institution.

Undivided back. This card is from a very early series distinguished by a number in the upper left margin.

◂ 87a

Caption: No. 49. Convent Garden, Penang

Imprint: A. Kaulfuss, Penang.

The Convent Light Street took pride in its gardens. This block was identified as 'The Old Wing'.

▾ 87b

Caption: No. 49. Convent garden. Penang.

Imprint: A. Kaulfuss, Penang. Undivided back.

◂ 87c

Caption: The Convent School, Penang.

Imprint: Federal Rubber Stamp Co. Real photo. Used in Denmark in 1932.

The three-storey 'A' Wing was built in 1929, with a new school hall.

Logan's Monument in the foreground is flanked by a pair of cannons.

◂ 87d

Caption: The Convent, Penang.

Imprint: Federal Rubber Stamp Co.

This part of the Convent was used as an orphanage.

◂ 139a

Caption: No. 184 Penang Hospital.

Imprint: A. Kauffuss, Penang.

Cows grazing on the Parade Ground in front of the General Hospital, showing the European Ward (centre) and Nurses' Quarters (right)

◂ 139b

Caption: Hospital, Penang

Printed in Germany.

Sent to France 7 MY 1910.

The European Ward at the corner of Residency Road and Hospital Road. The small brick building at the far left is the Lunatic Asylum, with only small air-holes high up in the wall, and an adjoining enclosed yard with a high wall.

Jail Road

▴ 139c

Caption: Goal Road, Penang

Imprint: M.J., Penang.

◂ 139d

Caption: Jail Road, Penang

Imprint: M.J., Penang.

The jail was first built in 1849 during the term of Governor Butterworth. The Criminal Prisons were put up in 1874 by the Public Works Department. The jail complex survives relatively intact today.

▲ 140a

Handwritten caption: 'The Lawn'. Penang Race Meeting. 1905.

Real photo card. Sepia finish.

Used to Scotland AU 18 1905.

'The Lawn' was the preserve of the European elite, while the 'natives' were largely confined to their own stands. The crowd is dressed in the Edwardian fashions of the day, the women with parasols and large hats, the men in straw hats.

The Victorian cast iron fountain donated by Chung Thye Pin in 1904 (see page 134) was reinstalled at the present Batu Gantong site.

The Turf Club

The Turf Club in Penang was founded in 1867 with David Brown of Gelugor as its first president. The first race course site at Macalister Road was granted by the government. The first stands and buildings were of wood and attap; they were rebuilt in 1900. In the early 20th century, the jockeys and griffins were largely imported from Australia. Race meetings were held under the auspices of the various Turf Clubs across Malaya. In Penang, two race meetings were held annually. As race days were observed as general holidays, the European elite turned up in full force, and in their finest attire.

(Wright & Cartwright, 1908: 198, 564-565)

140b ▶

Caption: Race Course, Penang

Imprint: M.J., Penang.

141a

Caption: Race Course and Grand Stand, Penang

Imprint: Co-operative Agency S.S. No. 11.

Used from E.&O. Hotel to Madras, April 1912.

The races in progress, cheered by spectators. The Penang Hills provide a marvellous backdrop.

'The prettily situated course, surrounded by a wealth of tropical verdure, presents an attractive spectacle on race-days, with its brightly-dressed crowd largely composed of natives.'

(Wright & Cartwright, 1908: 564-565)

141b

Caption: Races, Penang

Printed in Germany.

141c

Caption: Penang. The Race Course. Pritchard & Co., Penang, No. 26.

Undivided Back.

This postcard shows the grand stands and stables.

141d

Caption: No. 1 – Penang Grand Stand & Race Course

Imprint: T.C.B. Penang.

Used to France in 1910.

The new grand stands built in 1900.

142a ▸

Caption: Race Course Road, Penang

Imprint: M.J., Penang.

Notice the road sign for 'AYER RAJAH ROAD' above the stone gatepost of 'Spring Grove'. What is called 'Race Course Road' is actually a section of Macalister Road, at its junction with Ayer Rajah Road and Cantonment Road.

142b ▸

Caption: Race Course. Penang.

The Ford model 'T' taxi with a 'For Hire' sign is plying Macalister Road.

▴ 142c

Caption: Race Course Road, Penang 240

142d ▸

Caption: Race Course Road, Penang.

Imprint: K.M. Mahmed Esoof.

The old Race Course was located on Macalister Road. The Turf Club acquired a 230 acre site at Batu Gantong and moved there in 1939. The old race course site was given to the Maternity Hospital and the Education Department, which subsequently built the St. George's Girls' School and the Residency Road Girls' School there. What is now called Residency Road was formerly 'Race Course Road'.

The Beaches

▲ 143
Caption: No. 158 Sea Shore,
Tanjong Tokong, Penang

144a

Caption: Penang. North Beach.

Imprint: Co-operative Agency S.S.

'North Beach' usually referred to the beach along Light Street, Northam Road and Kelawai Road, originally lined with European bungalows. The jetty in this picture could be a private jetty belonging to a wealthy resident.

North Beach

144b

Caption: Malay Kampong, Penang.

Imprint: K.M. Mahmed Esoof.

An European bungalow on Northam Road, which appears as 'The Homestead', in an 1893 map (not to be confused with the present Homestead further down the road).

144c

Caption: Penang. Sea Shore.

Imprint: Co-operative Agency S.S.

A pedlar ascending the stone steps leading to the back garden of a Straits Chinese mansion at the end of Northam Road, adjacent to present-day Gurney Drive. The mansion belonged to the Chew family, which owned the Boon Pharmacy.

The bungalow featured in postcard 144b can be seen here, from the other side.

(Source: Lim Kean Chye)

Kelawai

Gurney Drive was non-existent then and, where it now is, stood a beautiful beach where Malay fishermen kept their boats and Indian fishermen dragged their huge nets.

> '... The fishermen's homes of attap and rickety planks dotted the sand here and there, reaching out towards the shore where the fishing boats, covered with the fronds of coconut palms to prevent the sun drying up their caulking, lay on their sides, waiting for the next fishing trip, and the long drag nets of Indian fishermen drying in the sun would cover portions of the shore up to the water's edge...'
>
> *(Lim Kean Siew, 1997: 129 138)*

▲ 145a

Caption: Malay Children at their Morning Meal, Penang

The man wearing a songkok is selling *nasi kandar* – rice and side dishes carried in two baskets by means of a shoulder yoke. The fishermen's children gather around.

145b ▶

Caption: No. 33. The Beach, Penang

Imprint: A. Kaulfuss, Penang.

The steps mark the compound of the Chung Thye Pin Mansion along Kelawai (present-day Gurney Drive). See page 134.

◀ 145c

Caption: Penang. A.S. Mohamed Assan & Co., Penang. No. 13.

The same stretch of beach as postcard 145b, taken from the other side of the house with a pyramidal roof.

145d ▶

Caption: Sea Beach, Penang

Printed in Germany.

▲ 146a

Caption: Malay Village, Penang

Imprint: No. 35.A. Beach Street, Penang.

This is possibly an early view of the houses along the coast of Kelawai (present-day Gurney Drive). The name Kelawai comes from *Kuala Awal* meaning the 'first estuary'. The village mosque was the Masjid Lama in Burmah Lane, founded around 1800.

The houses are raised on stilts, built right on the seashore. Note the steep slope of the attap roof, the simple window shutters, and some of the stilts made of mangrove trunks. The coconut trees were planted very closely together, probably as a means of mitigating erosion. Note another very large house in the background. These are Penang-style *rumah bumbung panjang*, the size of the houses reflecting the relative wealth of the inhabitants.

(Abdul Kahar, undated: unpaged)

◄ 146b

Caption: Malay Village, Penang

Imprint: M.J., Penang.

Note that both postcards 146a and 146b are exactly the same images but one is reversed left to right.

146c ►

Handwritten caption on reverse: 'Corner Club Penang'

Imprint: Real Photo Copyright The Federal Rubber Stamp Co., Booksellers etc S.S. & F.M.S.

The old Corner Club building at Gurney Drive. In the original postcard, the name 'Corner Club' is visible over the portico at the front of the building.

147a

Caption: No. 126 Malay Huts. Tanjong Tokong. Penang

Tanjong Tokong Village

Isma'il bin Hadji 'Abdoellah 'Oemar Effendi, a Mandailing from the Dutch Indies who visited Penang in 192[illegible], was impressed with the urban standards in George Town, but not with conditions in rural Tanjong Tokong.

> 'If you want to go to a Malay kampong which doesn't even have a single person of another race, go towards Tanjong Bungah. ... That village is Tanjong Tokong, go in through Bagan Jermal. It is situated on uneven ground... The houses are miserable, all of them have walls of nipah fronds and posts of wood. ... Those who live there are only the poor, whose livelihood consists of fishing at sea.
>
> Each village carries its own flag. In a quarrel, those who live in villages with a common flag will side with each other. There is the red flag and the white flag. The custom originates from the Chinese feud. Once upon a time, when Penang was overrun by bandits, it seems that the villages joined the secret societies of those bandits. The Chinese custom has persevered until today.'
>
> *(Isma'il, 1924: 51)*

147b

Caption: 2919 Tanjong Tongkong, Penang.

This photograph shows the well-known junction at Tanjong Tokong village. The road to the right looks newly made.

148a ▸

Caption: 370 – Tanjong Tokong, Penang.

Imprint: Federal Rubber Stamp Co.

The bridge looks newly built. A double-storey brick house stands at the curve in the road, amidst Malay houses of wood and attap.

Tanjong Tokong

148b ▸

Caption: Malay Villages & Fishing Stakes, Penang

Printed in Germany.

Probably a view of Tanjong Tokong – compare with the profile of the hills in postcard 148a.

▴ 148c

Caption: 2918 Sea-View of Tanjong Tokong, Penang.

▴ 148d

Caption: Penang. Tanjong Tokong. Penang. Pritchard & Co., Penang. No. 21.

Undivided back.

149a

Caption: Tanjong Tokong Road, Penang.

Imprint: Federal Rubber Stamp Co.

On the left, a woman going up the steps of a Malay house on stilts. On the right, three figures dressed in white walking down the road. Far right, possibly a brick house with a pyramidal roof.

149b

Caption: Malay Village, Penang.

Imprint: S.M. Manicum, Penang. No. 96.

This picture is taken from the shore just beyond the Tanjong Tokong promontory. It shows Malay fishing boats or 'koleh', in the foreground, and Chinese sampans in the distance. The photograph has been hand-coloured in such a way that the Malay houses look like brick houses with terracotta roofs.

The large brick structure on the left is Masjid Karwa Nina Mohamed, founded by a wealthy Indian Muslim money-changer in 1893 named Karwa, who lived in Muntri Street, and set up a money-changer's shop outside the Netherlands Trading Society in Beach Street.

(Abdul Kahar, undated: unpaged)

149c

Caption: Penang. Pulau Tikus Ketchil. Pritchard & Co., Penang. No. 34.

Undivided back. Late use in 1911.

The photographer apparently left his shoes on the rock so as not to get them wet.

Pulau Tikus

The island of Pulau Tikus (literally, Mouse Island), located off the coast of Tanjong Bungah, has a small lighthouse. The Malays call it Pulau Kechil which means 'small island'.

(Lo, 1900: 238)

150a ▸

Caption: A Shore View at Penang.

Published by Nikko-Studio.

The building in the distance is the Penang Swimming Club.

▴ 150b

Caption: Swimming Club, Penang

Imprint: Real Photo-Copyright
The Federal Rubber Stamp Co., Stationers and Booksellers, Penang, Ipoh, Kuala Lumpur & Singapore.

Used from Singapore to United Kingdom, 1929.

Penang Swimming Club

The Club was formed in 1903 by a group of 'young Europeans of Pinang'.

> 'The Pinang Swimming Club at Tanjong Bungah, 6 miles from the town, is approached by a road which skirts one of the loveliest stretches of sea beach on the island. The Club bungalow looks out over a charming little bay, hemmed in by fantastic rocks, and half hidden by varied tropical foliage. Perhaps it is seen at its best at one of the periodical moonlight fêtes, when the shore is dotted with hundreds of coloured lights and the strains from a band of music float across the water. These gatherings are always largely attended.'
>
> *(Wright & Cartwright, 1908: 585-6)*

150c ▸

Caption: Swimming Bath. Tanjong Bungha.

Imprint: Co-operative Agency, S.S.

The Penang Swimming Club can be seen at the end of the crescent-shaped bay.

151a

Caption: Swimming Club, Penang.

Imprint: Tuck's Super Glosso' by Whiteaway Laidlaw, Penang.

This photo shows the original club building of 1904 and the diving platform.

151b

Caption: No. 260 Swimming Pool of Penang Swimming Club. Tanjong Bungah

1930s series.

The salt-water swimming pool was constructed in 1930, as was the 'Snake Temple' – the nickname for the pavilion which catered to women and children, who were barred from the clubhouse proper.

151c

Caption: Penang Sea Beach.

Undivided back.

151c reverse

Used to Sweden, at correct rate, from TRONOH 12 AU 1908.

152a ▸

Caption: Penang.

Handwritten caption, 'Under the shade of the Palm'.

No imprint. Undivided back.

▾ 152a reverse

To Belgium at correct rate, dated 6 OC 1904.

▴ 152b

Caption: Penang

Imprint: A. Kaulfuss, Penang.

Vertically impressed, right margin.

Used to Hamburg 11.9.00.

◂ 152c

Caption: Sea Shore, S.S.

Imprint: Published by A. Kaulfuss, Penang.

▾ 152c reverse

A beach postcard posted from one hill station to another! Example of a fine local usage, Penang Hill JU 25 1906 via Penang to Taiping, addressed to 'The Nest', Taiping Hills.

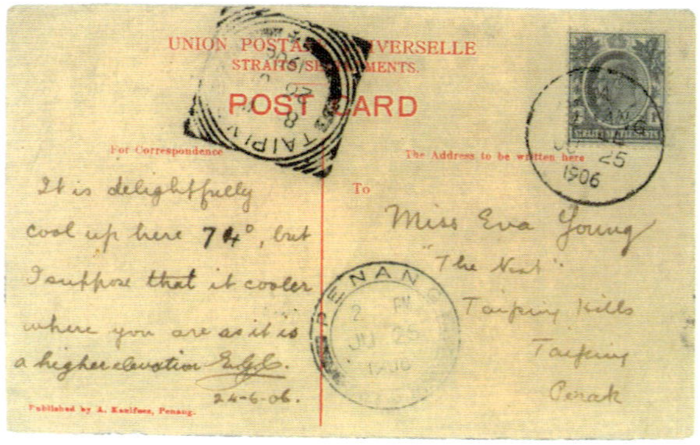

◂ 153a

Caption: Fishing Village, Penang.

Imprint: S.M. Manicum, Penang.

This picture shows Chinese fishing boats, the 'shoe-boat' or sampan.

Again, the hand-colouring of the photographs is somewhat misguided.

◂ 153b

Caption: No. 6. Native village, Penang.

Imprint: A. Kaulfuss, Penang.

A rickshaw ride through a village, beneath the shade of coconut trees.

◂ 153c

Caption: View of Penang

154a ▸

Caption: Tanjong <u>Boonga</u> Hill, Penang.

Imprint: S.M. Manicum, Penang. No. 108

▾ 154a reverse

Note the S.M. Manicum card with 'scissors' trade mark, and also a semi-circular mark under the words 'PATRONIZED BY H.M. THE KING EMPEROR OF INDIA'.

An underpaid card sent to an Italian working in Customs in Hokow. Underpaid by 1c, a T (tax) mark was applied in Penang but there is no evidence of a charge being made upon arrival.

154b ▸

Caption: Tanjong Bunga River, Penang.

Imprint: S.M. Manicum, Penang.

A family wading in a stream. The banks are grown with nipah palm which is used for making thatch (attap).

154c ▸

Caption: No. 11. Tanjong Bungah Village, Penang

Imprint: P.L.I. Da Silva, E.&O. Hotel, photograph by Photo Nikko.

Dated 1923 in handwriting.

Rather poor houses, the walls as well as the roofs are thatched.

◂ 155a

Caption: Norddeutscher Lloyd, Bremen. Penang – Tangjong Bungah.

Imprint: Ocean Comfort Company m.b.H., Bremen H34-4.

▾ 155a reverse

The only example of a Norddeutscher Lloyd card in this collection. It was probably on sale on board the ship. Example of a nice usage at the correct 'foreign' rate in 1912.

Tanjong Bungah

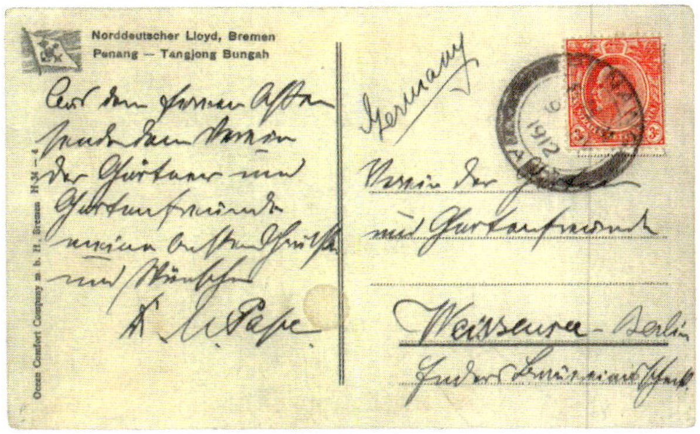

▾ 155b

Caption: Tanjong Bungah, Penang

The culvert in the distance, also seen in postcard 155a, helps to indicate the location of this village.

156a ▸

Caption: No. 259 Fishing Boats. Tanjong Bungah Village

1930s series.

This view shows seaside bungalows once popular with local tourists.

Tanjong Bungah Village

The coastal drive past Tanjong Bungah village proper brings one to a stretch of beach which is

> '... bristling with cafes, restaurants and bungalows. Here is the week-end centre for the sea-loving George Town residents and their outstation friends. The road continues to hug the coast right from Tanjong Bungah to the fishing villages of Batu Ferringhi and Telok Bahang, giving the tourists one long drive of delightful coastal scenes – sun-kissed waters gleaming on lovely bays and enchanting capes where scores of people sport all day.'
>
> *(Cheah, in Khaw, 1951: 21-22)*

▴ 156b

Caption: M.N. No. 68 Copyright. Tanjong Bungah Beach Penang

Real photo.

The viewing platform with handrail, in the distance, was part of Cheah Cheang Lim's seaside bungalow named 'Adorable'.

156c ▸

Caption: Sea Side, Penang

Imprint: S.M. Manicum, Penang.

Bamboo fishing-stakes at Tanjong Bungah.

▲ 157a

Caption: Tanjong Bunga

▲ 157b

Caption: Tanjong Bungah

Dated May 1934 on reverse.

This view shows the bungalow which is seen in postcard 157c. Note that the hill behind has been cleared.

◄ 157c

Caption: Tanjong Bungah

This section of Tanjong Bungah is popularly known as Miami Beach. This view was taken when the hill had just been cleared and a new road had been built.

◄ 157d

Caption: Tanjong Bungah, Penang

On the left, a sign reads, 'STOP. BATHE HERE. DRESSING ROOMS WITH FRESH WATER 20c. GALLON.'

On the right, a sign for 'MIAMI' beach is posted on a coconut tree.

158a ▸

Caption: Penang. T.N. Shaik Ismail No. 14.

Undivided back.

Bath houses, Malay coastal village. The location could not be determined.

▴ 158d

Caption: Penang Views. Sungei Pinang Waterfalls.

The waterfall at the 'other' Sungai Pinang, on the western side of Penang Island, is a popular picnic spot.

◂ 158b

Caption: Country Scene Penang

Real photo.

◂ 158c

No imprint. Undivided back.

Used from 'Pulo Penang', OC 31 1902, to Bohemia.

Waterfall Gardens & Penang Hill

▲ 159
Caption: No. 3 – Penang, Entrance to the Botanical Garden
Imprint: T.C.B. Penang.
Not the entrance, but one of the hill slopes.

160a ▸

Caption: Entrance to the Botanical Garden, Penang.

Imprint: No. 35.A. Beach Street.

This is definitely not the entrance, but the Middle Bridge, constructed in beam and plank in 1888 then reconstructed as an iron-framed, granite pillared structure with railings in 1892. Completion of this bridge also enabled the completion of the Lower Circular Road.

(Jones, 1998: 153)

Waterfall Gardens

The Penang Botanic Gardens, popularly called the Waterfall Gardens, is the third botanic gardens on Penang island – the first (1794) and the second (1822) were located in the Air Itam valley. The Penang Botanic Gardens was founded as a 'nursery for the planting of colonial products' by Charles Curtis, who was Assistant Superintendent of Forests and Gardens, Penang District, under the Straits Settlements administration.

The site of the gardens was formerly a nutmeg plantation, while part of it was an old quarry. Charles Curtis supervised the design and development of the gardens from 1884 to 1903 and established the Gardens as a botanical research centre. Economic and horticultural plants were regularly introduced from the Kew Gardens to the Singapore Botanic Gardens, and thereafter to the Penang Botanic Gardens. During the Straits Settlements days, the two botanic gardens came under the same Director, based in Singapore.

A variety of attractions have been developed such as the Formal Gardens with pergolas, the various plant houses for ferns and orchids, the band stand, the path to the Lily Pond and the fern rockery.

During the Japanese Occupation, the Japanese navy used the Botanic Gardens as their base. A shed was used for torpedo assembly and tunnels were dug into the hills from the path to the Lily Pond.

(Jones, 1998: 145-160; Pulau Pinang Magazine, Vol 1. No. 6: 20-23)

160b ▸

Caption: No. 16. Botanical Garden Entrance, Penang

Imprint: P.L.I Da Silva, E.&O. Hotel. Artist signed.

Twenty Rain Trees (*Samanea samans*) were planted along the Penang Botanic Gardens' entrance on 20 June 1887, marking Queen Victoria's Golden Jubilee. This one is still standing. On the right is Shed No. 1.

(Jones, 1998: 153)

161a ▸

Caption: No. 19. Scenery in the botanical Gardens

Imprint: A. Kaulfuss, Penang.

View of the Lower Circular Road and the Middle Bridge. Notice the garden seat and the broad stone path (bottom centre).

▾ 161b

Caption: No. 13 – Penang. Botanical Garden

Imprint: T.C.B. Penang.

Used in 1909.

▴ 161c

Caption: Penang No. 5. Botanical Gardens, Waterfall, and Penang Hill. British Empire Series.

Undivided back. Sent to Tasmania 16-7-08; Hobart arrival on picture side.

◂ 161d

Real photo.

An atmospheric view of the gardens from Lower Circular Road. The shelter in the distance is located across the road from the bandstand.

162a ▸

Caption: Penang. The Gardens. Pritchard & Co., Penang. No. 20.

Tuck's artist's easel trademark lower left.

Undivided back, late use, 21 JA 1911 from Taiping to the United Kingdom.

Probably a very early picture of Shed No. 1, roofed with Bertam chicks. In 1893 Curtis described it as 'an octagonal shed with a water tank, rockery and fountain in the centre, and is such as in an English nursery would be termed a show-house.' The shed was later extended with four wings.

(Jones, 1998: 153)

Plant Houses

162b ▸

Caption: Botanical Garden, Penang

Printed in Germany.

Shed No. 2. was 'principally devoted to aroids' among rockwork. Originally a span-roof structure, the shed was re-constructed in 1895-6 with 'light angle iron' and Bertam chicks, and re-roofed with corrugated iron in 1899.

(Jones, 1998: 154)

162c ▸

Caption: No. 116 Fernery.

Imprint: A. Kaulfuss, Penang.

This was probably the interior of 'Shed No. 2'.

163a

Caption: No. 122 Orchid House, Bot. Gardens.

Imprint: A. Kaulfuss Penang.

This was probably the timber orchid plant shed erected in 1887. It was reconstructed in 1889 using 'well-seasoned old timbers from the buildings removed to make room for the new Government Office' and roofed with Bertam chicks.

(Jones, 1998: 154)

163b

Caption: No. 9. Penang The Gardens.

Imprint: A. Kaulfuss, Penang.

Divided back. Used to France JY 7 1906.

163c

Caption: Penang the Gardens. Straits Photo Coy., Penang, No. 35

Undivided back.

This card is an indication that Kaulfuss supplied photos for other publishers.

A little European girl posing under a palm tree across the road from Shed No. 3. The cross-shaped double-span roof structure, first erected in 1892, was 'devoted to orchids and ferns in pots' grown among raised beds of rough granite stone interplanted with small ferns and mosses.

(Jones, 1998: 154)

163d

Caption: Penang. The gardens. A. Kaulfuss, Penang. No. 22

Undivided back. Used to Germany from Penang, 7 May 1901, Hamburg arrival 16.6.01.

◂ 164a

Caption: Botanical Garden. Penang.

No imprint. Undivided back.

This photograph shows the early appearance of the bandstand and the gardens. The span-roof structure on the left is the Shed No. 2 while the structure on the right is Shed No. 1.

▾ 164b

Caption: Botanical Gardens, Penang.

A view almost similar to postcard 164a above, but the gardens have matured by now, and the bandstand is railed in by bollards and chain. The 'V'-shaped stone path (left) leads to a shelter across the road, see postcard 161d. The stone quarry can be seen just outside the gardens.

The Bandstand

As soon as the Municipal Band was formed in 1890, a bandstand was erected in the Penang Botanic Gardens, and regular performances were put up as a strategy to help popularize the gardens.

The first bandstand was an artificial mound, in line with the landscape philosophy in which even the bandstand was supposed to blend into the natural terrain. A circular path and nine circular flower beds were formed around the bandstand. The granite steps were added in 1913.

(Jones, 1998: 154; *Pulau Pinang Magazine*, Vol 1. No. 6: 20-23)

▴ 164c

Caption: Botanical Gardens, Penang.

A still later view where the palm in postcard 164b has grown somewhat. The Waterfall appears like a silver stream in the background.

▴ 164d

Handwritten note: 'Grass cutters in Penang park.'

Indian gardeners in head-cloths and chequered sarong wielding scythes. The photograph is taken in the palm section of the gardens, with the Waterfall in the background.

165a

Caption: Monkeys Botanical Gardens Penang

Two women, the one on the left in kimono, feeding the monkeys.

Monkeys at the Waterfall Gardens

165b

Caption: The Botanical Garden Penang

Real photo.

The Long-Tailed Macaque *(Macaca fascicularis)*, native to the island, has always been a favourite subject for photographers.

165c

Handwritten note: 'Feeding Wild Monkey in the Park'

Message dated 1934.

During the days when cars were still allowed in the Waterfall Gardens, it was a popular recreational activity to go there for an evening drive, get out of the cars and feed the monkeys. This photo shows two early 1920s touring cars, probably rented by visitors to Penang.

166a ▸

Caption: The Botanic Gardens, Penang

Imprint: Co-operative Agency S.S. No. 24.

Looking from the centre of the gardens towards entrance; the bandstand is to the left of the river. As the postcards were mostly printed and hand-tinted in Europe, the colouring of the cards at times did not accurately reflect the hues of tropical foliage.

▾ 166a reverse

A nice local usage showing the E.&O. Hotel cancel in use from 1910 to 1924.

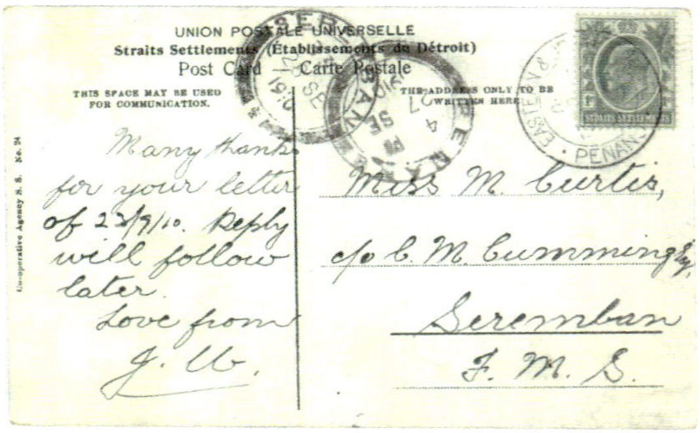

◂ 166b

Caption: Native Boys Gathering Flowers (Botanical Garden) Penang.

Imprint: M.J. Penang.

166c ▸

Caption: 339 – Botanical Gardens, Penang.

Imprint: Federal Rubber Stamp Co.

Perforated right hand side indicates it originated from a booklet.

The Nursery next to the Formal Gardens. The shed (right) covered with Bertam chicks, has probably been rebuilt in the same spot. Potted plant specimens are placed on raised benches supported by rough granite stone.

◂ 167a

Caption: Penang. Waterfallgarden.

Imprint: A. Kaulfuss, Penang. No. 11.

An early view of the Penang Botanic Gardens, taken from a high angle across the axis of the Middle Bridge. The meandering path (lower centre) no longer exists. The road to the right of the reservoir is the Upper North Road. The Waterfall (top right) flows down to the water reservoir marked by the pavilion. Crossing an area known as the Fern Rockery, and passing under a foot bridge, the stream descends along the rock-filled gully (right) to the small cascade (bottom), which can also be seen in postcard 167b.

▾ 167a reverse

The card was sent from the E.&O. Hotel, Penang DE 3 1900, and has a rare example of the fine E.&O. Hotel handstamp.

SARKIES BROTHERS, Proprietors.

E.&O. Hotel – Penang.

Raffles Hotel – Singapore.

Strand Hotel – Rangoon.

167b ▸

Caption: Penang the Gardens. A. Kaulfuss, Penang. No.

There is no number on this card, but it can be deduced from a later copy that this was Kaulfuss No. 21.

Undivided back. Though datelined Penang 13th Feb 1903, it must have missed the post in Penang, and was instead sent from Rangoon to the United Kingdom, 16 FE 03.

Just upstream from the Middle Bridge, this cascade was created by constructing a masonry dam across the river.

168a ▸

Caption: Water Supply Reservoir, Penang

No imprint. Undivided back.

The Municipal Reservoir in the Waterfall Gardens was built in 1892-4, supplying water to George Town. In the early 1900s, the water authorities considered enlarging this reservoir by blocking off the entrance of the gardens and flooding the valley. Fortunately, this plan was scrapped and the gardens were saved.

The domed structure behind the pavilion might be a store and valve tower.

(Jones, 1998: 150-151)

The Reservoir

◂ 168b

Caption: Penang, The Reservoir.

Undivided back. This card is from a very early series distinguished by a number in the upper left margin.

The Waterfall

The Waterfall has been depicted by many European painters since the early 19th century. One of them, Edward Cree, also described in 1845 how the 'stream tumbles down 30 to 40 feet amongst rocks and trees in a narrow glen – wooded with thick jungle.'

The Hindu shrine at the foot of the reservoir is said to have been erected by the convict labourers who built the early aquaduct from the Waterfall in 1804-1805. This used to be the destination of the annual Thaipusam procession, but when the waterfall was closed off to the public in 1904, the object of worship was moved to, and reconsecrated at, the Waterfall Hilltop Temple.

On his visit to Penang in 1872, Ibrahim Munshi remarked that the water and water supply in Penang were the best among the Straits Settlements. He described his trip to the 'Alexandra Baths', a hotel at Waterfall Road:

> We then got back into our carriage and went to the hill where the water-fall is situated. Near this hill we encountered some Hindus, male and female, young and old, gathered together at a temple to pray and bathe, for it was their feast day. On arrival at the hill, we had a look round and called in at an hotel with facilities for bathing, at the foot of the hill. ...
>
> The water, which is crystal-clear and consistently cold, flows rapidly down the hill between huge rocks. The pools are faced with stone. ... On the other side of the hotel with the bathing-pool, there is a place where the water plunges down the hill from a great height with a loud roar. This water never ceases flowing and is known as the water-fall.
>
> *(Lim, 1986: 176; Sweeney, 1975: 92)*

◂ 169a

Caption: No. 15. Waterfall, Botanical Gardens, Penang

Imprint: A. Kaulfuss, Penang.

Note the Hindu shrine at the foot of the reservoir.

▴ 169b

Caption: Water Fall, Penang.

Imprint: S.M. Manicum, Penang.

◂ 169c

Caption: Water Gush at Western Road, Penang.

Imprint: M.J., Penang.

Bathers at a cascade along Waterfall Road (an extension of Western Road), possibly during a Hindu festival.

170a ▸

Caption: Penang Quarry.

Imprint: No. 35.A. Beach Street, Penang.

Note the muscular Indian coolies, possibly convicts, and the emaciated bullocks.

The Quarries

Several quarries were found along the road to the Penang Botanic Gardens, including one just before the entrance. In the 1890s, prisoners were employed in the quarries and the stone was transported by the Penang Steam Tramways which ran from the Prison to the Waterfall Gardens.

(Source: Ric Francis)

170b ▸

Caption: Penang. Waterfall Road.

No imprint. Undivided back.

Bullock carts at a granite quarry, waiting to transport the stone to the tramline.

170c ▸

Caption: Quarry, Penang

Imprint: S.M. Manicum, Penang.

The eight men posing here are not the workers, but probably visitors to the Penang Botanic Gardens who stopped for a picture at the quarry. Notice how the stones are neatly cut into rectangular slabs and piled on one side.

◂ 171a

Caption: Penang, Weg zu den Hotels. Personenbeförderung.

No imprint. Undivided back.

German caption meaning 'Way to the Hotels. Personal conveyance'. Shows the various means of conveyance to the top of Penang Hill by the path from the entrance to the Botanic Gardens. They are by pony for gentlemen and by doolie for the ladies. A 'doolie' is a Hindi word for a chair slung on bamboo poles and carried by four porters. The rickshaws in the photo are waiting to carry people back to the passenger tram at Ayer Itam Road. The handcart may have been used to transport luggage.

The same image appears in photomontage postcards 178a, 284a and 284b.

The Ascent to Penang Hill

◂ 171b

Caption: 43 Road to Penang Hill

Imprint: A. Kaulfuss, Penang.

As early as 1787, a rough track had been cut through the forest. The track up the hill, starting from the vicinity of the Waterfall, became more accessible when the road to the Waterfall from the town was laid in 1792.

◂ 171c

Caption: 935. Chair Coolies going up Penang Hill.

British Empire Exhibition. 1924.

This photo shows a 'dooly' carried by four porters. On the right just behind the lead porter is a sign which reads; 'GOVERNMENT HILL & CRAG HOTEL'.

Not far from the entrance to the Botanic Gardens, along Waterfall Road, was the village of sedan-carriers. The village is called 'Nakali Thandal' or 'Sedan Mandur', after the sedan labour-contractor, who arranged housing for his workers.

172a ▸

Caption: Penang Hills Railway, Penang, Straits Settlements.

These are probably the two cars, No. 1 and No. 2, that ended up as chicken houses. It is not unreasonable to think that the Bengali *jaga* (a Punjabi security guard) lived in the hut shown in this picture!

▴ 172b

Caption: Penang Hills Railway, Penang, Straits Settlements

Imprint: Federal Rubber Stamp Co., Kuala Lumpur. No. 170.

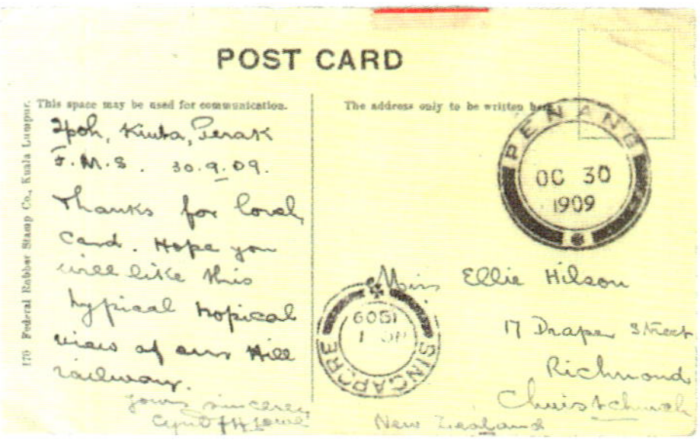

▴ 172b reverse

Nice 1909 usage to New Zealand.

The First Penang Hill Railway

The first attempt at constructing a funicular railway on Penang Hill began in 1897 with the formation of a limited company called the 'Penang Hill Railway Co. Ltd' by three men, D. Logan, J. Hein an A. Wilson. Construction commenced in 1898 and was completed in 1906, the railway comprising one section covering the whole distance, while the motive power was a water turbine situated in a winding house at the bottom of the Hill. The design, however, was faulty and no means was ever discovered to ensure that the cars could actually move on the rails. The company accordingly went into liquidiation causing the enterprise to be abandoned.

(Ric Francis, in Khor, 2002: 107)

An eye-witness account of this fiasco was reported in the *Pinang Gazette:*

When Private Enterprise and a few foolhardy friends took their places in the first car on the first day of the first Hill Railway, enthusiasm knew no bounds. The signal to start was given: The Bengali jaga saluted; a cock crew loudly on the station roof; the water power was turned on with a gentle hissing noise, the passengers waved their adieux to their less adventurous comrades on the platform and nothing happened! Let us draw a veil over the next two hours, when everyone got out and pushed, at first good-humouredly and then furiously, coolies sweated and the director of operations and his satellites cursed everyone. Private enterprise cursed him and them, till at last the gentle hissing of the power machinery joined the general turmoil and spat loudly water and oil; and the winding drums alone remain unmoved.

History has it that the empty car was eventually pushed by hand two yards up the track and then the manpower failed. Some more money was eventually raised and Charlie Patterson had a go at it till it (the money, not the railway) was finished, but the cars never moved again till they were made into fowl houses by the Bengali jaga who alone always retained his enthusiasm and his job, to the end.

(Pulau Pinang Magazine, Vol. 1, No. 4: 4-5)

An Experience of the Hill Railway

Parada Harahap, a famous journalist from the Dutch East Indies, who visited Penang in 1925, wrote about his experience of the funicular railway:

> Formerly, (Toejoeng) M. Arief wrote in *Bintang Hindia* (Dutch Indies newspaper) that whoever goes to Penang, but doesn't go up the hill with the funicular train, is like someone who eats a meal without gravy.
>
> Surely, we must try to get there.
>
> With Mr. Joenoes, we ascended to the top, with the climbing train, the height was not less than 3000 feet*.
>
> Penang with its port, ships and houses, looked tiny from above.
>
> It is the energy of the English that runs the electrical train up the mountain.
>
> In Hongkong the car just circles around the hill slopes, but this one goes right up to the top, until it frightens us to look down. The rail is full of spinning wheels like the pulleys of a well. At the top is a wagon, one in the middle and one at the bottom. If the one at the top descends, then that at the bottom ascends, meeting and crossing in the middle. If the one stops, so does the other, because the distance is already measured. If one reaches the bottom, the other reaches the top.
>
> It is not wrong for us to say that almost like coconut trees that are a little tilted, so is the railroad to the top – such is the power of humans, that we, just by paying 50 cents and sitting right down, in a little while find ourselves on top of such a lofty hill, without even feeling tired.
>
> At the top are pretty flower gardens, and the villas of the Europeans and the Chinese. There is a good restaurant, where one can stay overnight and dine. Since this (the funicular railway) came into existence, fewer Europeans are going to Brastagi – that is the news I hear.

(Parada, 1925: 55-56)

*The height is actually 2,722 ft. or 830m.

▲ 173

Caption: No. 120 Ayer Etam Valley.

Imprint: A. Kaulfuss, Penang.

A distant view of the coconut estates in Ayer Itam, the Paya Terubong Valley, the channel and Province Wellesley beyond.

The picture appears to be taken from one side of a cleared path, possibly from the railway track, showing a cross-section of the forest. As the Kaulfuss cards are pre-1910, this must be the first hill railway track laid around 1900.

▲ 223a

Caption: Chingay Procession 1928. Penang

Young girls posing on a modern Chap Goh Meh Chingay float, which is really a dressed-up automobile, with a tiger head in front flanked by two flying horses. This contingent hails from Anson Road and Logan Road, and displays the Anglophile tastes of the Straits Chinese sponsors.

Chingay Processions

A chingay float is called a 'chin-peh', meaning a decorated stage. Chingay floats were part of the Chap Goh Meh celebrations, held around the fifteenth day of the Chinese New Year. The floats cost quite a large sum to decorate, using rich silk transparent tissues, beautifully embroidered tapestry and variegated crêpe papers. Though not normally allowed out of the house, young girls from wealthy families were picked to be *chin-penh* girls. They were often dressed up like fairies and extravagantly decked with thousands of dollars worth of real jewellery.

(Source: Sunday Gazette, *February 3, 1974)*

◄ 223b

Handwritten note, 'Penang Chingay 1924'

The delegation is identified by the Chinese characters on the banner and two flanking lanterns, which read, *Phak Thih Kay* (Hokkien Chinese street name, meaning 'striking iron street'), referring to the part of Beach Street between Acheen Street and Malay Street, where there used to be a number of blacksmith shops.

The parade, consisting of large carnival figures and chingay flags, is passing through a rural area – judging from the tram wires overhead, it is probably the road to Ayer Itam. 1924 is the year of the 'Tua Pek Kong Chingay', normally held every 10 to 12 years.

▲ 224a

The delegation representing 'LEITH STREET AND MUNTRI STREET', posing for a photograph in the middle of Muntri Street.

They comprise three distinct groups, from right to left:

1) standard-bearers (some of them non-Chinese) carrying a silk embroidered banner and a pair of lanterns which identify the delegation representing 'Two Yuan Street' (it is not known which street(s) this name refers to).
2) a pony-drawn carriage conveying a decorated float with two small girls (notice the two small umbrellas with extended handles, used to shade the Chingay girls).
3) a chingay flag team made up of young men recruited from the neighbourhood. Partly legible from the flag: one of the sponsors could have been Cheah Ch(EANG LIM), a wealthy owner of tin-mines in Perak, who had his residence at Leith Street; see postcard 135b.

The following description by Mr. Lim Kean Chuan could well describe the young men in this photograph:

> 'The standard bearers of the chingay flags were all dressed alike, each section having its own colours... white cotton trousers (sometimes blue Chinese silk), a white or coloured cotton shirt, a hat or cap, and a towel tied round the waist to support the standard.'

(Source: Sunday Gazette, *February 3, 1974)*

224b ▸

Caption: Chinese Naga, Penang.

Imprint: K. M. Mahmed Esoof.

Used 1921.

A city street scene showing a Chinese dragon float and a crowd of spectators. The shop sign reads 'Wo Shing Loong & Co.'.

The picture has been somewhat distorted through inappropriate hand-colouring, depicting unlikely orange stripes and apple green shirts.

▲ 225a

Caption: Penang. Chinese Boy's School

The postcard was addressed to someone at St. George's School in Newport, presumably to allow some comparison of classroom set-ups. It contains the condescending message, 'Behold the visible intellects. They are really attractive little duffers' – the term 'visible intellects' could have been a sarcastic reference to the shaven foreheads.

▼ 225a reverse

This is a Penang card used from Hongkong to America in 1910.

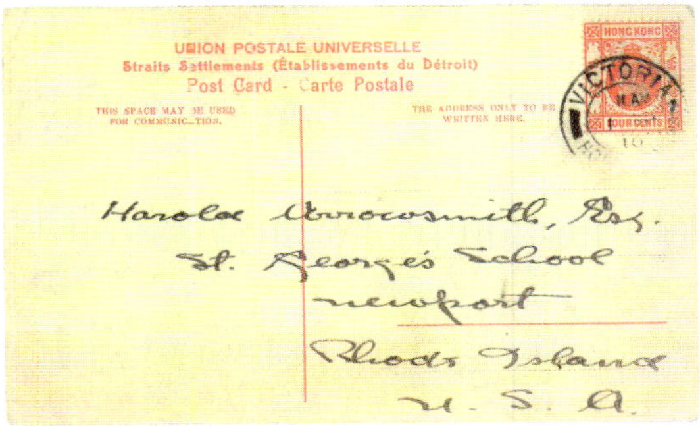

Chinese Classroom

Before the introduction of modern Chinese schools, traditional Chinese education was organised by Chinese associations, and this scene may have been taken at a clan kongsi. Note that the schoolchildren are wearing Manchu queues, but one of the teachers is already sporting a modern hairstyle. The Chinese teachers were at the forefront of the revolutionary movement in Penang, towards the 1911 Chinese Revolution.

◀ 225b

Caption: Chinese Wedding Musical, Penang,

Imprint: S.M. Manicum, Penang.

The surname lanterns announce a marriage between persons from the 'Goh' and 'Koay' clans. The wedding procession would indeed have been accompanied by a Chinese musical troupe, but what is shown here are just the standard-bearers. The latter are poor Indian boys dressed up in what look like Chinese clothes and French berets! The hand-tinting makes the clothes look a bit too dour for the occasion.

226a ▸

Caption: No. 124 Chinese Temple, Pitt Street, Penang

Real photo card. Used to the United Kingdom 14 FEB 1934. The double-storey building next to the Pitt Street Temple is the former building of the Chinese Town Hall.

No 124 CHINESE TEMPLE, PITT STREET, PENANG

Goddess of Mercy Temple, Pitt Street

A classic description of this temple was given by J.D. Vaughan, Superintendent of Police in Penang, in 'Manners and Customs of the Chinese in the Straits Settlements':

> This temple is in Pitt Street, built on a piece of land granted by the Government to the Chinese community in perpetuity for religious purposes. The older part consists of a hall forty feet square, having a paved terrace in front, on which stand two lions and an urn in which sacrificial paper is burnt. The lions are painted green, red and black. Before the entrance to the hall a substantial railing is placed to keep the mob out on great days when it is necessary for the priests alone to worship. Within the rail, on the right hand side, the names of the erectors of the temple, with the sums subscribed by each, are cut on a piece of granite which is let into the wall. The front of the building is decorated with carved work, gaudily painted. There are three doors leading into the hall; over the centre door is a black-board which bears the words "Kong Hok Keong" which indicates that the building was erected by Macao and Hokien men conjointly. In front of this house a hole about five feet square is left open from which the idols command a view of the sea. It is supposed that the gods are particularly gratified by a fine prospect, and the Chinese endeavoured to buy up the ground in front of the temple as far as the sea so as to keep it free of buildings. But some years ago the proprietor, not a Chinaman, of a plot of ground in Beach Street refused to sell his land and built a fine house thereon, intercepting the view of the sea and Province Wellesely from the temple. The Chinese console themselves by declaring the house unlucky and under the ban of the gods....'

(Vaughan, 1879: 59)

PENANG.

PRITCHARD & CO., PENANG. No. 8.

CHINESE TEMPLE.

226b ▸

Caption: Penang. Chinese Temple. Pritchard & Co., Penang. No. 8.

Undivided back.

227a
Caption: Chinese Temple Penang

Kuan Im Temple, Burmah Road

The lesser known Goddess of Mercy Temple is located on Burmah Road. It is one of the centres of the Nine Emperor Gods (Kiu Ong Iah) festival. During the nine-day festival, devotees observe a strict vegetarian diet. The temple is decorated with yellow bunting and flags, and temporary street stalls are set up in front of the temple to sell vegetarian food.

(T. Poh, undated: 41)

227b
Caption: Chinese Temple, Penang
Printed in Germany.
Miscaptioned, postcards 227b and 227d actually show the Thian Hock Keng in Telok Ayer Street, Singapore.

227c
Caption: No. 236 Penang Buddhist Association, Anson Road. Penang
1930s series.

227d
Caption: Penang. Chinese Temple. A. Kaulfuss, Penang. No. 2.
Undivided back.

Penang Buddhist Association

The Penang Buddhist Association was founded in 1925, for the study of Buddhism free of the influence of Taoism and folk beliefs, so prevalent in other Chinese Buddhist temples in Penang. The association building was built in 1931.

▲ 228a

Caption: Bird's Eye View, Penang

Imprint: M.J., Penang.

▼ 228b

Caption: Chinese Temple, Penang

Imprint: M.J., Penang.

Boey Kongsi

This view shows a spectacular roofscape, with a diversity of roof gables along Penang Street, near the junction with Church Street. The prominent Cantonese-style temple gable in the foreground belongs to the Boey Kongsi. This temple was designed by Barnett and Stark in 1906.

The small tower on the upper right, set against the greenery along Light Street, is part of the Foo Tye Sin Mansion at 1 Light Street. Refer to postcards 80a and 80b.

Seh Ong Kongsi

The Kai Meng Ong Beow on Penang Road, an association of Chinese with the surname Ong, was founded by three brothers in 1895. The Chinese character for 'Ong', which means 'king', appears on the pair of lanterns at the front verandah of the temple.

▲ 229a

Caption: Penang. Chulia Street.

Used 1908.

The postcard is miscaptioned 'Chulia Street', but is actually the junction where Church Street traverses King Street. On the left, a signboard with Chinese characters for 'oil and rice', and just below it, a chicken which may have escaped from the corner sundry shop! Note the four-storey building towards the end of King Street.

King Street Temples

Looking down King Street, we see an impressive row of Chinese temples with an assortment of gables. The temple in the foreground is Chong San Wooi Koon (association of a district originally called Heong San in Kwantung province) with a Cantonese-style gable and an arcaded verandah running along Church Street. Next to it is the Tua Pek Kong Temple of the Hakka Community, a branch of the temple in Tanjong Tokong. This is followed by the Toi San Nin Yong Hui Kwon, an association of the Sing Ling dialect group, Toi San District, Kwantung province, and its adjacent temple the Wu Ti Meow, dedicated to Kwan Kong, the god of war. The temple with the 'horse-head' gable is the Ng See Kah Meow, the Ng surname clan association. The photograph was taken before the alterations were made to the adjacent Toi San Nin Yong Hui Kwon and Wu Ti Meow by Barnett & Stark around 1913, creating 'horse-head' gables (like the Ng See Kah Meow) and providing back lanes according to municipal requirements. Refer to postcard 222a.

▼ 229b

Chinese Temple, Penang

Imprint: M.J., Penang.

Yeoh Kongsi

Founded around 1836, the Yeoh Kongsi is an association of Yeoh clansmen hailing from a clan village in Fujian province, China. The Yeoh Kongsi faces Victoria Street, but this photograph shows the side view of the temple along Chulia Street Ghaut. Many Yeoh clansmen from Penang were involved in the rice trade with Burma, and the Yeoh Kongsi in Rangoon is closely affiliated to this one.

230a ▸

Caption: Penang, No. 34-A Wayside Temple

British Empire Series. Artist signed 'Hood'.

This photograph shows the original 'Siew Thean Keng' with a wooden lean-to structure and a tree on the right.

▾ 230b

Caption: Wayside Shrine Penang

Real photo.

Compared to postcard 230a above, the tree on the right has grown big, and a permanent extension has been added to the left side, with a stone tablet commemorating the sponsors.

Siew Thean Keng

'Siew Thean Keng' (literally, Receiving Heaven Temple), still stands on Perak Road, facing the junction with Anson Road. The Francis Light School is in the background. The temple is believed to have been founded in 1812. It is dedicated to Tua Pek Kong (God of Prosperity) and is managed by the committee of the Kong Hock Keong at the Goddess of Mercy Temple at Pitt Street.

230c ▸

Caption: Chinese Temple, Bridge Street, Penang.

Imprint: Federal Rubber Stamp Co.

Seng Ong Bio

The 'Temple of the City God' is a Taoist Temple patronised by the Hokkien community. Located in the 19th century Hokkien working-class area, one of the benefactors in 1879 was Khoo Thean Teik, leader of the Tua Pek Kong 'secret society'. The deity is said to 'take his appointment from Yama, the ruler of hell, to whom he has to report the doings, good and evil, of the people in the town under his jurisdiction. The Chinese consider this temple to be the most appropriate one for taking oaths, such as that of cutting off cock's heads, etc.'

(Lo, 1900: 229)

231a ▸

Caption: No 172 Tanjong Tokong Temple, Penang

A late 1920s touring car parked in front of the Tua Pek Kong Temple.

▾ 231b

Caption: No. 151 Tanjong Tokong Beach, Penang

Tanjong Tokong was a popular seaside resort among the Chinese. It featured a small lookout tower, seating areas among the rocks, and a Chinese pavilion sponsored by Aw Boon Haw of Tiger Balm fame.

Tua Pek Kong Temple

The place name Tanjong Tokong itself means 'Temple Cape'. The historic temple here is the 'Sea Pearl Temple', dedicated to Tua Pek Kong, regarded as the God of Prosperity and the foremost tutelary deity among the Penang Hokkien Chinese. Both the Hokkien community and Hakka community in Penang have laid historical claims to this temple, and take turns to gather at the temple for celebrations of Tua Pek Kong's birthday during the Chinese New Year period.

231c ▸

Caption: No. 112 Chinese Burial ground.

Imprint: A. Kaulfuss, Penang.

The Chinese cemeteries along Mount Erskine, some of them more than two centuries old, to the interior of Tanjong Tokong.

232a ▸

Imprint: Federal Rubber Stamp Co.

The Snake Temple originally stood in a forested setting, surrounded by coconut trees. It was a natural snake sanctuary before the Sungai Kluang area was developed into an industrial park.

The Nobel Prize winning poet Pablo Neruda visited the Snake Temple around 1930, as a young man working with the Chilean Consulate for Singapore and Batavia. He wondered, 'Were these snakes brought here? How did they adjust? Our questions are answered with a smile, we are told that they came on their own, and will go on their own when they feel like it.'

(Neruda, 1978: 80)

▴ 232b

Caption: Snake Temple, Sungei Kluang, Penang.

Imprint: Federal Rubber Stamp Co.

▴ 232c

Handwritten caption on reverse: 'Snake Temple'

Imprint: Federal Rubber Stamp Co., Real Photo.

Snake Temple

The temple of the 'Pure Water Tutelary Deity' (Cheng Chooi Chor Soo) is popularly called the 'Snake Temple' (Chuar Biow). The temple was built in the mid-19th century on land donated by pioneer planter David Brown of Glugor.

George Bilainkin, editor of the *Straits Echo*, wrote in 1932 about a visit by the playwright Noel Coward and his friend the Earl of Amherst to the Snake Temple. At first they were disappointed to see nothing more than a few Straits Chinese women praying, but:

> Suddenly Coward and Amherst recognized that parts of the "furniture" were snakes, dark green in colour, five, six and seven feet long, with triangular heads. They were coiled round candle sticks, hanging loosely from bells, entwined about sundry small gods, surrounding the earthenware pots in which joss sticks are placed after prayer. Coward stroked the body of one snake while Amherst showed more normal respect for unknown reptiles, and watched Towkay walking about the stone floor swinging his cane.

The 'Towkay' mentioned here was Bilainkin's boss, Lim Seng Hooi, owner of The Criterion Press and publisher of *The Straits Echo* (refer to postcard 58a). He was also chairman of the Snake Temple's trustee board. Coming out of the temple, Bilainkin related that:

> We stepped into the sleeping quarters of the priests in the Temple and were shown the rest room for pilgrims. Here there was real monastic simplicity, a few chairs, planks, walls covered with oriental picture postcards.

(Bilainkin, 1932: 206)

◂ 233a

Caption: Two Means of Conveyance in the Straits Settlements.

Imprint: Methodist Publishing House, Singapore (MPH today).

Used to Holland in 1917. The Edwardian-style car and bullock cart are posed in front of the 'Snake Temple'. Notice the 'bungalow' structure next to the temple, possibly used as a stable or cattle shed. See postcard 253a.

◂ 233b

The main attraction of the snake temple were the live snakes coiled around the altar. The photo was taken by 'Chan Fook, Penang', who must have been one of the early Chinese (probably Cantonese) photographers.

▾ 233b reverse

Although the photograph was printed on a card with a 'Post Card' back, no space was provided to write an address. Instead, there is a request for donations to the temple. The Chinese characters read:

> Penang 'Pang-ka-lang' (the Chinese name for Sungai Kluang is 'pangkalan', a Malay word for river port);
>
> Hock Heng Keong (Hokkien temple); Cheng Chooi Chor Soo Kong (name of deity);
>
> With compliments from Master Lur Si.

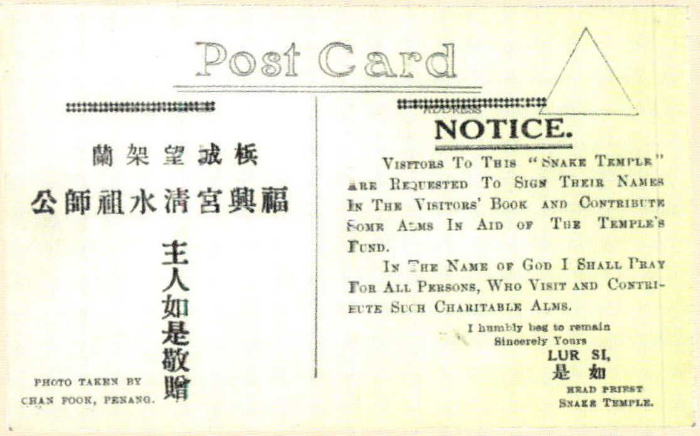

A Temple Postcard

With a publisher tycoon as the temple's chairman, and priests collecting 'oriental picture postcards', it is not surprising that the Snake Temple published its own postcards for fund-raising purposes. The following account by Bilainkin indicates that this method of soliciting funds met with good response among the English-educated Straits Chinese:

> 'Passing out we noticed the visitors' book. In this were written and scribbled the names of callers and the amounts they had apparently contributed. All the names were in English and the sums they had given were immense, ranging from ten dollars to five hundred (about £57)!
>
> *(Bilainkin, 1932: 206)*

Province Wellesley

▲ 259
Caption: Railway Prye
Imprint: S.M. Manicum, Penang.
Used to the United Kingdom in 1916.

▲ 260a

Caption: Butterworth, Main Road, Penang.

Imprint: K.M. Mahmed Esoof.

Two Chinese signboards are legible, both advertising medical halls. The Mahamariamman Temple can be seen at the far end of the street.

Butterworth, Province Wellesley

Butterworth, the main town in Province Wellesley, was named after William J. Butterworth, the Colonial Governor of the Straits Settlements (1843-1855). The town was described by G.W. Earl in 1861:

> Butterworth is situated close to the sea immediately opposite to the Town of Pinang, the Strait being here a mile and three quarters in breadth. As the sandy beach shelves off into deep water, passengers can land conveniently at all times of the tide. ... The beach herebouts is lined with a row of fine casuarina trees, which afford an agreeable shade, without intercepting the view of the island and shipping. As the sea-breeze blows home without interruption, while there is always a cool current of air from the land side during the night, the climate is generally considered to be better than that of the plain of Penang.
>
> *(Earl, 1861: 6)*

260b ▶

Caption: Penang Harbour from Butterworth

Very high gloss photo.

▲ 261a

Caption: Landing Bridge, Butter Worth, Penang. Photo by Nikko-Studio, Penang.

The 'Old Jetty' at Butterworth, Province Wellesley, was a main entry point to the peninsula. Like Victoria Pier in George Town directly across the channel, this was a public jetty used by small boats.

At the end of the landing bridge was the Butterworth Mahamariamman Temple, also seen in postcard 260a. Originally this area was a coconut plantation settled by South Indians. In 1901, the Straits Trading Company set up smelting operations at Bagan Luar, recruiting many local Indians as employees. The Butterworth Mahamariamman Temple was built on land granted to the community leader and later placed under the Hindu Endowments Board.

(Source: K. Ramanathan)

◂ 261b

Caption: 322 Bagan Lur Wharf. P.W.

Imprint: 'B' of Bodom.

Sepia tinted real photo card. Attributed to H. Bodom, proprietor of the Northam House Photographic Studio at 15 Northam Road, Penang, circa 1910-1920.

Mitchell Pier at Bagan Luar was the main entry point to Butterworth by car ferry steamers which plied from the Church Street Pier at Weld Quay.

262a ▸

Caption: Penang. Butterworth. Pritchard & Co., Penang. No. 9.

Artist signed. Undivided Back.

The bungalows look like European officers' residences or rest houses near the Butterworth beach.

◂ 262b

Caption: Sea Shore, Butterworth, P.W.

Imprint: Co-operative Agency S.S. No. 2.

On the right is the famous stretch of Butterworth beach lined with casuarina trees.

▴ 262c

Caption: Fishing village. Butterworth. P.W.

Imprint: Federal Rubber Stamp Co.

◂ 263a

Caption: Eastern Smelting Company, Butterworth.

Imprint: K.M. Mahmed Esoof.

Miscaptioned Eastern Smelting Company, this postcard actually shows the Straits Trading Company.

▾ 263b

Caption: Tin Refinery, No. 127 Tinslobs ready for shipping

Imprint: A. Kaulfuss, Penang.

These photos were probably taken at the Straits Trading Company in Bagan Luar, Province Wellesley.

Straits Trading Company

The Penang branch of the Straits Trading Company started operations in 1901 in Bagan Luar, Province Wellesley, next to the town of Butterworth.

> A jetty, built on screw piles, enables coasting steamers and native vessels to discharge the ore direct, and it is then run on trucks to the smelting works. The ore is obtained from Perak and the Siamese Malay States, and is also bought up locally.
>
> *(Wright & Cartwright, 1908: 534, 644, 806)*

▴ 263c

Caption: No. 126 Chinese method of smelting tin.

Imprint: A. Kaulfuss, Penang. The stamp does not belong to the postcard.

The Relau Tongkah or Siamese furnaces stand on a tripod and the fire is fanned with bellows. Used widely by the Chinese in Perak in the 19th century, they consumed ordinary firewood and were considered to be more efficient than other types of furnaces.

(Wong, 1965: 158-160)

264a ▸

Caption: No. 35. Native dwelling boats

Imprint: A. Kaulfuss, Penang.

A scene along the Prai River, where a gantry pulley and chain were used to pull the river ferry across the channel. The place is called 'Chain Ferry' to this day.

▾ 264b

Caption: Penang. A. Kaulfuss, Penang. No. 35.

Undivided back.

Handwritten date 5.4.05 and note, 'It is hotter here than it usually is in Aberdeen.'

264c ▸

Caption: Penang, <u>Goodstraffie</u> on Rivers.

Undivided back. Used to England, 21.9.04.

Probably the earliest version of Kaulfuss No. 35, but bears no imprint.

▴ 264d

Caption: Scene on the Prye River, P.W.

Printed in Germany.

◂ 264e

Caption: Scene on the Prye River, P.W.

Children on a raft which serves as a river ferry, pulled by a cable across the channel. In the foreground, a half-submerged granite embankment. Straits Steamship ferry steamers can be seen docking near the Prai Railway Station and Prai Harbour at the opposite bank.

▲ 265a

Caption: No. 42. Group of Natives, Penang

Imprint: A. Kaulfuss, Penang.

An interesting group posing in front of a charming spot with a fig tree and a granite terrace, overlooking what must be the Prai River. The Malays wearing conical hats (trendak) are probably boatmen waiting to take passengers across in their ferry boats (sampan penambang). One man wears a head-cloth, while another has a cloth pulled over his head. On the right, the three children with half-shaven heads could be Burmese children working on coastal vessels.

265b ▶

Caption: Penang

Imprint: A. Kaulfuss, Penang. Undivided back.

The postcard has Kaulfuss' name and number (12) handstamped in the left margin and is thus rare.

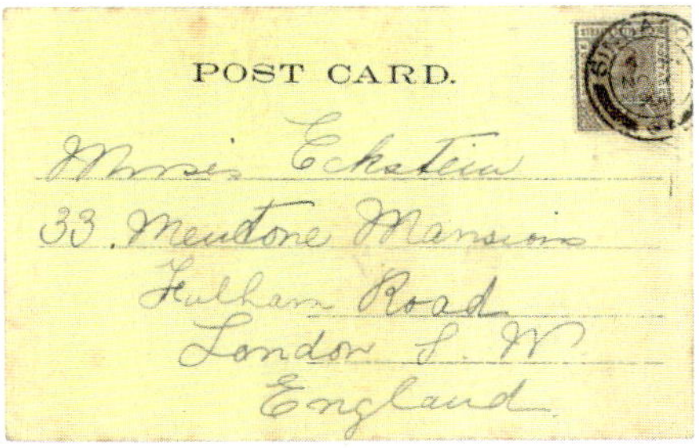

▲ 265b reverse

An undivided back card used November 1900 at the 3c Britain and Empire rate.

266a ▸

Caption: Prai Dock.

Imprint: Printed in Germany.

The Prai Dock consisted of a screw pile wharf, a dry dock for ship repairs and a coal depot.

▴ 266b

Caption: Penang. Prye River Dock. Pritchard & Co., Penang. No. 33

Prai River

The Prai River is an important waterway to the interior of Province Wellesley. In earlier times, elephants were being exported via the Prai River to the Coromandel Coast in South India.

> The Pry River, whose mouth is nearly opposite to the town of Pinang, is accessible to ships of burthen, as there is no bar at its mouth owing to the protection afforded from the swell of the ocean by the island ... its sources are only a few miles inland. It is in fact a mere arm of the sea ... The banks of this river are exceedingly monotonous, the mangrove being everywhere abundant.
>
> *(Earl, 1861: 3)*

The river clay was suitable for making bricks, and in 1836, James Low reported that 'There are brick kilns on the bank of the Pry river, where bricks and tiles are manufactured'. These brick factories were the main suppliers for Penang's building industry until recent times.

(Low, 1836: 230)

266c ▸

Caption: 5149 Prai Wharf, Province Wellesley

The main wharf for ocean-going steamers was 1,100 feet long by 142 feet wide, constructed entirely of reinforced concrete and founded on concrete cylinders sunk to a hard foundation about 40 feet below mud level. The landward side of this wharf was dredged to form a basin for lighters. In addition there was another 1,000 feet of wharf frontage.

267a ▸

Caption: Prye Harbour, Penang

Imprint: S.M. Manicum, Penang. No 103.

The Straits Steamship ferry steamer 'PERAK' waiting to take passengers across the North Channel.

▾ 267b

Caption: Prye River, Penang.

Imprint: S.M. Manicum, Penang.

Railway Ferry Steamers

Travellers from the Federated Malay States heading for George Town had to take a ferry to complete their journey.

> The F.M.S. Railway terminus is at Prai, on the mainland. Passengers detrain and pass under covered approaches to the Railway Ferry Steamers which cross the harbour to the Penang Railway Jetty. Railway tickets issued to and from Penang include the fare on the Ferry Steamers. The time taken by the Railway Ferry Steamers crossing the harbour is about 25 minutes.
>
> *(Thorpe, 1939: 6)*

Prai Wharves

With the development of the railway along the west coast of Malaya, it became advantageous to develop a railway to ship connection at Prai itself. In 1914, the F.M.S. Railway authority took over the Prye River Dock to extend its railway facilities and to construct the deep-water Prai Wharves (1916-23). However, the project proved too ambitious, chalking up a cost of Straits Dollars $18 million. Due to rapid silting at the mouth of the Prai River, the low water depth required could not be maintained by dredging. The Prai Wharf ultimately proved quite unsuitable for ocean-going vessels, and could only serve as a lighterage facility.

(Allen, 1950: 22-23; Fifty Years of Railways in Malaya, 1935: 52-53)

▴ 267c

Caption: Province Wellesley

Part of caption is illegible, but this picture shows the Prai Wharf.

▲ 268

Caption: Railway Station, P.W.

A railway station in Province Wellesley, with a distinguished group gathered here for some occasion. Seen here is the 'G' class Locomotive, a general utility engine introduced by the Perak state railway in 1899.

F.M.S. Railway, Prai

The Prai Railway Station marked the northern terminus of the F.M.S. railway system. The first section of the Prai Railway was from Prai to Bukit Mertajam. The opening of the railway ferry service from Penang and the section of line in Province Wellesley was officiated on 29 June 1899, by Lieutenant-Colonel Sir C.B.H. Mitchell, Governor and High Commissioner. The Governor hoped that the line, when complete, 'may prove a bond of union between the Straits Settlements and the Federated Malay States'. In this connection, Sir Frank Swettenham wrote in *British Malaya*:

> At the time when federation was adopted there were disconnected sections of railway in all the States, and the most important work then in view was to join them up and secure a main line from the Prai River, in Province Wellesley, right through the greatest agricultural and mining districts of Perak, to join the Selangor main line and continue it to Seramban ...
>
> The Malay States made, and paid for, the Province Wellesley Railway, and no benefit so great has ever been conferred on Pinang in the history of that Settlement, but the people of this place were slow to appreciate the fact, and have never been demonstrative in thanks to the Malay States, which also lent them a large sum of money to complete their steamer pier, another public work the advantages of which escaped their foresight.

(Swettenham, 1906: 278, 279-280; Fifty Years of Railways in Malaya: 16, 31-33, 52-53, 79; Wright & Cartwright, 1908: 369)

◂ 269a

Caption: F.M.S. R'way Station Prye, P.W.

Imprint: S.M. Manicum, Penang. No. 7.

This postcard shows a train stopping at the Prai Railway Station built right along the Prai River. The letters 'F.M.S.R.' can be seen written large across the station roof.

The early railway station facility included a passenger pontoon jetty constructed on the river bank for use of the railway passenger ferries, as well as two timber jetties for general merchandise.

▴ 269b

Caption: Prye Rubber Estate.

Imprint: S.M. Manicum, Penang. No. 34.

The Prye Estate was bordered by the Prai River, the Juru River and the sea. Originally a sugar plantation, the estate was replanted with rubber in the early 20th century. The Prai Railway Station was built adjacent to the Prye Estate and the railway line ran through the centre of it. This photo shows young rubber trees along the railway track.

The Prye Estate was earlier owned by Brown, Scott, Vermont and other partners, and then was passed on in 1907 to the Pinang Syndicate Ltd., whose agents were Messrs. Huttenbach Brothers & Co..

(Wright & Cartwright, 1908: 369)

◂ 269c

Caption: Pry Pier. Pry Station. A 48 – Station Building, Penang.

Imprint: Nikko-Studio, Penang, S.S. Printed in Saxony.

A postcard that shows each part of the F.M.S. Railway service in Penang – the 'Station Building' at China Street Ghaut, Penang island, the 'Pry Pier' and the 'Pry Station' in Province Wellesley.

270a

Caption: Malay Junks

Printed in Germany.

An excellent view of river boats with attap cover, carrying sacks of goods down the Krian River.

The pontoon bridge over the Krian River was later replaced by the 'Railway Bridge' as seen in postcards 271a and 271b.

270b

Caption: Malay River Junks, P.W.

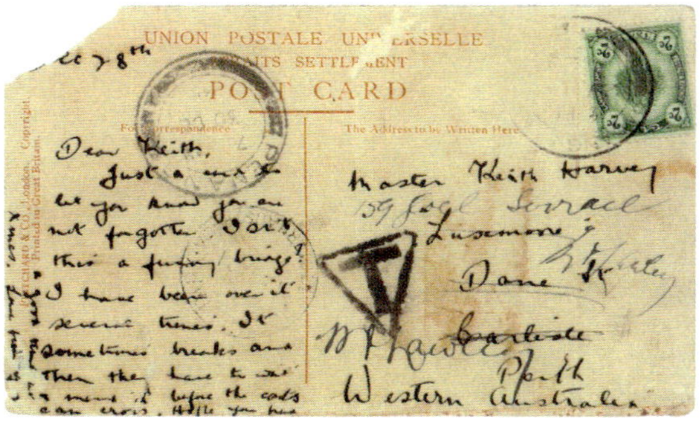

270c reverse

This postcard, though damaged, is an unusual usage from Padang Serai in Kedah in 1920. As it was 2c underpaid, a T (tax) mark unique to this post office was applied (this is one of only two examples recorded). It appears to have been delivered without charge to Australia.

270c

Caption: Pontoon Bridge, Nebong Tebal.

Imprint: Pritchard & Co. London. Copyright. Printed in Great Britain.

The pontoon bridge crossed the Krian River, joining Nibong Tebal in Province Wellesley and Parit Buntar in Perak.

◂ 271a

Caption: Railway Bridge – Nebong Tebal P.W.

Imprint: Co-operative Agency S.S.

▾ 271b

Caption: Railway Bridge Nebong Tebal, P.W.

A slightly different photograph, with only one figure instead of two. The dug-out boat can be seen clearly.

Krian Bridge

The Prai Railway was soon extended to Nibong Tebal, where the Krian Bridge had to be constructed (1898-1900) for it to connect up to Parit Buntar and the Perak Railway. At first the temporary bridge was supported with pontoons or hollow metal cylinders.

> The Krian River at the bridge site is approximately 400 feet in width and the surrounding country only a few feet above high tide level. There was considerable traffic on this river in the late (1890s), and it was in consequence necessary that the bridge should provide sufficient head room for the craft then using the river. … The Krian River bridge was founded on cylinders which had to be sunk through 40 feet of mud before they reached sufficiently reliable strata. … A novel method of erection was employed for the steelwork; a method which today is frequently adopted in tidal rivers. It consisted of erecting the main girders of each span on barges moored to the bank of the river. When all the riveting was complete the girders were floated out into the stream at such a state of the tide that the bearings were a few feet above the level of the tops of the cylinders on which they were finally to rest.

The Krian River crossing was made possible by this engineering feat, and the line to Parit Buntar was opened in 1901.

(Fifty Years of Railways in Malaya, 1935: 60-61)

271c ▸

Caption: Penang. T. N. Shaik Ismail No. 18.

Undivided back. Dated January 12 1904.

Possibly the approach to the pontoon bridge at Nibong Tebal.

272a ▸

Caption: Malay Former Houses, Penang.

Imprint: K.M. Mahmed Esoof, Penang.

A typical scene of farmer's houses in Province Wellesley.

272b ▸

Caption: Malay House, Penang.

Imprint: No. 35.A. Beach Street, Penang.

Padi-Farming

The proportion of Malays is greater in the northern district (of Province Wellesley) than elsewhere, as the nature of the country is peculiarly favourable to the mode of life in which they most delight. Their dwellings are erected on the permatangs or sand-ridges, under the shade of the cocoanut trees with which they are thickly studded, and the bulk of the male population is employed during the intervals of planting and reaping the paddy lands in forming and tending the fishing weirs which extend far out to sea on the bank that lines the shore, and which yield an abundant harvest of excellent fish at all seasons of the year.

(Earl, 1861: 4)

272c ▸

Caption: Paddy Cutting, Penang.

Imprint: K.M. Mahmed Esoof, Penang.

In Penang, paddy was mainly grown in Province Wellesley, but there was also some smaller-scale cultivation in the southern parts of Penang Island.

◂ 273a
Caption: No. 124 Fruit plantation.
Imprint: A. Kaulfuss, Penang.
Two baskets of durians and some mangosteens amidst a harvest of coconuts in a coconut plantation.

▾ 273b
Caption: Coconuts pressing, Penang
A pre-industrial coconut press using bullocks to turn the mill.

Copra

Coconut was one of the earliest cash crops, grown extensively in the estates of Ayer Itam and Province Wellesley and exported to the Burmese and Siamese ports. Coconuts were also prepared for export as copra by sun-drying or kiln-drying the coconut kernels. By the early 20th century, less copra and more oil was exported, as local entrepreneurs had begun to establish oil mills, using European machinery such as hydraulic oil presses to extract coconut oil from the copra.

▴ 273c
Caption: No. 123 Cutting & drying copra.
Imprint: A. Kaulfuss, Penang.

▴ 273d
Caption: Cocoanut plantation, Penang
Imprint: S.M. Manicum, Penang.

Left: **Crossroads** *etching*

Above: **Interior of Pear Tree Cottage 1992** *mixed media*

for her hip replacement so there is little she can do. He is losing weight alarmingly fast.

A few days later neighbours noticed his back door was wide open and nobody was at home. This was unusual. They discussed it among themselves trying to decide what to do about it. They didn't go inside. They shouted through the door but there was no response. They hadn't crossed the doorstep for ten years. They closed the door. His Roberta persona was embarrassing and they have tried to ignore it. They have solidly maintained their Norfolk reserve.

Percy was in hospital. He had been admitted as an emergency. Throat cancer had been diagnosed. He had a major emergency operation but it was too late to remove the tumour. Joan sent stamps, flowers and food. She was desperate to help but was immobile. She telephoned and wrote. He made feeble attempts to reply. For the first time his letters were written on scrappy lined paper and placed in small mean envelopes. Although his handwriting was small and shaky he still managed to address the envelopes in strong letters with a prominent postcode. His years as a postal worker were deeply ingrained.

Above: **Still Life with Lemon** *mixed media*

None of his immediate neighbours came to visit him. He will never return to Pear Tree Cottage which sits empty and sad. Ena visits and Jacquie and David Ralli – a gentleman farmer and his wife who live a few miles away who have always kept a friendly eye on him and given him help when needed. They take him food, writing materials and crayons as does David Hankin a more recent friend who brings in shopping.

On 1st June, having been transferred to a convalescent home at Holt which he hated, he had a big surprise. Joan had telephoned his twin brother John in Workington and given him the news. They joined the army together in 1939 but Percy was quickly transferred to the Royal Signals and their paths had barely crossed since then. Joan had filled him in with the situation and suggested that Percy might like to see him. John told her that Percy's only child Brian might also like to come. This was news to Joan. She was not aware he had a son. He had never referred to his family in all those letters to her. Percy hadn't seen Brian for 27 years and he had never mentioned him. In millions of words he had never made any reference to his only child. Nor had Brian ever made any attempt to see his father. He is not a man of action unlike John who immediately organised the trip bringing Brian and his wife Doreen with him. Brian was the car man and did the driving but he had little sense of direction, nor did he read maps. John avers he would never have even found Norfolk on his own. He had rarely left his own little patch on the Solway coast in West Cumbria. After years, nay a lifetime, of estrangement, Percy was genuinely pleased to see them. He asked Brian, now aged forty seven, if he'd come on the bus still thinking of him as the child he never noticed and on finding out he had an old Jaguar car struggled to the window to look down on it in the car park. For the first time in his life he took an interest in his son. Too late, they had discovered a point of contact.

On the 12th June, he wrote his last letter to Joan and managed to do a few small shaky pencil drawings of birds seen on the window sill of his room. He was still optimistically planning his return to Pear Tree Cottage.

At the end of June he was sent back to a private room in the Norfolk and Norwich hospital where he died in the night on 3rd July 1993 with David Ralli at his bedside.

Above: **Below Naddle Fell** *mixed media*

chapter 2

Shadows Fall Dark

The Rallis organised the funeral at the Norwich Crematorium. These kind busy people who lived nearby had worked tirelessly in the last few months of Percy's life to make him comfortable. They had ferried possessions between Pear Tree and the hospital. They had listened attentively to his requests. He had asked for his ashes to be scattered at Loweswater – his favourite place on earth and he had made it very clear that when the time came he wished to be cremated as Roberta Penelope Kelly.

Everything was arranged according to plan. The coffin decked with simple foxgloves was waiting outside when John and Brian with his wife Doreen turned up at the crematorium. The Rallis had no idea they were coming. They weren't great communicators. Realising that the family had no inkling

of his gender confusion, they quickly decided that a service in the name of someone called Roberta Penelope could be difficult for them. They would soon realise anyway when they got to Pear Tree Cottage but it would be better to explain to them gently afterwards. They quickly changed the name on the vicar's prepared eulogy. There were only two other mourners and they didn't seem to notice. The other request about the scattering of his ashes took years to fulfil and none of us are certain it was ever fulfilled. It will remain a mystery.

After the funeral, the Rallis drove the family to Pear Tree Cottage. It is hard to imagine their thoughts as they approached this tumbledown place. John was thinking sadly of the brother with whom he had grown up but never felt close. Percy was so much cleverer than him and as a child had shaken him off impatiently to wander off alone. John had always looked up to him, admired his extraordinary talent and enjoyed seeing him steal the limelight. He basked in reflected glory. He was shocked at the state of the house but pleased to see all the paintings. He always knew his brother had a remarkable talent.

Left: **Winter Sun** *watercolour and ink*
Above: **Foxgloves** *mixed media*

Above: **Early drawing of Buttermere** *pencil and chalk*

Brian was wondering how much the house was worth. He was not a man of property. He was wondering if he would inherit anything. He hadn't ever really known his father. He was a man devoid of curiosity. He knew nothing about friends, wives, children or step children. He would take his usual stance, the line of least resistance. He would wait and see. Doreen his wife had no idea what was going on. Brian had never talked about his father in the years they had been together. She eyed up the untidy garden. She wandered round the house appalled at the mess and dirt. She suspected that she would be the one sorting this out. She usually did. She was a practical, sensible woman – and observant. She soon realised that there was something strange when she got upstairs. Jacquie Ralli had mentioned in the car that Brian's father liked dressing up which she thought a strange comment but this was more than that. There were wigs and make up strewn around the bedroom; high heeled shoes and dresses; female underwear. She called to Brian and pointed this out to him. He stood impassive in the bedroom door.

'He was my dad.' he said. 'That's who he was – my dad.'

Only one Will was found among the detritus of Pear Tree Cottage and it was invalid. It was not signed or dated and had no official counter signature or witness. The solicitor had helped him draft several Wills but he had kept changing his mind, crossing things out and amending things by hand and was worried about the cost. He didn't like solicitors. Their advice was expensive, they strung things out interminably and they had no patience with him. The solicitor had urged him to finalise it; get it signed and witnessed but, like hundreds of other things, he had failed to do so.

This unofficial will left seventy five percent of the estate to his son Brian and divided the rest between his brother John, The Salvation Army and his eldest step daughter Kim. Brian showed no reaction as the solicitor carefully explained that the will was not valid in law and Brian, as the legal heir could do as he wished. He could inherit it all or fulfil his father's wishes. Brian had great difficulty expressing himself, making decisions and particularly giving anything away. It was never clear whether he had understood what was being said. He just kept quiet. He always worked by the maxim

Above: **Cumbrian Cottage** *watercolour and ink*
Right: **Bridge at Allonby** *mixed media*

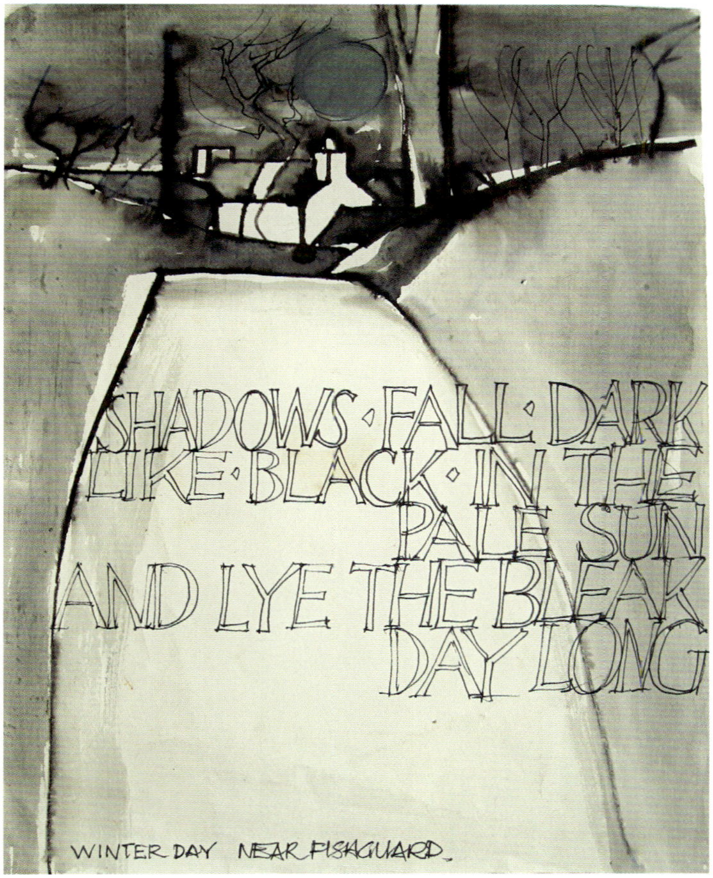

If in doubt do nowt and say nowt and that is exactly what he did. He said nowt.

He was glad to inherit his father's **estate** because to him that meant property and he knew that property carried value. He didn't understand then that the house would take years to sell because it was in such a bad condition. He failed to realise that his biggest value in the inheritance was the art work. To him it was jumbled heaps of paper. That wasn't an estate it was all rubbish which had to be cleared before he could sell the cottage. To be fair most other people walking into that place would think exactly the same thing.

Above: **Shadows Fall Dark** *watercolour and ink*

chapter 3

Educating Percy

3rd November 1918

Martha Kelly was exhausted. It had been a long and difficult labour despite being her fourth and she now slept. When she woke, she peered over the side of the bed into the drawer on the floor and looked anxiously at the two tiny forms lying swaddled side by side. Twins! She wondered how they were going to manage. They had three children already, a boy Hugh named after her father, next Muriel and then Sally, a quiet morose child. She was unprepared for twins. The terrace house, 113 Corporation Road Workington had just three small bedrooms, a lean-to kitchen and a shared privy across the yard. The house belonged to her father, Hugh Grey. She and Oscar had lived with him since their marriage ten years ago – and now there were eight of them in the house. It was November 1918, the end of a debilitating war and this industrial town on the west coast of Cumberland was depressed and depressing. It depended on heavy industry; iron and steel and coal mining. The people worked hard and were poor. Her eye lit on the tract on the bedroom wall; *God is love*. She smiled weakly. It must be god's will. The twins must have been sent for a reason. He would see them through. She looked down on them sleeping peacefully and wondered what they would make of their lives. Would they have an easier life than she and her husband Oscar. She hoped so.

It was a good thing that she didn't know then that there would be two more babies after the twins; Douglas six years later and Kenneth two years after that. In the present circumstances and in a future with no prospects, a family this size was not uncommon but unsustainable. She had years of gruelling hard work in front of her with no relief, no help, no labour saving machines; just grinding poverty.

If she had a crystal ball she would have been surprised to learn that one of these tiny sleeping scraps was going to dine with royalty, converse with a Prime Minister and be befriended by influential people in Government and industry. He would have a life of success and depression and die in poverty and loneliness.

The father, Oscar Kelly, was a Manxman, a carpenter and Martha was a Scot, a handsome young woman with compelling cornflower blue eyes her daughter in law remembers. They were married in September 1908 at the Methodist church in Cockermouth. They were practising Plymouth Brethren and Primitive Methodist – both austere religions. In those hard times when people had nothing, they either turned

Top left: **Martha Kelly**
Left: **The twins, Robert Percy and John Arthur**
Above: **Dockside** *etching*

to god or alcohol for comfort. God cost nothing and gave a promise of a better life hereafter so was the option they chose. Her father was even more religious following the strict Plymouth Brethren evangelical creed. He was a steel worker who read only the Bible and the Daily Herald. He hated Roman Catholics and Trade Unions, smoking, alcohol and all other newspapers.

They christened the twins Robert Percy and John Arthur. Percy was not a common name at that time but it had aristocratic overtones. A search through relatives' names yields nothing so there is no clue as to why such an improbable name was chosen for him. The other children were given ordinary names which did not stand out. Percy, as he was known, was the first born and the dominant twin. John was a good natured quiet follower.

Even in those early days, Martha realised there was something very different about Percy. He was bright and alert and learned to hold a pencil before he could walk. By the time he was two he was drawing things; the teapot, a jug and other objects his brother remembers. He never drew like a child - the drawings were mature from the start. There is a strong possibility that he was autistic but that was not a recognised condition then. His mother was astounded and treated him differently from the others. She knew he was special in a different way from that all mothers feel. She watched him develop quite differently from the rest. His father was puzzled. There was no-one else in the family like this. There were no pictures on the walls of the house – only religious tracts. There were no books. These were luxuries never even contemplated. Their life evolved around work and chapel.

Many artists have some connecting link with an artistic parent or relative. I had none and this was a source of puzzlement to my father Percy wrote in a later memoir.

'I was fortunate to be born with a love of nature and to be brought up in a home where the Christian faith was paramount. Any pictures on the walls were religious tracts' Percy wrote later in life comparing this with his present home. ***'How different today for where I sit there is all around me a multitude of images painted and printed – engines, boats, churches, villages, flowers, fruit and lettering. A clutter of much loved objects; my mind embraces a whole world of love and beauty.***

When Percy and John were five, Martha was pregnant again with Douglas so they had a lot of freedom to roam, something denied to children these days. Workington Docks were a very short distance from their house. Percy would wander off alone and spend hours observing and drawing ships and cranes. There were never any questions asked about where he had been. Although he was a twin, he was a loner, preferring his own company to the hullabaloo of a big family. His twin recalls with pride that he would often return with marvellous drawings. ***I suppose most of my work is derived from childhood obsessions*** Percy wrote in a diary. ***I love boats and have vivid memories of countless days spent by the harbour at Workington watching the steam cranes unloading tramp steamers with chipped black hulls, raw sienna painted superstructure, red oxide decks and long tall smokestacks of innumerable colours.***

I have always loved birds, butterflies, flowers and bees. What a world it was between the shore, hills and the slagbanks - butterflies of all shapes and colours flitted about on lazy summer days.

Every child is able to draw in their early years. They enjoy colour and work without inhibitions or preconceived ideas. Parents are proud and admire the infant scribblings then at about the age of eleven they lose that freshness of approach, become inhibited and give up or try to portray things as they think the world wants them to be portrayed. Percy was not like this. Long before going to school he was making drawings in an adult and academic manner. It was obvious to anyone whoever they were that this was an exceptional child; a prodigy, a genius. His brothers were in awe of such a gift. His younger brother Douglas remembers that while the others breakfasted on bread, Percy would often have a half grapefruit and coffee. His mother often went hungry to give Percy the best. They all had second hand clothes but Percy was dressed better than they were. This was not said with any envy. He emphasised that none of them were jealous – they were proud that they had a brother who was different and special.

Maybe it was this that set the seeds of narcissism in Percy that developed in his adult life. He knew he had an exceptional talent and felt he merited this special treatment. He was made to feel superior to the rest of his family. He craved admiration and recognition and he got it. In a middle class family his obvious talent would have been encouraged and nurtured but not worshipped. In a family who had never seen genius he was treated with reverence; he was their hope for better things. He always in any subsequent stories and escapades, saw himself as the hero, the saviour, the centre of attention.

His first school, Victoria Road, was just a few streets away round the corner of Corporation Road, so he and John toddled off there together when they reached the age of five. John recalls that their head teacher Mr Allison was a kindly man with a long grey beard but he quietly talks himself down. Percy was the clever one. John was glad to stay in the background and see his brother grab the attention time and time again.

Percy wrote in his memoir ***I loved Mr Allison for he was kind and encouraging. He even called at my home and spoke about my artistic powers to mother and father.***

Mr Allison called to see his father again as Percy approached the landmark age of eleven. Percy had won a national handwriting competition

Far left: **Bridge at Workington** *watercolour and ink*
Left: **Workington harbour** *watercolour and ink*
Above: **Red Sail** *watercolour and ink*

and brought rare honour to the school and Mr Allison thought he was definitely Grammar School material and should have the chance to go. He had been coaching him and setting him to work apart from his classmates. He suggested the idea to Oscar. It would be Percy's big chance and he knew he could handle it and benefit. His father, who was earning £2 a week at the time which didn't go far with seven children, reluctantly said it was out of the question.

There was little privacy and no luxuries whatsoever in the Kelly family's lives. In 1927 when Percy was eight, grandfather Hugh died and they moved to a council house at Salterbeck about a mile away from Corporation Road. Although this is now a huge urban sprawling estate, it was surrounded by open country then. The sea was in view, still not far away. Another harbour, Harrington, was close by so there was plenty to interest him within walking distance. The Oval where they lived was on the edge of a cricket field. Percy had excellent coordination of hand and eye and excelled in all kind of sport so this was an added bonus apart from his being able to wander alone for hours.

Their Uncle Walter, Oscar's brother, had a farm – Larkhill at Abbeylands on the Isle of Man – and the family would enjoy the occasional luxury of a holiday over there. They all loved the change and freedom they had there. In a letter to Sami* he proudly recalls ***My great great grandfather was a lengthsman in the Isle of Man long before tarmac was invented. His length of road was two miles and was believed to be the best on the island. I seem to have inherited his talent for placing stones perfectly. This has crept into my work because I am conscious of placing objects, be it boats or houses in a precise manner in what I imagine to be the perfect spot.***

Percy and John went on to the Central School for Boys; a newly built school in the town. Of course Percy excelled there as well. We have his school reports 1930 – 1931 and in each he came first in both Art and Handicrafts every time. He was a good all rounder because in a class of forty he came seventh twice and eighth once . In those three years he was only recorded with two days absence and never once late. He was captain of the football and cricket teams and the favourite of his art teacher Mr Cobb who was delighted to have such a talented pupil. He had never seen talent such as this before. Mr Cobb also went to see his father to plead the case for Art School. Percy ruefully wrote in his memoir that his father said he was not interested, making the excuse that it would be giving preferential treatment over his brothers and sisters. This was obviously a face saver because Percy had been treated differently all along. The truth was that they needed another income. The three older siblings had left school at fourteen and Hugh the eldest was now contributing to the family finances. The two girls were probably in service or helping Martha with the smaller children. Percy commented on the decision; ***odd reasoning but there it was. I never felt any animosity over his decision.*** After the talk with Mr Cobb, his father sent him to a local artist Albert Rosser for watercolour lessons but there was only one lesson because Percy found the stylised form of the exercises he was given left him uneasy – his words. So his father recognised the talent but the family needed the extra wage to survive.

The Salterbeck days were good for Percy. He began to explore further afield. He could disappear for a whole day and nobody would worry.

The River Salter is a very small stream which flows into Harrington harbour. At the end of the garden was a hayfield and unrestricted views south west to Whitehaven. It was a new and

Far left: **Deep Snow, West Cumberland** *watercolour and ink*
Left: **Whitehaven harbour** *mixed media*
Above: **Keeping chickens, Workington** *charcoal*

wonderful world to an enthusiastic boy with an insatiable curiosity. It is hard to realise that five years later I did my first townscape drawing from the cricket field with Harrington stretched out below.

He was thirteen then. Other townscapes followed some years later when he could travel further; Whitehaven, Maryport, Parton and Kendal. These were made on rolls of wallpaper lining paper fifty inches by twenty seven inches – monumental and beautiful pieces of work.

It was then that he discovered the Lake District whose western boundary was about eight miles away. He recalled to Joan.

The nearest lake to my home town is Loweswater. I walked the road only once before my tenth birthday but walked the road to Ullock many times. On the outward journey I kept to the road but on the return I always took to the fields cutting corners as it was easier on ones feet. This proved useful on poaching expeditions. This is when I met my first trip wire. The gamekeepers were a sly lot. One of my friends got peppered with buckshot and when we were in the clear I tried to poke it out of his backside with a penknife. I always stuffed newspaper down my trousers. I was once chased from Branthwaite to my home at Salterbeck. I sneaked into the bathroom as the policeman knocked at the door. My dear old father answered and he covered for me. Imagine all that bother over a few pheasant eggs. The police were awful during the depression. In the streets men could not stop and talk in a group.

As a matter of interest there was a Meeting House (Plymouth Brethren) to the left of the Harrington church. It was demolished some time ago. I often wonder if the depressive part of me is not due to the influence of that building I attended classes three times a week during my early years and even as a child I found it all so miserable. Whenever I could I escaped to the fields and woods. This was my private world of flowers, birds, bees, streams, butterflies, trees. Corporation Road where I was born is a horrible depressive place still and my father still lives in the house on a housing estate where I lived most of my life on and off until I was 28. Whenever I go to see him depression seeps into my very bones... this is not good. No wonder I depict deserted villages and towns and sad dead weeds. You reach out and holding my hand you take me back to the sunlit woods, bird song, the sound of bees, a world of myriads of exquisite butterflies and nodding flowers.

So at the age of fourteen Percy sat an entrance examination to join the postal service. There was much competition in 1932 for any job at all – unemployment was endemic in the area. He came out top in both the entrance and handwriting examination and he was appointed Telegraph boy messenger first in Workington and subsequently in Kendal to work on the counter and sorting office.

I don't know how I did it but I managed to pass the clerical exams with a very high mark he wrote to Rosanna* many years later *so I became a clerical officer and began a six month training course. Oddly enough from fourteen and earlier I was always drawing and painting and this gave me hope and something to lean on. I spent the last two months of my training in Liverpool one of a class of six. Another boy from Workington myself and four delightful girls. This boy Jock eventually became a customs officer and died of TB in 1965. He shared digs with me and when we all got to know each other we became inseparable. That summer the Wirral was wonderful. I fell in love with my favourite girl Barbara – walks, swimming, supper all together in the girls' digs. What fun we had. People, especially historians, run down the Thirties but to me it was a wonderful time. When we could Barbara and I would sneak off alone if the weather was warm and sunbathe in the nude. Her kisses were wonderful but the thought of making love physically never entered my head – probably due to my strict religious upbringing. Had this been the Sixties I am sure we would have married. Unfortunately my wage*

was ridiculously low and it meant waiting until the age of twenty eight for sufficient wages to support two – and the practice was for long engagements.

Not long after this my parents forced me to return to Workington. I was so happy in Kendal. I was a member of the cycling club and Fred Hodgson an amateur artist and I were inseparable. I cycled weekends and raced during the season. At eighteen I was reported in the National papers because of a fantastic ride I did. An old time trialist took me under his wing and quite a future was predicted.

When he was transferred to Workington he still kept in touch with Fred* and his Kendal interests by cycling the fifty miles between them in his time off. Kendal was a prosperous town with no unemployment. Workington was a different scene. He had learned a lot in Kendal and now applied it to the industrial landscape he loved so much. Mr Gilespie, Head Postmaster, like everybody else who ever dealt with Percy, soon became aware of his exceptional talent. He was so impressed by the neatness of his ledgers that he circulated them to the rest of the staff as an example of how things should be done. He was interested in painting and would summon Percy to his office and talk for hours. This hardly endeared him to his colleagues. For the first time in his life Percy experienced jealousy and resentment.

16th March 1995

Dear Mrs David

Many thanks for your letter and of course the enclosures re my late friend and colleague Percy.

I first met him when he took over my post as Boy Messenger in the Post Office at Workington. There were three such posts and two of us had just been appointed as Sorting Clerk and Telegraphist. Percy lived in the same area of town and came from the same school. Other than that we were unaware of each others' existence.

He first came to my notice after the war (WWII) when the office boasted a football team.(PO Regional games only). He was a stalwart playing as the mainstay at centre half (unknown today) obviously far better than the rest of us. Later he organised walks into the area around Keswick and Buttermere and it says much for his enthusiasm

Left: **Percy Kelly,** *Easter 1938*

Above: **Telegraph boys,** *1932 Workington, Percy Kelly on left*

that Post Office folks, and that included some postmen, joined him for walks. About forty of us would go by coach to some point then hike over the fells stopping say at a farm house for a real home made tea then be picked up by the coach again. It was a Sunday treat still remembered by my two boys now fifty two and forty seven.

Another of his sporting activities was cycling, road racing etc. On one occasion he took me for a spin on a tandem which is not the ideal method of transport in the Lake District. I was used to getting off the machine at an early stage of a hill but not dear old Percy. He would continue even if I stopped pedalling on the back.

Although all who knew him were aware in his interest and indeed his prowess as an artist, his desire to paint or draw rather than do wages etc; his disenchantment with work, was considered to be due more to his lack of interest in clerical work rather than his calling as an artist.

Of course I knew him during his spell at Great Broughton Sub Post Office. Even then I recall he had an easel set up behind the counter the customers being merely a form of interruption. Later he and his family moved to Glen Cottage Allonby which gave him the opportunity to devote more time to his painting. His wife Audrey working at Dovenby seemed to keep things going.

As pals we knew nothing of his domestic life and, although my wife and I called to see him quite frequently he always sent us a home made Christmas card of some particular view dear to him and he continued to send until after I was made Head Postmaster at Sudbury Suffolk in 1959.

One of the most sad moments of my life was when I heard that he had died and that for at least ten years he had lived within a stone's throw of our home. How dearly we would both have tried to see him but I suppose that is life.

I am sorry I have no greater details for you but grand memories.

Yours sincerely

Stan Wilson.

* *Sami was the nickname of Jane who lived next door to Joan David in Kendal. When she fell seriously ill in 1983 Joan mentioned it to PK and he began to write to her.*

* *A friend he met in his first term at Carlisle College of Art.*

* *Rosanna was a young woman Percy met in his first term at Carlisle College of Art.*

Left: **Christmas card** *mixed media*

Above: **Bridge at Allonby** *etching*

Above: **Dereham Village,** *1950s mixed media*

chapter 4

The Still Sad Music of Humanity

September 1939.

This was a day any mother would dread. Martha Kelly was standing on the doorstep of their house in Salterbeck waving her twin sons off trying hard not to let them see her cry. Her favourite, talented, handsome son Percy who had been transferred from the Post Office to the Ministry of Works had done so well. Her son John, equally tall, but quietly shy was with him. John who was training to be a plumber and plasterer was kind and solidly loyal and described the scene that day. They were walking to the station and out of her life possibly. Once again she wondered what lay ahead. If only they had gone to work in the steel works nearby they wouldn't have been conscripted. They were excited about the adventure ahead. Her two boys had been born at the end of the first war but she remembered the carnage. Would she ever see either of them again? Tears were now rolling down her cheeks from her big blue eyes as the figures receded with a final turn and wave. She had desperately wanted to go to the station with them and wave them off but they had protested and said their goodbyes privately at home. She turned and went back into the house heartbroken.

John described how they travelled together to Belle Vue, Manchester where, along with hundreds of other young men they were allocated their future. They were excited by it all. John was posted to the Royal Artillery in Liverpool and Percy was sent to the Border Regiment in Kendal. To them it was the beginning of a great adventure. They wished each other luck, shook hands and parted. It was at this point that Percy wrote in his memoir that the reality of the situation dawned and he remembered the odds of surviving in the Royal Artillery in the last war and feared for his brother.

He recorded that in February 1940 after the initial training he was compulsorily transferred to the Royal Signals in Derby. His ability to draw had been discovered. How could it not be? He was drawing all the time. He was asked to make exploded drawings of weapons on the blackboard. He made maps and diagrams. He also wrote letters for fellow soldiers who were unable to write or express themselves. This continued for the next six years wherever he was and whatever he was doing. Once again he was lucky. One of his officers called Hazard owned a Rolls Royce which Percy took great pleasure in drawing. All his life he loved cars. Hazard saw this drawing and was impressed. He was an old Reptonian, a public school near Derby, and he took Kelly there, met his old headmaster who was naturally also impressed by Percy and introduced him to the art master, Arthur Norris, who eagerly cleared a space in the art room for him to use in any spare time he had. Percy describes him as being rather like Mr Chips. He would call at his billet in a Morris saloon and drive him to the school. And he would often end up in his study with tea and toasted crumpets. This is unbelievable – but it happened. Percy had the ability to impress, to charm and to communicate with anybody. They perceived his genius and admired it.

This happy interlude as he refers to it came to an end when he was transferred to GHQ Home forces in London. Fire bombs were falling on

Above: **Brown farm** *charcoal*

London. The Germans had walked into France and had then targeted Britain by trying to wipe out our air power. They had failed and decided in revenge to try a new tactic – demoralisation. They would systematically bomb civilians in the capital - and so began the Blitz.

Under Whitehall, in a small room next to the Cabinet War Rooms, a soldier in Khaki uniform was sitting on his small camp bed with a drawing board on his knee. The only other furniture in the room was a simple wooden table. The soldier, Private Percy Kelly, was laboriously drawing a teleprinter - an encrypter and typewriter - a precursor of the fax machine which stood on the table. It was an intricate drawing because the machine was complicated. This was no problem to Private Kelly, he loved the challenge. He was a born draughtsman. He was concentrating so hard that he was unaware of a portly figure in a dark plum velvet siren suit standing in the doorway watching him.

'That's very good,' said the man in a rich deep voice,' Where did you learn to draw like that?'

The soldier started and turned. He dropped his pencil and stood up and saluted. Winston Churchill motioned to him to sit down again and joined him on the bed. They spent several hours talking about art and drawing while the air raid continued faintly rumbling above them. When the raid finished at four in the morning, Churchill left.

Letter to Joan David November 1992

In the war in Whitehall, I used a small room to sleep in which was right at the end of the underground complex and next door to Mr Churchill's room – incidentally where he made some historic speeches. I met him when he came to my room during a heavy bombing raid to see if I was OK. I was doing a detailed sketch of a teleprinter carriage at the time he knocked and entered. It was typical of me to be quite unconcerned and to carry on drawing but when I saw who it was I stood up and said 'Good evening sir.'

They had very little in common apart from painting and a liking for cigars but that was enough because art was the major interest in both their lives. They forgot the war for a few short hours and talked about art. Kelly believed that drawing chased away fear. Churchill has been quoted as saying ***When I get to heaven I intend to spend a considerable portion of the first million years in painting. ... Whatever the worries of the hour or the threats of the future, once the picture has begun to flow along they pass out into shadow and darkness. Just to paint is great fun. The colours are lovely to look at and delicious to squeeze out.***

This was the first of several visits when the Prime Minister couldn't get back to Downing Street because of bad air raids above ground and Kelly couldn't get back to headquarters at Kew so would use the temporary camp bed provided for such situations. Churchill encouraged Kelly to visit the National Gallery which was just up the road in Trafalgar Square. Although many of the treasures had been evacuated to the safety of a redundant Welsh slate mine, there were still good things to look at. Percy

had never been to an art gallery before and found a world of stimulation and excitement there. He saw paintings by Constable and Gainsborough, French Impressionists and Italian Renaissance painters. More importantly Sir Kenneth Clarke who had been appointed to nurture the arts in this time of war laid on a series of events and exhibitions in the National Gallery which people flocked to see and enjoy in the dark days. Percy recorded seeing an exhibition of Sutherland's early Pembrokeshire landscapes. He saw Stanley Spencer's large paintings of Glasgow Docks and Henry Moore's underground shelter drawings made on site. These all made an impact on his fresh mind. He had no idea who these artists were but he made it his business to find out more.

Years later in a letter to Sir David Eccles with a margin of brilliant red poppies in a milk bottle he wrote;

I collected these poppies on a visit to the local waste tip a reminder that in the most unlikely places beauty can be found. Bright red when picked they fade like tinted tissue paper exposed to strong sunlight. During poppy season I am reminded of Mondrian and his single red flower in a white room. And I remember a Turner in Edinburgh, a seascape, a boat with the most exquisite red sail. From afar the colour floated delicately over the surface and drew me towards it like a magnet. During the war years in London I saw a Constable and a Renoir; they stunned me by the sheer beauty of the paint. Made life very difficult. In recent years two painters who affected me deeply were Degas and old Wallis – especially the latter.

Churchill arranged for his standard army camp bed to be replaced by a better one which arrived the day after that first meeting. Churchill also encouraged him to submit three watercolours to an exhibition of servicemen's work in the National Gallery. All three were accepted and he was given a day's leave to attend the Private View where he met King George VI. As a mere private, he was already making friends way above his station. His letters back to his family must have caused a great deal of pride. None of them had ever been to London which was impressive enough but to have a member of the family shake hands with the King and talk with the Prime Minister was unbelievable. They were overawed and proud.

Far left: **Farmstead** *watercolour and ink*
Left: **Army football team** *Percy Kelly far left front row*
Above: **Letter to David Eccles** *watercolour and ink*

Kelly couldn't conceive of a day in which he didn't draw or paint. Several of his small sketchbooks have survived with drawings of soldiers and aircraft as well as places which plot his movements during those six years; Salisbury Cathedral, Durham Cathedral, Edgware, Virginia Water, Wentworth. Figures and portraits, well drawn, are prominent in many of these sketches but many drawings were sent home to his Workington fiancée, Audrey James, and carelessly destroyed. But life was not all drawing and painting; during the London period he played quite a lot of cricket and also played football for the Army Eleven against Derby County.

It all ended with a move to Wentworth with a small detachment of signals where he stayed for a year on light duties. He had a measure of independence and managed to fit in a lot of time for painting. It was here that he met Lord and Lady Webb. Laura Webb was an amateur painter and collector. She saw him drawing one day near the golf course and, seeing the quality of his work, invited him to their home, Windlesham Cottage, for tea. She and her husband, Lord Webb became his lifelong friends. When he moved on to Oxford, Thetford and Bath, he still kept on painting but more covertly. He was disciplined for it several times and even arrested outside Admiralty Headquarters until he was given a war office permit to draw and paint.

Doing secret exercises along the River Severn based at Bradford on Avon he wrote to Lord Eccles in a later letter. ***I was drawing in Bath sketching the cathedral sitting on a pile of sandbags by the wall of a building which turned out to be the Navy Headquarters.*** He was surprised when the Military Police came hurtling up and arrested him on suspicion of spying. His CO eventually explained and bailed him out. To save further embarrassment the CO asked the War Office for a pass allowing him to draw. This was issued but he was not allowed to use a camera. He didn't want to! The word went round and he was then treated with enormous respect and his talent was utilised when he got to France.

He seems to have done quite well despite the fact that he deplored the army discipline. He was not army material. He was a loner and non conformist and didn't want to follow instructions which seemed pointless to him and this got him into trouble with his superiors and with his peers. He had no problem with the physical challenges – he was very fit and well coordinated so he enjoyed the drills and 'square bashing'. He was highly competitive and allegedly broke the army record on an assault course near Aldershot. But he was arrested when he designed a poster with a large pair of scissors cutting through a piece of red tape. Someone pinned it to the noticeboard at GCHQ and he was arrested. The creator of a drawing as good as that was easily identified.

He wrote in his diary; ***There were times when I was ordered by contemptible officers to pack up my books and paints and send them home. But I always found a way out. My favourite hiding place was a spare red cross box.***

He was in trouble several more times for indiscipline. He had this self centred belief that he was always right. Probably this had been inculcated by the admiration he had enjoyed up to that point; always being treated as special particularly by his mother. He was put into solitary confinement and sent to Coventry. This is probably why he remained a corporal. He was again unpopular with his own ranks. He must have been annoying and irritating to live with – boasting, insensitive and opinionated. They sent him to Coventry and one signalman whom Percy describes as weird tried to shoot him. On another occasion a private came into his twelve bed dormitory and tried to bayonet him but missed and went through the blanket.

I entered the service a wonderful happy virile person continuously full of fun. I kept letters from cycling friends who, if I missed an outing would write telling me of the void because of my absence, Days were full of laughter and it was infectious. The first year of army life was happy enough but my colleagues soon deteriorated. This is inevitable when working and sleeping together day after day. I neither swore nor drank, smoked a pipe a little and my character was such, being introspective, a perfect target for slings and arrows. I suppose I was fortunate in that I made friends with one or two titled folk and high

Left: **Percy Kelly,** *1943*
Above: **Winter Fells** *lithograph*

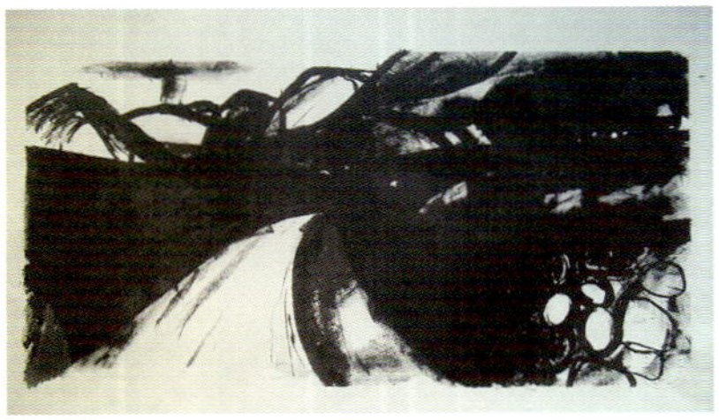

ranking officers – this saved me from total extinction. I was victimised so often that on three occasions I had to see my commanding officer – in each case the officer concerned was 'deported'. Then there was the awful time when they stripped me and slung me in a cell. I became a nervous wreck.

When I resumed civilian life it was hard to fit into office routine.

He sailed for France in 1944 where his drawing ability became even more sought after. With the Germans in occupation security was tight. Maps and Road signs had been removed from the roads. No cameras were allowed. He was loaned out to other units to make detailed maps and drawings.

This was a nice experience he continued ***because when I arrived at a unit that wanted a particular place sketched I was treated with enormous respect. I was made to feel comfortable and I felt like royalty.***

I think I was the only one to be excited when the French coast came into view. The fields and woods looked beautiful in the sunlight, even the sight of bursting shells sending the brown earth upwards had a certain beauty. In the 2 years that followed I did a mass of work. I was loaned out to various units to do drawings of road accidents. I painted insignia on trucks and draughted (sic) railway layouts.

He was involved in the D Day landings. He described this to Lord Eccles in another reminiscing letter.

On D Day or thereabouts I found myself on a Manx boat bound for the Normandy beaches. The section disembarked without incident but all ill-tempered and edgy. I found solace in the excitement of seeing a new landscape. As soon as the British and Canadian troops landed .... we were sent to set up a signal office on the main railway station. We were bogged down by heavy shelling but when it was clear I went off to sketch principally ruined churches which I found fascinating. I stayed in a chateau and made drawings of telegraph and railway layouts. There was a hut with a teleprinter near the station and a twenty line switchboard.

When the section moved on he was sent to Neumagen in Holland and then down the Rhine to Germany. He records that he did very little painting in Germany because as soon as he crossed the border there was an 'aura' that prevented him and remained with him until he was back in England. He was very patriotic. There was no way he could even draw in that country. He was too stressed.

Even though I was very much in love with Audrey during the war I had a very bad time. I remember I became so downcast I refused to look at myself in the mirror. After I was twenty one I worried about growing old and became a bundle of nerves. Although I was a civil servant I always painted and sketched when I could so I always had a dread of losing my hands. Firing guns, doing manual work made my hands shake.

He ended up working with a soldier called Bill Hutton in Munster. He was better with a one to one partnership. Maybe the army recognised this and gave him these postings away from ridicule where he could use his individual talents. The town and station there were devastated and the two of them lived underground for three months. This must have been like the cabinet war rooms. It was from this bunker that they heard Churchill's VE day speech. The war was over.

He was repatriated and demobbed in 1946. His release certificate said;

Corporal Kelly is an asset to both his section and the company ..... His chief hobby is art on which he spends practically the whole of his spare time.... Truthful, sober and clean, he can be thoroughly relied on.

Above: **To the Fells** *lithograph*

Right: **There is hope in honest error** *watercolour and ink*

THERE · IS · HOPE
IN · HONEST · ERROR
NONE · IN · THE
ICY · PERFECTIONS
OF · THE · MERE
STYLIST
CHAS · R · MACKINTOSH · GLASGOW 1901

chapter 5

The Obscure Fells and Silent Tarn

Today a piece of charcoal or chalk is like an extension of my forefinger. Drawing is as natural as walking.

1942 St John's Church Workington

Audrey James and Percy Kelly made a handsome couple as they emerged from the church as Mr and Mrs Kelly. Percy in army uniform was on leave from the Royal Signals. They had been courting for some time since before the war. Percy was a good footballer playing for the local team before he joined up in the army and Audrey had her eye on him. The arrangement was that if Workington FC won the match the following Saturday, they would go out together. It is bizarre that their future lives were decided on the results of a football match. The team won and they went on a date. If the team had lost, Percy's life would have followed an entirely different course and Audrey's life would probably have been happier. Her mother Ada took an immediate dislike to Percy and tried to discourage her daughter seeing him but she took no notice of her and carried on 'walking out' with him as it was so quaintly put in those days. Ada felt he and his family were beneath them. There were many layers of status even within the working classes. Audrey's father John worked in the steel works. The James lived in Frostroms Road which Audrey's mother considered a cut above a council house at Salterbeck. The family had always owned cars. Audrey proudly says her father had the first car in Workington and she passed her driving test aged sixteen in a Hillman Minx. In pre-war Britain the car was the ultimate status symbol.

The Kelly's had no hope of ever owning a car. When Audrey left school she did what so many girls did at the time, a typing and shorthand course to fill the gap between school, marriage and babies. When Percy proposed marriage, Ada opposed it so vehemently that his father Oscar, a normally mild quiet man, went round to her house and confronted her with her prejudices. A big row ensued. She obdurately refused to attend the wedding and after they were married Audrey moved into the Kelly family home at Salterbeck. Her mother would not tolerate Percy in her house even on leave.

Just before the war started I was twenty and I got marching orders from Audrey's mother. To Audrey's credit she went with me ignoring her mother's plea to exclude her from her will. So she gave up hundreds of pounds, got a job in Kendal and I moved compulsorily to train in the Border Regiment for some months before moving to more distant parts. After training I left and Audrey was ultimately

Above: **Audrey and Percy's wedding day**
Left: **Audrey** *1939*

Above: **Letter to Joan 28th March 1984 illustrating Glen Cottage, Allonby** *watercolour and ink*

conscripted herself. My love waned in spite of writing most days. I could not understand life. I painted a great deal and scribbled poetry and prose.

Audrey was conscripted to the ATS which she did not enjoy at all. She was always a smart fashionable woman and the scratchy uniform displeased her. She hated Khaki which didn't suit her complexion. After training she was deployed as a secretary at the Coal Board much to her disgust – she had fancied a driving job – she could see herself driving a colonel (no less) round London in a big car.

The war over, Audrey now replaced Percy's mother as the most influential woman in his life. She was attractive and stylish – she was the first young woman in Workington to sport the 'New Look' – a reaction to the austerity of the war years. She had no appreciation of the arts.

Percy had a way with words. How his vocabulary developed isn't clear but he quoted and used the language of poetry and boy's books of the time using words like chump, super, horrid. chums and jolly good - not terms found in common usage in the back streets of Workington. There is no evidence of extensive reading. His habit of writing descriptive letters began during the war when he was far away from home. He wrote almost daily to Audrey telling her everything he could that wasn't censored including little drawings and love tokens. These letters continued even more intensively after they were married until 1946 when he returned home. They would have made excellent reference material because Percy could describe things so graphically but Audrey kept them in a hat box and her mother burnt it in a fit of pique - however, if she hadn't Audrey most certainly would have done at a later date.

Their relationship was shaky from the start. They both had enormous egos, they both craved attention. It was a marriage of competitiveness in which each felt superior to the other. While her husband was fighting for his country Audrey felt proud. He was tall and athletic with broad shoulders and light wavy hair. He looked so good when he came home on leave in his uniform. Once he was back in civilian life however, Audrey wanted Percy to 'make something of himself' and couldn't see any future in his constant drawing. She felt it should be his hobby. She was ambitious for him - she wanted him to earn a decent living, have a family and go on outings with her. She wanted them to enjoy a 'normal' weekend like other people – shop together and entertain. When he was demobbed from the army he applied for teacher training. This would give them status. There was a shortage of teachers post war and an emergency training course was set up by the government but Percy was already trained in the Royal Mail who also needed skilled people so he was cursorily ordered to resume his civilian duties and return to his old job. There was a shortage of staff in the Post Office. He was trained and fit. He was put on the Region Acting list and was sent on periods of supervisory duties. After his freedom in the army this was onerous. He was working long hours with no time to draw or paint and these things were essential for his mental and physical well being.

He went through bouts of deep depression. Drawing was a compulsion. If he couldn't draw or paint because of work commitments he became very unsettled and sad. Audrey was affronted by his need to go off on his own to paint. She felt his future was in the Post Office. One of his attractions

Top left: **Early painting** *watercolour and ink*
Left: **Bridge, white cottage, Skiddaw, Allonby, Cumberland** *watercolour and ink*
Above: **Glen Cottage letter** *watercolour and ink*

for her had always been his white collar job. He wore a suit to work and looked very handsome. He was fit and sporty reaching professional football standard under the manager at Workington, one Bill Shankley. But she had failed to understand that painting and drawing were the centre of his life. Art was as necessary to his well being as eating and drinking. It sustained him.

He was popular but bored with the job. In 1962 he recounted one of his escapades to his friend Rosanna

Although the Post Office was a soul destroying job – if I got on the counter with two or three fairly human types (girls) it was possible to have quite a crazy session. I don't know why but when I sat under the counter-well smoking my pipe it always appeared funny to the others. On the request for a dog licence I would say with poker face 'Is it for yourself?' and the reply would inevitably be 'Oh yes'. One girl used to make herself ill with laughing. On one occasion I got into the letter box and as the letters and packets were popped in I would pop em out again,. – rather like candid camera.

It was into this competitive marriage that Brian was born in 1946 in a private nursing home in Vulcan's Lane Workington. He didn't stand a chance. These two adults were so caught up in their own problems they had no time for him at all. Percy was becoming introspective and unhappy – a backlash from his war years. He became self absorbed and was frequently in the doctors' surgery. Until this time he had capitalised on his natural ability to draw and produced many topographically correct drawings and watercolours of the landscape. These were pale and accurate and got him accepted into the Lake Artists' Society. They were his practice ground. He submitted them to exhibitions in the Royal Academy, The Royal Glasgow Institute and the Royal Scottish Academy and they were all accepted. He spent time painting with a well known local artist Heaton Cooper from whom he learned a lot about watercolour tecbnique. He even began to sign his landscapes in the same way as he did with spaced out capital letters. They were good and competent but they alone were not going to change his world. They lacked the simple strength and individuality of his later work. They were exercises in mastering watercolours. If he had continued to work like this he would not be making the waves that he is today.

They were the pictures-in-waiting for the big step forward. Remember he was self taught, he had not yet been to art college and this was part of the process of learning. He hungrily sought out knowledge. He was building on what he had seen in London. His depression grew blacker and he had to get out of the Post Office or go mad. In 1951 aged thirty two, he resigned and he and Audrey took over the sub post office in the small village of Great Broughton a few miles west of Cockermouth. He would never be formally employed again. Brian was six. They sold not only stamps but groceries and stationery. Percy did grocery deliveries and sometimes helped out with postal deliveries if the local sorting office was short staffed. Audrey was happy about this to begin with because they now had their own business. But trouble loomed large. Percy disappeared a lot to draw and paint. Audrey was left to mind the shop far more than she had ever anticipated. While she ground her teeth over this Percy reached rock bottom. Both were totally absorbed in their own situation resenting the other and not listening to each others' problems. Audrey felt she was doing all the work and it was unfair and it probably was. Brian sat in the room upstairs above the shop by himself listening to all this being played out. Percy went off to draw. In 1996, three years after his father's death, Channel 4 made a half hour programme about Kelly in which Brian, in a rare burst of words and insight, said ***'My dad was a genius. He just wanted to draw and paint but my mother wanted him to be Postmaster General.'***

It is no surprise then to find that in all his letters and the numerous accounts of his life, Percy never referred to the birth of his son. It was as though he never existed. So Brian began to grow up as a passive disinterested boy. He was a loner. His language and social skills were undeveloped. His cousin Val, younger brother Douglas' daughter, remembers him as physically tall and strong like his father but bullied and pushed about by the other cousins. He never fought back. He just allowed himself to be hit and knocked over. She tried to defend him but as the only girl she failed. She felt sorry for him.

Meanwhile Percy disappeared for hours drawing and painting frantically. He almost painted himself to a standstill it was so intense. An old postal slip was found among his effects dated 1957 on which he had written

I find I am seeing colour with such intensity that it is making it difficult to adjust my colour sense. It is a wonderful experience and were I not an artist it would give me untold pleasure. But I can never walk the countryside relaxed. I am forever searching and my mind races like a turbulent stream. Perhaps, like the stream, I shall find peace when the water flows more placid.

He saw doctors who gave him 'happy pills' and sent him away. He found a book on yoga in the library and calmed himself down with the exercises. He got through it by frantic drawing and painting. It passed. But he was hard to live with. Audrey was keeping the business going and working too hard and resenting it. She didn't believe he was ill. She thought he was lazy and work shy.

After a lot of 'discussion' Percy decided to resign as sub postmaster. The house went with the post so there was a great upheaval in their lives. Audrey got a secretarial job at Dovenby Hall, a psychiatric hospital near Cockermouth. Once again she was the breadwinner taking the financial load on herself albeit unwillingly. They found Glen Cottage in Allonby on the coast north of Maryport and bought it allegedly with Audrey's money.

Top left: **Percy Kelly in his studio at Glen Cottage, Allonby**
Left: **Maryport Harbour from the Settlement** *watercolour and charcoal*
Above: **Windy day, Cumberland** *charcoal*

They moved there in 1958. This marked a massive turning point in Percy's life and work. Allonby is on the Solway coast and he could walk for miles along the beach. It was restorative and calmed his mind. He spent his days walking, drawing and painting. At some point round about 1958 Percy bought or acquired a ream (500 sheets) of large Imperial size paper. He had never worked on anything this big before. He also got charcoal; black, brown, fine and chunky and he worked unremittingly, producing a series of drawings unsurpassed by any other artist in the Lake District. It was an enormous breakthrough. He referred to it many times as being born again.

He described this in a letter to Joan David

In 1958 I had to resign from the postal service because of my nervous breakdown and we went to live in Allonby. I took masses of pills and then I discovered Yoga. Mentally and physically I was reborn. I began to think deeply about my work and literally overnight gone were the delicate watercolours. I discovered the symbolic nature of things and this induced a degree of simplification. I realised the value of form and the mistake in copying nature. My perception of true values gathered momentum but the physical nature of things was sadly out of gear. Wisely or unwisely I decided to DRAW for a period of two years. This I did with unrelenting enthusiasm but the hand and eye were constantly out of tune. However one day after hundreds of 30 x 22 inch full Imperial sheets I sensed a perfect rhythm and touch. Apart from one spell in 1969 this state remained constant. Today a piece of charcoal or chalk is like an extension of my forefinger. Drawing is as natural as walking.

This series which took several years of work but is concentrated between 1958 - 1962 is magnificent. He travelled miles in the lakes and in the West Cumberland villages and coast recording what he saw in a fresh, almost abstract way. He saw shapes and tones rather than objects. He reduced everything to its essentials. There are many white roads winding out of sight, there are bridges and telegraph poles. He introduced strong verticals and triangles to ground the composition. He filled sketch books with drawings and ideas. Looking at them today one can sense the compulsive urgency which motivated him.

To me a street was once a place of bricks and mortar but … it became a place of near miracles. Around every corner they unfolded. The play of light, the faded paintwork, decaying masonry and broken pavement. One's mind inevitably begins to cogitate on the men who built these houses and those who lived and died in them. What manner of people were they?

Above: **Three stones** *charcoal*

Right: **Blue moon, Maryport** *mixed media*

He covered many miles each day and filled many sketch books and large sheets of paper. It is sometimes possible to track the route he followed by the location of these sketches. It was a phenomenal output.

In a letter to Joan David in 1987 he made a rough sketch of Dearham, a village a few miles west of Cockermouth and on the other side he wrote

The sketch overleaf was executed on a day which is still so vivid in my mind. The light on the road was fabulous so I just had to stop and make a sketch. On a later day I returned and using a piece of paper 30 x 22" I did a very satisfying drawing with no attempt at being arty, just a simple visual essay because I had just been reborn and learning. For me it was right to keep things unsophisticated and simple for a two year period. Imagine 1959/60 I used 1000 30" x 22" sheets of cheap cartridge paper one penny a sheet. Eventually I retained about 40 drawings and destroyed the remainder. This forty was later reduced to about twenty.

I set out to use two sheets a day. It was a marvellous and fulfilling moment when I found my hand and eye and mind were in perfect unison permanently. There was a long period when things went well but then my hand acted stupid but I kept my resolve and I crossed the barrier. When I began to play tennis and golf it was not dissimilar. The day came when the touch happened. My tennis tutor called Kirkpatrick knew exactly when it happened. On that day I was quite unplayable.

As regards drawing and painting I have not lost that particular mastery nor has there been a single lapse since 1960.

Writing in The Spectator 15th January 2011, Art Critic Andrew Lambirth wrote of the exhibition at Messums, Cork Street;

The best of Kelly's output is the grand series of powerfully mesmeric charcoal drawings he made in the late fifties - mostly of landscape. They bear comparison with the cream of Sheila Fell's work but have a solidity and conviction, an earthbound magic which is all his own.

Top: **Fishing boat** *charcoal*
Above: **Allonby bridge** *watercolour and charcoal*

chapter 6

A Place of the Imagination

By 1959 the born-again Percy was lapping up knowledge like a starving cat with a saucer of cream. His breakthrough had turned everything on its head. His uncertainty had turned into conviction. He now knew he could go forward. The prospect excited him. He was open to new ideas.

It was a life-changing exhibition of French printmakers at The Settlement in Maryport that led him to the next big step in his development as an artist. This Georgian house on the cliff top was run by The Workers' Educational Association who were formed in 1903 to provide higher education for working people. They ran courses, evening classes and exhibitions. Since his demob from the army Percy had seen no international art exhibitions and he missed the stimulation. He was fascinated that day. He knew nothing about etching but he was thirsty for knowledge particularly about art and artists. He walked slowly round trying to work out how this technique was achieved. His recent development into charcoal, with clear black lines resonated with these pieces. His work would translate into this medium. It appealed to him. It reduced the subject to pure lines. He was just puzzling it out when his friend the poet Norman Nicholson arrived.

He had first met Norman in 1957 in Edinburgh. He had submitted a pen and wash drawing of Thistles and Cow Parsley to the Royal Scottish Academy Summer Exhibition and it had been accepted. It attracted a lot of attention and when Nicholson saw the quality of the drawings Percy was producing he was seduced by them just as everyone else had been. He then met Kelly and a friendship had built up.

At The Settlement they chatted about the exhibition over coffee. They had a lot in common. Nicholson was the son of a tailor still living in the terrace house in Millom where he was born and in which he lived until he died. His gritty northern poetry was gaining him national recognition. This working class poet who was now successful and respected, helped and supported other working class artists. He was particularly interested in the visual arts. Listening to Percy bubbling with excitement over the printmaking and speculating about the process method, he realised he needed a Mentor. His friend Helen Sutherland whom he admired was just the right person. Before he left he handed Percy a letter of introduction addressed to her at her home in Dockray near Ullswater. He urged him to write and make an appointment to go and see her. Percy promised he would.

The day at The Settlement had stimulated him on several levels. First having seen the impressive exhibition of printmaking he wanted to do it. He had not had a formal art lesson since leaving school. Everything had been instinctive. There was no way he could teach himself printmaking. He realised that – it was much too technical. But he knew he would be able to produce some good work. Etching lends itself to his clean shapes and demands an inbuilt sense of design as well as precision craftsmanship. It combines chemistry and art; machinery and design. It begins with a drawing on a piece of metal in an acid resistant material, then dipping it in an acid bath for a variable length of time depending on the required effect. The plate is withdrawn and worked on again and the process is repeated many

Above: **The road to Penrith** *watercolour and ink*

times to produce the finished plate from which an edition of prints can be made. Percy was utterly seduced by the process and the results This was a medium designed for him. But he needed equipment and expertise; he needed someone to show him what to do. He seriously set about finding an evening class or a daytime course where he could learn the craft . He drew a blank. There were no part time courses which was what he needed. Apart from his drawing and painting he had to do some paid work. He had been painting signs. He had just done one for the local garage in Allonby. He painted coffin plates and pub signs as well. He had to contribute to the household expenses to some extent to keep Audrey quiet. He persisted in the search. He was determined to do this. He called in at the council education department. They informed him after some diligent searching that the only course in the county was a full time four year NDD at Carlisle College of Art. He couldn't even consider it. Not only had he to earn something to help the household maintenance but it would cost too much as well. He had always wanted to go to art college ever since the suggestion had been made by his art teacher at the Central School but he was now forty and had missed the opportunity. He was wistfully thinking about the exhibition in Maryport again when he remembered Norman Nicholson's letter. Downcast, he wrote to Helen Sutherland pouring out his frustration. He put a little drawing in the envelope attached to Norman's letter. She invited him for lunch.

A few days later he was on his way to a farmhouse called Cockley Moor near Dockray. He had no idea that this would be a life changing experience. It took some finding. This traditional stone built farmhouse was way out of the village up a steep and narrow no-through lane. A maid answered the door and led him to Miss Sutherland – and Paradise. He had never in all his life been in a house like this before. He stepped out of a grey January day into a different world. It was Wonderland to him. This was no ordinary farmhouse and Helen Sutherland was no ordinary woman. In her late seventies, she greeted him formally in the drawing room which was a large modern split-level room with a south facing wall of windows. On the top level of the pale wooden floor there was a pure white Grand piano and to offset this lovely shape, an old gramophone. It too was pure white. The ceiling was strips of

ash and coloured birch and the floor strips of wood like hickory. The floor to ceiling windows revealed a breathtaking view of the Ullswater Valley and the surrounding fells across to the High Street range. The room was full of books and paintings. There were paintings on the floor leaning against the wall, paintings in racks and paintings above the book shelves. He spotted a Henry Moore. He hadn't seen anything like this since his days spent in the National Gallery during the war and never in a private house.

She led him through to lunch in the formal dining room, a small exquisite room with dark coloured walls on which hung huge pieces of lettering by David Jones and Ben Nicholson's paintings and white reliefs. This house was full of modern works of art, sculpture and tapestries. His mind was racing, his eyes darting about the room. A framed piece of exquisite lettering took his eye. He loved calligraphy. He had been making signs for some time now at a commercial level to earn money but these were works of art. '*David Jones*,' she said noticing his gaze. '*He comes to stay here. He draws and paints as well. He's suffered several breakdowns.*' Percy could identify with that.

He noticed how beautifully dressed she was. Everything she wore was pale and understated but as a man interested in clothes he could appreciate

the detail of the pale blue silk chiffon blouse with tiny pin-tuck pleats, the soft grey wool skirt, the grey silk jacket – all hand stitched. This was a woman of style and substance. Her face was stern, her standards exacting but he felt comfortable in her presence. He had never met a woman like this before. After lunch they looked at some of her vast collection of paintings – paintings which made his heart and mind race. They discussed them in depth. She was interested in his opinion and he respected hers.

This first visit was an education for Kelly They got on well just as Norman Nicholson knew they would.

Helen Sutherland was a wealthy woman – an heiress - whose life focussed on the arts. She was one of the major patrons of the arts of her day, quietly amassing a collection of artists of the time which in today's terms would be worth hundreds of millions of pounds. They weren't expensive at the time. She moved to Cockley Moor in 1939 leaving a huge stately home, Rock Hall near Alnwick in Northumberland. She had no family – her parents died decades before and her two brothers were killed in the wars.

She was a great supporter of The Pitmen Painters, a group of miners who worked down the Ashington pit a few miles south of her former home. Through the aegis of the Workers Education Association, in 1934, they had set up an evening group for self improvement in a YMCA hut. They had wanted to study economics but no tutor could be found so they accepted Art Appreciation instead. Robert Lyon, Master of Painting at Newcastle University, was their tutor. The miners were keen. Every Monday, after a gruelling day down the pit they came home had their tea and a bath, changed into shirt and tie, and went off to learn and discuss modern art. In order to understand it Lyon encouraged them to paint - and theory turned into practice. They painted from their own experiences; scenes underground, domestic scenes, greyhounds and back terraces. Their work can be seen today in the Woodhorn Colliery Museum. Helen Sutherland got to hear about this from her friend Lyons and became involved. At first the pitmen were suspicious of a woman of her class but she won them over, invited them to Rock Hall to see and discuss her art collection and then paid for them to go to London on the train and visit The National Gallery, The Royal Academy and The Tate Gallery. She supported them in any way she could

Left: **Helen Sutherland at Cockley Moor with the evacuee boys from Newcastle**
Above: **Near Dockray** *mixed media*

and when she moved to Cockley Moor in 1939 they were invited there as well. She was a passionate supporter of working class, self taught artists.

That first meeting with Kelly was a great success. She encouraged him to come back and use her library and look at the paintings. This was an adventure in Twentieth Century British and European art. It was a crash course which built on what he had learned at the National Gallery during the war years in Whitehall. With a mind like blotting paper he absorbed it all quietly while sitting in that wonderful place. With the dramatic landscape outside and the knowledge within – written and visual – this was enlightenment. Wherever his eye fell there was stimulation. It was just what Kelly needed and loved. He absorbed everything. She had the largest private collection of works by Ben Nicholson at that time. Winifred Nicholson and the poet Kathleen Raine were frequent visitors. There were textiles by Edinburgh Weavers, sculpture by Barbara Hepworth, Nahum Gabo and Henry Moore as well as paintings by Mondrian, and Courbet. She got two Picassos out of a cupboard which she said she didn't much care for but she recognised him as a great artist who should not be excluded from her collection. He was overwhelmed. He subsequently did lots of drawings in and around Cockley Moor, Dockray, Stainton and Penrith and later when he had learned printmaking he made a striking small etching and a larger lithograph from one of the sketches entitled Helen Sutherland's Barn. This was a tribute to the part she had played in his education and life changing decisions.

After that first visit he did some beautiful pieces of lettering in brown ink on a potassium died board inspired by David Jones and he was now embracing abstraction.

In a letter to David Eccles in July 1974 he remembered her

I have two pieces of lettering decorating the walls and they were very much admired in fact I had difficulty keeping them. I was asked (by Helen Sutherland) to letter a poem by David Jones and another piece intended for Manchester Education Committees Schools' Collection. This delighted me because I have never sold any lettering.

Helen Sutherland was a controversial figure in the village of Dockray She caused a lot of interest in the neighbourhood when she bought Cockley Moor because it was isolated for a woman on her own but very soon a stream of architects and builders began to arrive and some avant garde alterations were made to the old farmhouse. The villagers were agog. She was often the main subject for discussion and speculation in the village pub and shop. First there were the builders and strange alterations to gossip about. Farmhouses in the Lake District traditionally have thick walls and few windows which are small and rarely face south for good reason; the strong capricious South Westerly winds. To knock out the whole of the south west facing wall and replace it with glass was considered the height of folly. The woman must be mad. She appeared to have unlimited money and ran a large car which was driven by her chauffeur. She added more bathrooms to the house – one of them with a bidet which caused endless speculation. She was small, not beautiful, with a nervous manner which belied a strong will. She was stylish, exciting and unpredictable. She brought a maid with her from Northumberland and soon added two local sisters to her staff, one

Above: **Helen Sutherland's barn** *etching*

Above: **Lettering** *in brown ink on a potassium stained board*

of them a cook. Her friends were her family and she had befriended many young artists, poets, musicians and writers over the years who visited. There were many exotic visitors. After the outbreak of war she arrived one day with a car crammed with a motley group of unruly noisy boys - evacuees from the slums of Newcastle who had never seen a rabbit, owl or badger and they roared about the district enjoying the open spaces creating noise and havoc.

She took poet Kathleen Raine under her wing who remembers in her autobiography her first visit to Cockley Moor when Helen Sutherland met her at Penrith and she was driven to the house.

There for the first time since the outbreak of war I found myself in a house which seemed to me more like a place of the imagination – some castle in Spenser - one of those places of arrival where treasures are shown to traveller or pilgrim and wounds are healed ... I had come from the world of nature to the world of art, another universe. In this house ... whose famous collection of paintings, Seurat and Ben Nicholson , Courbet and Mondrian, David Jones and Christopher Wood and even (in a cupboard because she did not care for them) two Picassos. I was lifted as by a tide above the mean struggle of poverty to wake next morning in the peace of a spotless white room.

Helen Sutherland stayed at Cockley Moor for twenty five years finally selling it to Fred Hoyle the Astronomer Royal in 1965. Percy wrote in a letter to a friend

The last letter she wrote to me before she died was written in her favourite garden of flowers in Rome. Simple words but so touching. Helen uplifted my soul and made me think with a rare sense of purity. I shall never meet her like again.

The experience of Cockley Moor and Helen Sutherland's influence hardened Percy's desire to go to college and earn more. It showed him the broader spectrum of art and all that went with it. He was exploding with ideas. He discussed future possibilities with Helen and she urged him to do the four year NDD printmaking course at Carlisle. He applied for a grant and was turned down. The committee felt that, at the age of forty one he would not stay the course. He was too old.

This was like a slap in the face. He was getting plenty of those at home as well. Audrey thought the idea preposterous. He had given up a secure job with a pension years ago. He had no ambition. He was always out painting and drawing but never seemed to achieve anything but useless bits of paper which littered the cottage. While she was working he saw friends, drove the car long distances and often came back with a tan on pleasant summer days. It was unfair. If he wanted to go to college he must finance it himself. She was not going to share her wages and pay all their expenses. She was working at Dovenby Hospital and she got him a job there as a night nurse. He stuck at this for a year and was popular with the patients. Combined with all the other odd jobs he got enough money together to apply again for a place at the Art College the following year. He was accepted but again, appearing before the same committee, he was not awarded a grant. They had not changed their resolve. Nor had Percy Kelly. He would finance it himself.

Above: **Red Field** *mixed media*

chapter 7

This will take you to Heaven

September 1961

Tullie House in Castle Street Carlisle was milling with students. This austere old Victorian building situated between the soaring Early English cathedral and the massive Norman castle is situated on the remains of Hadrian's Wall. The Romans had been here and now Percy Kelly was here trembling in anticipation and resolute in his intention to get everything he could out of this course. He was not there to socialise – he was there to learn. It was a hard won opportunity. He was desperate for knowledge. As he nervously glanced around he noticed everyone in the room seemed ridiculously young and frivolous chatting away to friends, making assignations. He felt out of place and not a little insecure. He felt old.

It was the first day of term for the freshers. The Principal, Tennant Moon arrived, gave a short talk and introduced the course tutors and then they broke for coffee. The majority of students were aged between sixteen and eighteen. Percy Kelly was forty one. He was there to enrol on the four year NDD course. As well as the night duties at Dovenby Hall he had also

managed to get some teaching work at Tomlinson School in Wigton as well as an evening class for adults in Cockermouth. He had prepared himself during that year and taken loads of books on art history out of Maryport library and studied them while on duty when things were quiet. He had 'sweet talked' the Maryport librarian and she let him take as many books as he wanted. He had spent time at Cockley Moor talking to Helen Sutherland and using her library. He wrote in his memoirs

It was very exciting and enlightening and in the twelve months I accumulated a mass of knowledge covering the whole aspect of painting, architecture, sculpture, techniques and psychology. This study was of great help when a student and my own work and attitiudes benefited. I became aware that my path lay in some quiet backwater, personal and private.

This is the first indication that he was going to reject teaching and be secretive and possessive regarding his work. He was a loner - the army had quickly worked that out. But now he was here in the place he had so much wanted since childhood. He was nervous.

He got his coffee and caught the eye of a young woman sitting alone at one of the tables who indicated a spare place next to her. He was thrilled because he felt a little out of place. She offered him a fresh fig (an exotic gesture for Carlisle!) with a smile and introduced herself. Her name was Rosanna and she was seventeen. She was well spoken with a soft well modulated voice and she confessed that she was also feeling very insecure.

Left: **Percy Kelly and printing press**
Right: **Blue Moon** *screenprint*

She looked younger than her years and she knew nobody. She lived in a remote valley near Keswick but her family had no car or money so she had to take lodgings in Carlisle. She didn't have a grant either. She had no idea how the grants system worked and her family and school weren't any help so she hadn't applied for one. She was one of a family of nine children. Her mother ran a boarding house for actors and artists. She had not made many friends at Keswick School. Like the rest of her big family the Vergowan children were 'different' and ostracised by the other pupils, often taunted for their southern accent, strange clothes, matted hair and untidy appearance. Both her parents were artistic, intellectual and lived unconventional lives which was possibly what had put the idea of art college into her head. She needed to escape but she didn't know how. Percy was thrilled to find that they were both in the lithography class. They were drawn together because they neither of them fitted in.

The main subject at Carlisle College of Art was Printed Textiles. This was a compulsory subject. The city had a tradition of making and printing cloth and supplied many designers to the local firms. In the first year they studied a broad range of subjects with an intermediate exam at the end of the second year. Percy was there to learn printmaking but he enjoyed the painting and drawing classes as well at first although he needed no tuition. It was novel to have people telling him how to observe and draw. He had been able to do that since birth. He'd never realised that it was something you needed to learn.

He and Rosanna stuck together in that first term. They formed a friendship based on art and their studies. Percy had a car so he was mobile. He was popular. He gave lifts to other students who lived in the same direction down the west coast. He could easily cope with the work and soon gained the respect of the tutors. Audrey was NOT happy. He was dressing like a student in tight jeans and brightly coloured scarves; not what she wanted in her husband. She was ashamed of him. He was working with a frenzied enthusiasm. His output was impressive. He really valued this chance of higher education. He arrived at college early and stayed on in the print room as long as he could, sometimes until 9 o'clock at night until the cleaners complained and the principal asked him to leave earlier. He spent weekends out painting and enjoyed every minute. When he was home he was full of talk about his course and the people on it and of course he innocently mentioned Rosanna. Audrey was on to that straight away. She thought he was having an affair using the college as an alibi for his long hours away. She was wrong.

That first Christmas since becoming a student in 1961 was a frosty affair. Their son Brian was nearly fifteen and decisions about his future had to be made. He was not academic and had no idea what to do in the future. He had nobody to advise him, nobody who took any interest at all. He had kept out of trouble – just passively got through school. He was in the Army Cadets so it looked as though he would be chanelled into joining the armed forces. Apart from ferrying him to and from the cadets and drawing and painting while waiting for him to emerge, Percy showed no interest in his future. Audrey was full of resentment because she didn't understand Percy's new life. College term had ended so she was looking forward to a conventional Christmas visiting and entertaining family. Percy had other plans. He had to get some money together for next term's fees so he got a temporary job with the Post Office delivering and sorting the Christmas

Above: **Spiral bound** *sketch book, 1956*

mail so she never saw him. He started work very early and when he finished he went out drawing or was working out ideas in the little room he used as a studio so she felt neglected - and she was. Glen Cottage was very small and his art materials were scattered everywhere. He took no interest at all in his family. Audrey, being alienated from her own family, visited his parents, remembered family birthdays and kept in touch with his brothers and sisters and their partners. She returned from these visits with news and gossip but it didn't interest him at all. She always went away on a summer package holiday and would have liked to go as a couple but she wouldn't pay for her husband. Why should she? This was her hard earned money and he didn't want to come anyway.

Percy was relieved to get away from the tension back to college for his second term in January 1962. He was looking forward to meeting up with Rosanna again and exchanging news but when he got to the print room he had a shock; she wasn't there. He was devastated. After a little more than a week he was told she wasn't coming back - no reason was given. He knew where she lived. Rigg Beck, well known in the area, was a tall clapboard house way up the Newlands Valley. It had been built in 1881

Above: **Sunflowers** *mixed media*
Right: **Building Site sketch** *drawing*

by a local man who had lived in Canada and came back and built himself the first wooden house in the area. She had told him in coffee breaks how her family had moved up from London in the mid fifties when the Greater London Council could no longer house them. There were five small children by then living in a flat in Gower Street in Bloomsbury – their father worked in the British Museum. Percy could identify with that. As the eldest girl in the family Rosanna had spent her life so far looking after babies – her own siblings - while her mother languished in bed or talked to interesting lodgers. She did the washing and cooking. It was endless and soul destroying. She was the Cinderella of the family. There was no money apart from what the lodging house brought in and the house was bitterly cold. There was no electricity or running water at first; they relied on oil lamps, an old wood stove and fetched water from the stream in buckets. Her father came and went mysteriously but after each visit there was usually another baby on the way. Her mother Varya had a liking for the colour purple, so soon after they had moved into this four storey house she persuaded a group of climbers to paint it purple ostensibly to blend in with the heather. They belayed from the chimneys and abseiled down the walls splashing purple paint everywhere. The result was dramatic and the house became a landmark.

So Percy called to see Rosanna at Rigg Beck taking a toy train he had made as a gift for her young siblings. She was delighted to see him as he poured out his disappointment at not seeing her after his terrible Christmas break. She was desperate to get away from home but she couldn't raise the money for lodgings, transport, food and fees. It was impossible. She had no idea how the grants system worked and her mother was too preoccuptied with interesting and artistic guests to give her mind to this. Surprisingly Percy offered no help or advice either, he was too caught up in his own problems. He couldn't deal with Rosanna's. He was in need of his own female figure to lean on, to listen to his problems. Helen Sutherland wouldn't always be there at Cockley Moor for him. She was old now and looking to move away from the harsh winters and isolation. Was Rosanna that person?

Sadly not. If she had been he would undoubtedly have left Audrey then but he couldn't move out into insecurity. He would fall off the edge of the cliff. He was falling in love with Rosanna but his 'love' was not reciprocated. It was a self centred love of himself. She had too many problems. The age gap was too great. She saw him as an old man. She needed friendship and support. He needed a strong woman to lean on, to listen to him, to understand his problems. It was stalemate.

But he loved to visit Rigg Beck. It was his sort of place. It was a total contrast to the ordered life at Cockley Moor and untidy, chaotic Varya Vergauwen was no Helen Sutherland but before long he was really at home. She welcomed him to the changing community there. Interesting people came and went. It was open and relaxed. He fitted in. Mrs V had studied art at Westminster Art Scool under Henry Moore, Mervyn Peake and Mark Gertler - David Jones had studied there as a contemporary. They had lots to talk about. This was a different step forward in his education. He left late that first night having given Rosanna his address and telephone number urging her to come to Allonby on a reciprocal visit. He promised to keep in touch and tell her what was going on in college and on their course, telling her to keep on drawing and painting.

This resulted in a marvellous series of letters, most of them illustrated with little drawings.

She wrote her first letter to him in January 1962 after his surprise visit to Rigg Beck This was Percy's response in which he refers back to their meeting in September that first day in College.

I am glad you feel life has been kind to you in spite of ups and downs. I feel the same way. We have come close together more than we imagine which in itself is a blessing. It was destined our paths should cross. I do believe this.

How kind to think me handsome. I felt quite strange that particular day. I did sense your companionship and was really thrilled when I learned you were to take up litho. It pains me to think of those post Christmas days when you failed to appear. The future was very black – I still haven't got over it.

On Wednesdays I wanted to be so much friendlier but I kept thinking I might be intruding even though the years between us never seemed to matter. When you asked me to join you for coffee again I thought you were just being kind. The figs, the tomatoes little things

Above: **Car Mechanic sketch book page** *charcoal*

but I remember them all and won't ever forget. I loved the all-too-short day at your home. Although I wanted the children to have the train set it was part excuse to see you again.

Of all the students I thought you would be the one who would go places. Your first litho was really excellent and I was impressed with your figure drawing when you used a heavy black line.

He then went on to boldly suggest she do a drawing of him. He offered to pose for her *(au naturelle of course)*. This was all in the cause of keeping her working but one immediately senses a rather obvious double motive - no doubt she did as well.

I must show you the book of Permeke's work when you come to Allonby. I would love life drawing if I could have absolute freedom and not be directed.

Although Rosanna wanted a totally platonic friendship, she was pleased at the attention she was getting. She had been unnoticed by everyone all her life, working in the background, the invisible skivvy, just taken for granted. She had never felt valued.

In his next letters he again suggested that he would like to come over to Rigg Beck to do some life drawing in her bedroom. He was getting bolder, more confident. He said he would bring a heater. He arrived the following Saturday with an oil stove, brushes, inks, paper and her mother told him she'd gone off walking to Winlatter! What a disappointment. But he was frightening her with these advances. She didn't know how to deal with the situation. She was only seventeen and totally inexperienced.

Here were two needy people who clung together for different reasons. Percy needed an audience; he craved admiration and praise. He didn't get that from Audrey. Quite the opposite. He also wanted to talk about college which was so new and exciting. He needed a woman's sympathetic ear.

Rosanna was very young for her years; she needed guidance and stability. She recognised Percy's massive talent and wanted help and advice from him. She imagined he, with his independent transport, could show her the way out of Rigg Beck. She didn't want a sexual relationship with him. She wanted unconditional friendship and support.

Percy's storm of letters which followed, while valuable to a biographer, must have been upsetting for her because they were full of all the exciting things happening at college from which she was excluded. Maybe she enjoyed the vicarious experience. None of her letters to him were kept. Maybe he was worried Audrey might find them so they were destroyed on reading though they were probably innocuous.

26th February 1962

Dear Rosie

It was very nice to receive your second letter and happy to learn I was of some help.

.... I write this because the past week has been quite exciting and some of my drawings have turned out well. On Tuesday Mr Barnes really praised a drawing I did of cow parsley, teazles and dead thistles (coloured inks and wash on brown paper).

Letter after letter goes into details of his successes and failures in the print room with anecdotes and criticisms of fellow students.

Friday 28th March 1962

Re Brian – he seems to have inherited nothing from me except

stubbornness. He is hoping to go into the RAF when he is 16. If he does, Mrs K suggested that I go away for a year or so to work. I am difficult to live with always painting and struggling in a world of my own. One tends to drift away from a normal way of life. I have moved away from my family who cannot understand me. Still, I can now cope with loneliness.

I don't want fame and success Rose, I simply want to develop and mature, to be able to put down my experiences with lucid simplicity. It is what one feels that matters.

I put a chalk to paper and make a mark.

Rosanna visited Glen Cottage in the Easter holidays at Percy's invitation. Although others of his fellow students had called in, this visit was probably ill-advised and was not a success. Audrey sensed their closeness and felt excluded from their conversation about things of which she knew nothing and had no interest in finding out. After Rosanna left things blew up.

I have tried to do some work today but it is hopeless and I really can't see the point of carrying on. Alternative employment has reared its ugly head and the result is utter misery.

He was losing his reliance on Audrey and was frantic for someone to understand him. Audrey's accusations of an affair with Rosanna were unfounded but he began to wish they were true. Despite the massive age difference he began to woo her with words.

Easter Tuesday

..... I felt terribly lonely. The landscape had evolved around you. Dark, lovely and dark moons – my mind was hurting me. Yesterday in the lovely lovely sunlight I saw part of the landscape suddenly become lyrical. I attempted to catch a mauve road and sky light grey and greens but it ended in failure. As if I was trying to catch a gay mood. On Saturday sitting in my chair I suddenly flung something heavy at a frame on the floor. I hated the struggle and the landscape seemed to mock me.

Left: **To Rosanna** *back of Whitehaven envelope*
Above: **George** *Illustrated in a letter to Loard Eccles*
Right: **Percy Kelly and Charles Breaker,** *Cornwall 1969*

Saturday 27th April 1962
Have just sent off my college fees which leaves my bank balance at 7/6d. don't know how I shall travel next week so I thought I had better send the money in case they thought I might be leaving. This happened at the beginning of last term. Something will probably turn up but the future looks really hopeless.

Friday May 12th 8pm
Location. A black wet night in a dingy street in Workington.

I am back here again by the harbour Workington having delivered Brian to the cadets. It is a lovely evening but in spite of the sun this place fills me with gloom. Why do I come then? There is some hidden pull and always has been. I think the people are wonderful because they have always had a difficult time. It is no wonder that I have a miserable side to my nature. The whole place smells of decay – crumbling harbour walls, rails overgrown with weeds and scruffy boats. The water is a dark dirty green – and yet people cling.

I painted an abstract 14 x 11 in thick luscious paint – how stimulating and exciting. I have a feeling for the freedom of abstract design and I am sure it will be the path I will follow. In landscape one is tied to earth colours. No wonder the expressionists revolted so violently. My yellow and red hens are a reaction against these earth colours. I shall find much restriction at the art college. Mr Cardwell wouldn't let me print the blue and mauve cow landscape. I wish I had a press and a few pounds in fivers.

Monday 21st May 1962
Dearest Rose

I received your letter before setting off for Middlesbrough on Saturday. Odd place to go you might think. It rained the whole day but in spite of this it was quite enjoyable. Barry had to do some business in Richmond and Darlington en route but the real motive was to view Sheila Fell's exhibition in the Municipal Art Gallery. First time I have seen her work en masse. The enormous splash of colour did not fool me nor the physical make up of Sheila. Large works can look impressive. One or two were interesting but most lacked a painterly sense of creation and were quite insincere. There seems to be a deterioration in her recent work. Her scrap book for me and all to see was to me in very bad taste. I can understand cuttings taken

Far left: **Cornish harbour** *mixed media*
Left: **Boats, Cornwall** *watercolour and ink*
Above: **Zennor** *mixed media*

from the Times and Telegraph or Studio etc but from the Woman's Own an article in heavy black type 'Mother's food parcels kept Sheila going' is really the end.

... Time really does fly for it is now Friday, a bitter cold day. I spent Tuesday drawing Rhododendrons at Mr Barnes' request in pencilled detail – horrible. Wednesday was litho day which I enjoyed. I brought the dredger cum harbour design almost to completion. Unfortunately plates are in short supply. I can see quite clearly, probably due to my drift towards simplification that there is an abstract element creeping into most things – this is where the college is going to be an hindrance.

Cars were a source of fascination to Percy. In a letter to Rosanna he told her he was scouring the small ads for an MG but it was his college friend Barry Dunglinson who found one for him in Penrith. He sought him out while he was painting by the harbour in Maryport to give him the news. It was a 1932 MG Midget and the asking price was £125 which Percy hadn't got but Barry insisted they go straight away to see it. Percy recalls

It was five O'clock on Saturday. I left my Austin van by the harbour and off we sped in Barry's souped up Mini at 70 – 80 mph. We reached the garage – Tinklers – just a few minutes before closing time. The salesman was still there and we discussed the car for a couple of hours and went for a trial run. I wasn't at all impressed but eventually the price dropped to £70. Barry scribbled a cheque – he'd just inherited a quarter of a million pounds – and I found myself driving the MG back to Allonby with Barry trailing behind. Later he took me back to Maryport to pick up the Austin.

The following Monday, Barry suggested they drive to Penrith in the lunch break because he said the cheque hadn't been accepted and he had to write another. Percy was still worrying about paying it back. He had enough trouble raising his college fees. Barry went into the office and came out with the receipt which PK quickly pocketed without looking at it. When he looked at it later it was for £20. ***All my worldly wealth, about a hundred pounds, was in a Post Office savings account so in a few days I was able to pay him back.***

All his cars were given names. The MG - GR57 was called George. He had a few hair raising adventures in George - his brakes once failed on Cartmel Fell with a friend Charles as passenger as they were coming up to a T junction on to main road with a halt sign. PK said a prayer which he claimed was answered and they merged in and turned the corner just missing a stone wall. Percy was aggrieved when Charles would never ride in George again.

In the next few decades other cars came and went, broke down and were repaired, were towed and pushed and exchanged for other wrecks but George lived on and made his television debut on Anglia TV in November 1983. Although he referred to him as his pride and joy he had by then been subjected to some humiliating Kelly specials. PK had made a detachable top from a piece of old canvas and also fitted a hard top using oak, ash and bits of wood from a boat as well as litho plates and lengths of alloy angle struts. He'd been indulging in one of his favourite occupations plundering skips and tips and making do.

Since the late fifties, Percy had driven down to Cornwall in the summer. He went every year as a tutor on holiday painting courses run by Charles Breaker. The journey south was always spread over several days. He was easily distracted. He had a small primus stove and stopped frequently for a brew as well as making many detours and sleeping in the car. Once there

Above: **Letter to Rosanna** *with Maryport Harbour drawing as a heading*

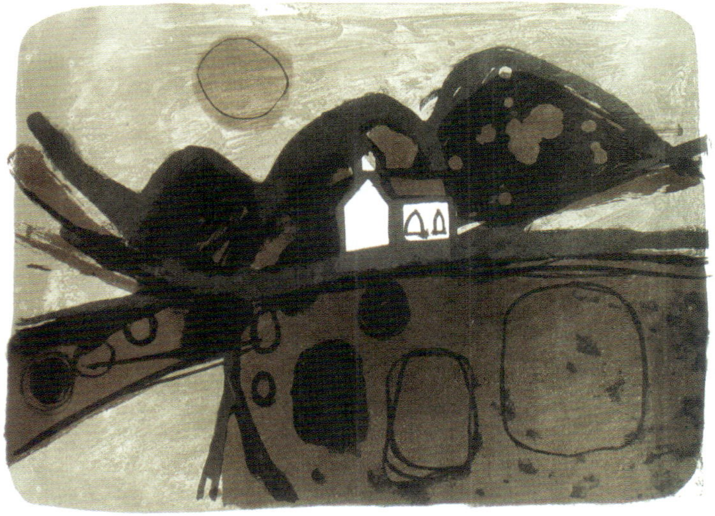

Top: **Newlands Church** *watercolour*
Above: **Newlands Church** *lithograph*

he didn't waste a second. He got up early and stayed up late working all the time; filling sketch books and painting en plein air. He did some magnificent paintings of boats and harbours; Mousehole, Newlyn, Penzance. In 1962 he asked Audrey to accompany him because they spent so little time together but it was not a success. He felt his time at college had inhibited him and he took time to get back into his painting. Audrey wanted a seaside holiday and she wanted her husband with her doing the same thing. Percy in an attempt to engage her interest presented her with a sketch book and pencils and tried to encourage her to use them. It was a failure. She didn't want to – she had no interest. He was trying to keep their marriage together but their objectives were poles apart. ***Any periods of silence or depression were of course interpreted the wrong way.*** he reported back to Rosanna. He recognised his need to get away from Audrey's constant reproaches. He decided to persuade Rosanna to come with him next year. All the time he wanted a companion who would share his love of painting, someone who would quietly recognise his worth, someone he could guide and teach.

20 August 1962

Dear Rosi

Audrey and I went to Cornwall for a few days and I managed to fill a large pad (16 x 12 made at the college) with lots of ideas – most are moderate but odd ones are not too bad. A second pad the same size will also be filled by the end of the holidays – in fact it is half way there. I am trying to concentrate on shop, pit heads, wagons etc anything that may be useful at the college.

The letters between Percy and Rosanna were now frequent and intense. Although Percy was careful to intercept the postman, Audrey was furiously jealous – certain that something was going on. She was changing her routine. It was turning into a race to the letterbox. She issued an ultimatum - he had to stop writing to Rosanna. He found a way round it. On 4th December 1962, having now completed four terms at the college while also doing a little part time teaching in Wigton, he once again had a Christmas Post job. He sent his address at work to Rosanna. suggesting she write to him there.

P Kelly Temporary Sorter Head Post Office Workington Cumberland.

At the end of his fourth term he appeared to be losing his enthusiasm for college and his enthusiasm for life. He was now forty three – older than several tutors. He felt he wasn't learning new skills. He was bored with drawing plants in the greenhouse. He was being discouraged from stretching out into abstraction. The tutors seemed to be working to a fixed syllabus with no flexibilty and a mature student like Percy needed to be stimulated, pushed, encouraged. This was probably beyond their capabilities. He was way beyond most if not all of them in talent, application, imagination and energy. Once he had grasped the fundamentals of printmaking he pushed it to a higher level. No wonder Percy's final report from the college said he had changed the face of printmaking in the college. He had far surpassed his tutors.

Another reason for his period of absence from college was that money was tight and he couldn't afford petrol. Both his and Audrey's cars were breaking down and her need to get to work took precedence over his. He began his fifth term badly. He wrote to Rosanna.

Each tutor gave me a pep talk during the first week. 'Bring the human figure into your work' – even Mr Cardwell despite the freedom given me in the litho test (figures are not required) chuntered away about it. Mr Barnes was depressing too about plant drawing so what spirit there was disappeared. The programme because of the new diploma course was drastically altered and so began more stupid talks and lectures. Needless to say I stayed away. Around the beginning of November friend Cardwell ticked me off because I used the etching press without permission (he had suggested using it earlier). Mr Barker was very nasty to me during a lettering session and Allen called me into his office and spoke at length about absenteeism - the bad influence that I have on others. ... I believe they all feel I am being rather big-headed about staying away whereas in actual fact it was all forced upon me. Brian has left school and is without a job so he is a worry. Audrey started to use Hetty (the other car) *when I bought the dear old MG which later was always breaking down. Built 1932 fitted with a Ford engine. The ride good for a liver or constipation really jolting but with a certain amount of witchcraft – wouldn't sell it for £100 – cost me twenty pounds and probably £10 to get it really shipshape. Whenever I go out in it something happens – a puncture, electrics, dynamo, fan belt breaks or something other than these situations.*

Anyhow, shortly after the Allen episode I began to feel terribly depressed and felt I wanted a long rest primarily because my old trouble started to rear its ugly head. My doctor happened to call to see me 3 weeks ago for some information about a Dutch artist so I asked him for a certificate. He gave me one so I have been absent ever since. For the first time since April I have been able to do some Yoga and this is bringing me round. Mind you I had to stay in bed for a week with a cold brought on I think through lack of food. When we last met I weighed almost 12 stone – now I am about 10.5. This is partly due to starting weight lifting exercises in October to develop my top half. Lack of fat and the development of muscle has certainly made me light on my feet and when well I feel wonderfully fit. My waist is 29" and 2 years ago it was 35". Living on a meagre diet has helped to shed the weight and I think is responsible for my present decline. However I am glad to say that I am returning to normal again and dispelled the depression.

The compliments are taken lightly because there is a long way to go. I am aware that certain ideas are becoming fixed which is a good thing. The charcoal drawings which you saw seem quite immature now which is understandable because they were done two years ago. By the way Allen said I have no endurance hence the plant drawing

Far left: **Percy's little notebook, 1962. Carlisle station** *drawing*
Left: **Grain store, Carlisle Brewery** *drawing*
Above: **The Lighthouse, Cornwall** *mixed media*

instead of life. He ought to see the work I have turned out the last week. I don't think he is particularly observant and recently has gone right down in my estimation.

By the way, the painting I sold was a landscape with Newlands church. I used some lovely colour and considering I used dyes it is quite the most intense painting I have done. I did a series, some not so good I am afraid. But my future lies in townscape – 5 already done (3 of them 36" x 18") of the Maryport area strengthen this feeling. Black chalk with burnt umber, raw umber and white washes. I can see before me a world of design. I know wherever I go the painting will be the same. I think that has got to be.

Pray you are well

Love Percy

Audrey was now violently objecting to his way of life. She refused to hand over any money and complained about the state of the cottage and who could blame her. Percy had not had a 'proper job' since 1951 and all this drawing and painting had not made any money at all, he was just filling up every available space with art. It was an obsession. He rarely sold any of his work. She decided she wanted a new kitchen and he set about doing all the work himself to keep her quiet. He went off to Cornwall during this frenzied bout of building work and painted frantically all the time. The only good news was that at last he had been awarded a grant for the next year. He appeared before the grants committee again expecting nothing and immediately noticed that the Chairman was absent. Based on his college reports rather than his age, the committee decided unanimously without hesitation that he should be awarded a grant. At last justice had been done.

Term started and he hadn't finished the kitchen. Audrey was on the warpath and his grant was late arriving. He couldn't afford the petrol to take him the fifty mile round trip to Carlisle every day. He had lost Rosanna's attention. He had too many problems. But having had some months off 'sick' he returned to college and concentrated hard on working for his intermediate examinations. His depression had lifted. He wrote to Rosanna.

Monday morning

Dashed down a quick drawing similar to the heading before setting off for Wigton.

It is a gorgeous morning, the sky is clear and the sun shining radiantly. The Scotch side is wonderfully clear in fact one can see the farms and cottages amidst the pattern of fields. I prefer the dull lonely days but now and again the brightness can stir ones heart in a wonderful elation. Especially when everything is so crisp and clear. I have 2 ½ hours break for lunch so Rusty and I shall go into the lanes and look for some drawing. I may be able to jot down a few words I wasn't able to do any writing because Rusty prefers to be on the move.

To sanity. The sky began to get quite cloudy whilst out walking and much of the landscape was dark in the shadows. The telegraph poles which I love were jet black and really fascinating. Remarkable the number of different types when one studies them objectively. Lots of people deplore them but not me because they form part of the design. Came across a wonderfully painted farm house and I really regretted not having my paints with me. The railings were picked out in different colours and the door was painted red. May sound horrible but it looked exciting to yours truly

I have started a sketch book for this type of subject because the assortment of colours are endless.

I was disappointed to have the postman pass by this morning but really I was expecting too much.

About to take my last class before leaving for home.

Lots of affection

Percy

The correspondence had resumed out of mutual need. Rosanna had met someone and the Cornwall idea had been dropped. She was turning to Percy as an older father figure for guidance. His only solution was to advise her to do lots of drawing. He was madly trying to work out a strategy to win her love against a younger suitor. She didn't see him as a contender. This was an impossible situation. Percy needed a woman to lean on. Audrey was hostile. Helen Sutherland had moved away from Cockley Moor. He was desperate for Rosanna's love and approval. She was not in a position to give that. She wasn't strong enough or settled and secure. In the summer of 1964 Percy Kelly, having returned to the college, sat the Intermediate examination which would then set his path through the rest of the NDD course. Apart from his entry exam for the Post Office when he was fourteen, he had

Left: **Harbour** *mixed media*
Above: **Long white road** *watercolour and ink*
Right: **Pierre, Brittany** *mixed media*

not had any other experience of such things. However, his confidence was high despite his term's AWOL because he knew he was good and able to achieve.

He described the architectural drawing paper in great detail both to Rosanna and some years later in a letter to Lord Eccles. It was an exam paper which seemed tailor made for Percy Kelly. The students were given the choice of making a drawing of one of three locations in Carlisle - the independent brewery; the railway station or the crescent. He wrote;

I elected to work at The Brewery and because I wanted to look down on the subject. I got permission to work high up on a tower used for brewing beer. It was a marvellous view which involved a host of detail including the main railway lines. I was going great guns when I was enveloped in hot steam which had a strong aroma of hops. It was impossible to see a thing so after a long wait hoping the steam would stop. I decided to pack up and make for The Station. I had lost a lot of valuable time because the deadline was five o'clock and it must have been about two when I packed up. I made my stand just outside the entrance to the station and the view was very interesting so I began to work with enthusiasm and completed the drawing in about two hours. The tutor arrived and told me the rest of the group had decided to make the town square (The Crescent) their subject so I went along with him to see how things were going. I had an hour to the deadline so I made an interesting drawing using a loose technique with some wash. We then made our way to college to hand in our work before going home. Next morning when I walked into the textile room my fellow students seemed to be unusually quiet. I thought there was something wrong. Then the tutor came to tell me the principle Mr Moon wanted to see me. Which deepened the mystery.

I walked into his room to find him most antagonistic. My drawing of The Crescent was on his desk.

'Kelly, I want to speak to you about this drawing. Is it your drawing?'

'Of course it is mine; my signature is plain to see.' I replied.

'Are you sure? He went on. 'If it is your drawing there wasn't sufficient time to do such a drawing.'

This was so stupid I just turned and walked out of the room.

Back in the textile room I discovered that one of the tutors saw it and gathered the students together telling them it was really beautiful. This was why the students had been so quiet when I entered. I then realised why Moon had questioned the authenticity of the drawing.

I always tried to keep my work secret when at college. I led a Jeckel and Hyde existence. The Crescent drawing was the first time I worked publicly as PK. Actually it did a world of good with my group who looked up to me as a sort of tutor. But it had the reverse effect on the college staff with the exception of two decent tutors they became jealous and unpleasant. The head of painting did his best to get me expelled. A short while after leaving I met the county art advisor. He said 'They wanted you out of the college but because of my support you finished your course.' He was a decent man. He bought three of my watercolours at an exhibition long before I went to college and said

'I'm buying your work whilst it is cheap for you have a marvellous future so it will become too expensive for me'

Left: **Zennor** *scraperboard*
Above: **Allonby** *lithograph*

How right he was. Kelly got an excellent report and assessment. There is no record of the result of the intermediate examination but he was awarded a travelling scholarship for the summer of 1964. Strangely all three of the drawings he had submitted for the architectural drawing exam were never returned to him. His sketchbooks with 'roughs' for the brewery and station have survived. Both of them have figures in them as he had constantly been exhorted to do. There are no sketches for The Crescent. He probably did that straight off without planning it out as a sketch because the remaining time was so short.

He decided to go to Brittany with his travel award. He had not been abroad since his war time days and chose France because of his early impressions of the landscape in war time. He loved Brittany because its craggy coastline and huddled villages reminded him of Cornwall. His Brittany paintings are much freer in style. He loosened up possibly in the warmer climate which he loved. He visited galleries who were impressed with the work and offered exhibitions but these are referred to in letters and then forgotten once again.

His third year report was a preponderance of A's with his lithography tutor making the comment ***Excellent work. Has done much to raise the standard of lithography in the college.***

He chose his own village of Allonby as the subject for his three day final litho exam.

... colours black, grey, brown and an orange sun shape. The mock-up was executed very accurately. I managed to do all this on the first day 9-1 and 2-4 - five hours in all..(Actually it adds up to six!)

The second day I concentrated on the third question and did several drawings of Allonby working up to the full scale colour study.. I put on liquid ground colours. When dry I scumbled colour on fairly thickly. The sky was a medley of greens and blues. The distant hill (Criffel), shore and part of the foreground were a fiery orange. The village area a loose area of lemon yellow and the green, a darkish green, down which I allowed the yellow to dribble. The cottage and boats were drawn in simply using black. Some stones and seaweed shapes were added with a suggestion of long grasses in the immediate foreground. There wasn't really time to work it all out properly So I felt it was a bit inadequate. Still as long as I passed that is the main thing. Textiles begin on Monday and is three days duration. I hope this goes as well as the litho test.

He did well in the litho test with his print of Allonby - so much so that many staff and students wanted a copy ***but I only part with my work reluctantly so I was rather mean*** he wrote.

Textile Design was Kelly's least favourite subject at college but his dissertation for his final examination in Printed Textiles, a beautiful grey hessian bound volume dated 1965, is a study of the history and fabrics produced by the Edinburgh Weavers. In this he was guided by Helen Sutherland. His introduction emphasises the importance of drawing and relates his own experience. ***I have spent the greater part of my life performing clerical work but perhaps I was an exception to the rule in the sense that I was constantly in revolt, painting and drawing whenever I could even during business hours......***

It was at Miss Helen Sutherland, Cockley Moor, Dockray that I first saw and became acquainted with a collection of Edinburgh Weavers' fabrics.

I live in a small village on the Solway and my journey to Dockray

led me Eastwards through the Cumberland fells. It was a dark winter morning, the kind which I really enjoy. Forking right at Troutbeck the road winds over a an expanse of lonely moor and then drops in a long steady decline towards the Ullswater valley. The fells overcast and dark were patched with old snow.

I finally reached Cockley Moor and when the door was opened the effect was quite overwhelming. From the dark world outside to a world of exquisite and sublime colour...

After reviewing and discussing the paintings Miss Sutherland showed me some samples of woven fabrics that she had just received from Edinburgh Weavers. I was so interested because because hitherto I had known nothing about this firm. In fact it was a discovery and a very stimulating one. I felt how compatible they were with the (Ben) Nicholson paintings and especially the white plaster reliefs with their purity of form and design.

This is illustrated with a Nicholson relief made out of white card mounted on the next page and a sample of the 1939 fabric based on his design on the following page. There are also samples of designs by William Scott, Alan Reynolds and Graham Sutherland. The next page, oh joy of joys, there is the small lithograph of Helen Sutherland's barn made by PK in 1963. It is darkly abstract with powerful black shapes and strong verticals. It is fitting because she was the person encouraging him to take the NDD course and he must have gone along and shown her this on one of his many visits. Maybe he gave her one of the edition. Maybe she gave him the Nicholson relief in return.

The end of term atmosphere saddened him. He had made many friends and learnt a lot despite his reservations. There was a camaraderie that he was going to miss. During sunny weather they all used to go off to the pub in typical student fashion or pile into cars and make for the river at Warwick Bridge. He wistfully wrote ***There were talks of parties but the enthusiasm has waned and little is left except a feeling of sadness. Although I have had pleasant days there, there is a feeling now of urgency to get away from it all. The period I shall dislike will be winter – being shut in by gales and rain and the resulting feeling of loneliness.***

Left: **Cottages and boats, Cornwall** *mixed media*
Above: **Cliffs, Brittany** *mixed media*

Last week I took a day off and went into the fields around Ennerdale. The sun was warm, the wind barmy so I wandered about without clothes enjoying the complete freedom of it all.

I am to meet Sir Nicholas Sekers this week now to discuss the exhibition in September so this will keep me occupied for a time. I only regret that I haven't more time to get things together. However it is best I think to hide one or two highlights for future occasions – not try to make too much of an impression. The way I feel at the moment is the near impossibility of putting on a show. This is no doubt due to having forsaken the landscape and drawing for such a long time (12 months)
After seeing Sir Nicholas I am going to Cornwall to try to pick up the threads once again. To be free to let ideas formulate.

He did well in the final exams. His final report was exemplary
Colin Allen - drawing tutor wrote ***An unusually talented and observant draughtsman. His interests are wide and his sense of colour excellent.***

William Cauldwell lithography tutor said ***Has continued to make progress. He is most enthusiastic in his approach and efficient in the craft. He has a real understanding and feeling for print making.***

The Principal Tennant Moon with whom Percy had so often clashed wrote

Mr Kelly is a dedicated and resourceful artist designer. He will I know make a first class teacher not only because of his talent, ability and experience but also because of his personal qualities. Congratulations on NDD success.

But Percy Kelly's future as a teacher never happened. When he left the army in 1946 that was what he wanted to do. In the intervening years he had gained experience teaching art in Cornwall and in local schools and evening classes. This had given him much needed money but had interfered with his own work which was more important to him. While teaching at Wigton he had spent every lunch time and free period drawing in the surrounding area. Many of his big charcoal drawings started there.

Now the circumstances had changed. He was 47 and had spent four precious years gaining the education he had earlier craved and had found it disappointing. He now had a first class paper qualification but he had never doubted himself and had found the drawing exercises onerous and much of the work unchallenging. The main benefit was learning printmaking which was his reason for applying originally. The prospect now of another year, another struggle to raise the money to get a teaching diploma was depressing.

Jean Gordon head of textiles wrote –

A prolific worker who devotes himself entirely to his studies and who is totally involved in his work. A serious mature approach to design which is readily sparked off and who reacts spontaneously to a vital environment. A perfect pass. This will take you to heaven

His forte was drawing. His skill as a draughtsman was phenomenal. He was living on the industrial coast of West Cumbria. All he wanted was to be an artist. That was the personal heaven he craved.

Above: **Brittany** *mixed media*

chapter 8

The Silk Purse

Bill Hamilton, works Manager for Sekers Silk looked out of his office window down into the factory car park. It was Saturday lunch time and it was empty. Everyone had gone. He was just preparing himself to go home for lunch – a short walk away in Hensingham - when a small white van drove in and stopped. Bill went out, locked up and walked over to see what the driver wanted. He remembered then, it must be the artist who'd written to his boss. He'd said he'd see him at noon today. It wouldn't take long. He'd come to see if he could do some drawings of the Mill. The Mill was a modern, purpose built industrial building. Bill couldn't see the point. The man must have some other agenda. Miki had passed the letter on and told him to deal with it. He wasn't interested.

Bill went down aiming to get rid of him quickly and go home but as they were talking Percy walked round to the back of the van and opened the doors to reveal a pile of paintings and drawings. The devastating Kelly magic kicked in and Bill was transfixed. Kelly had done many paintings and drawings along that bit of coast so familiar to him but not like anything he had seen before. The style was original and distinctive. Bill was transfixed; he was seeing familiar things with new eyes. Percy had made several large paintings of Whitehaven Harbour from the Loop Road above looking down on it and seeing it as two arms embracing all the shipping that came into its protection. He loved to paint and draw in Parton, a run down mining village tucked under the cliffs below Rosehill dwarfed by the Lowca pit on the hillside. He had drawn the little coastal railway which clung to the coast with a tiny engine chugging round the corner under the cliffs bound for Whitehaven. Bill impulsively bought a painting 'from the back of the van'

In 1986 in a letter to Joan David, Percy recalls;

I wrote to the steelworks, the docks, the mines and the Silk Mills to ask permission to have access to do on the spot drawings. The steelworks and the docks refused permission but I received a much more favourable response from the Silk Mills. My letter was addressed to Sir Nicholas Sekers Esq but I found later that Miki fobbed me off to Bill who was to see me and give me the polite push – kind of do the dirty work. The meeting with Bill was noon on a Saturday – well instead of a quick ten minutes, came 6.00 pm we were still together

Left: **Moresby Church and Lowca Pit** *mixed media*
Above: **Winter moonlight** *mixed media*

all because Bill happened to see one of my paintings in the back of my A35 van which had knocked him for six and he recognised my talent.

Sekers Silk Mills in Whitehaven was an unusual business. In 1937 two Hungarian entrepreneurs, Nicolas Sekers and his cousin Tomi de Gara, seeing the political climate in Europe changing towards Jews, arrived in England on a government scheme to encourage the start-up of new industries in areas of high unemployment. 'Miki' Sekers had studied textiles at Krefeld in Germany and went on to become a director of a silk mill in Bucharest though his primary interest was music and theatre. In Whitehaven he and de Gara trained local workers in the basement of an old school in Hensingham while the factory was being built with the help of a government grant. With the outbreak of war against Germany, they secured a government contract for making parachute silk for the RAF which put the business on a solid financial footing. After the war they moved into sumptuous dress fabrics and then fabric for theatre costumes supplying Covent Garden and Glyndebourne. Sekers had always wanted to work in the theatre. He was a patron of the arts with many connections in music and theatre and in 1959 he decided to build a theatre in an old barn in the grounds of his house at Rosehill. Built on a hillside north of Whitehaven just a short distance away from his factory, it looked out over the Irish sea to the Isle of Man.

Bill Hamilton was so impressed with Percy's work that he kept in touch and set up a one day only exhibition in his own house in Hensingham Road, Whitehaven. Although he and his wife Kitty invited their friends and acquaintances, the main purpose was to get the work in front of Miki Sekers. It was planned for a Saturday but at the last moment Sekers cancelled because he couldn't get back from London in time. Bill and Kitty quickly extended the show and said he could come the following day Sunday - which he did and bought two paintings – one for himself and the other for the Lever Art Gallery where he was on the board. Bill was thrilled when Sekers began to consider a bigger exhibition, which would reach a wider audience.

Percy wrote to Rosanna in 1964

A friend of ours, a director of the Silk Mills at Whitehaven saw my work a fortnight ago for the first time in 4 years although we have met quite often in the meantime. He was overwhelmed by my progress and rang Audrey the day after to tell her what enormous talent I possess (He also bought a painting) and he thinks I am a fool to carry on at the college. 'He should never teach' he told her. I don't think I will teach quite frankly and I never really thought I ever would. Anyway, a private showing of my work at Sekers' home is in the offing – if possible when the next London party comes North to the theatre. A television appearance is planned too so all in all things are moving in the right direction as regards making money.

This was good news. By now Rosehill Theatre was thriving and the charismatic Miki Sekers was on the board of Glyndebourne, the Royal Opera House Covent Garden, on the council of the Shakespeare Theatre Trust and governor of the Yehudi Menhuin School as well as Chairman of the London Mozart Players and London Philharmonic Orchestra. He was an impressive figure, a leader of the arts and had connections with many influential people including royalty. He was attracting famous performers to Rosehill and threw great dinner parties after the show in his grand house. He was granted a knighthood in 1965. If PK needed an agent and a mentor he couldn't do much better than this.

Sekers immediately liked Kelly and he liked his work and commissioned him to make some paintings of the factory. This was what PK had been hoping

Left: **The Silk Mills, Hensingham** *mixed media*
Above: **Lowry's steps, Maryport** *ink*

for and he set to work painting and drawing the looms and the machinery with colour and rhythm – something where he knew he could excel. Sekers bought fifteen which he hung in the boardroom at Hensingham. In the end, despite his ability to draw machinery the task became onerous and gave PK an inbuilt caution from then on against working to commission; working directly for money. It was too stultifying and proscriptive. As he found in the army, and to a lesser degree at college, he wasn't built for discipline. He described this to Rosanna in a letter

Allonby Tuesday 26 October 1966
Dear Rosanna

I took my work to Whitehaven yesterday and so ended my long involvement with the Jacquard project. Apart from the nine I was asked to do I took along a few others so Micky (sic) bought them all. They are now on the way to London to be framed. Bill Hamilton was in London last week and he said they have started off publicising my work. I suppose if I had Miss Fell's agent I would appear on radio, TV and in Women's magazines.

On my way home I felt as if I had shed a huge load and all night I sat overawed by a sense of freedom. After all the whole thing has been in my mind since January last when I first started the original sketches. Although I was never keen on the work I am glad I did it. A certain professionalism developed and also my powers of observation as well as drawing. I don't think one can do enough. Funny in spite of all this and the competence of the work, I felt on the journey to Whitehaven as if I had a date with the dentist. My heart sank when the factory buildings came into view.

All that remains now is the price. I am to see Sir Nicholas on Monday re payment. I ought to do very well.

A cheque for £200 was sent with a letter of thanks for thirteen asking for an invoice for the other two. This was found among his effects.
Decades later he recalls it – somewhat inaccurately, in a letter to Joan.

When I went into the extension today I came across the first exploratory drawing inside the Silk Mill Whitehaven. Miki asked me to do three interior paintings. I ended up doing fifteen and he

purchased eleven but I never allowed him to see the original effort and a number of others, I remember walking out of the mill with Miki after selecting eleven paintings and he nudged me playfully and said 'I bet you kept the best Percy!'

And he had of course.

Sekers then offered him an exhibition in the Foyer of Rosehill Theatre. This was his first solo exhibition at the age of forty eight. He had submitted single pieces in large group exhibitions but had been very secretive about his work. He had never approached galleries. Lowry had visited him several times at Allonby when he was out with Sheila Fell and PK had hidden his work away. He had always feared being copied. It had happened because his work looks transparently simple and easy to copy – it isn't. Simplicity is hard to achieve.

To be fair to Audrey she had no proof of his outstanding ability. With no exhibitions, no sales and this secrecy about his work there was no wonder that she doubted him. They had now been married for twenty five years and she had been the major wage earner for at least half that time. He had not had a single solo exhibition. Helen Sutherland had an exhibition of her lifetime collection at the newly opened Abbot Hall gallery in Kendal. It was a beautiful setting and an intimate space. She introduced Percy to the first Director Helen Capp in the hope that he might consider a show there at some point. He allowed Helen Capp to see some of his work – she came to Allonby to see him and they got on very well and she was impressed but although she tried, she never persuaded him to have the exhibition.

Miki Sekers fared much better. The Rosehill exhibition took place in 1966 with a simple catalogue designed by the artist. He showed seventeen paintings - nine oils and eight watercolours. These were local scenes of Cumbrian coastal villages and towns as well as Cornwall and Brittany. Number 7 titled ***Segment of an ash tip Broughton Moor Cumberland 25 x 20 inches*** sold for £25.10d. The most expensive was a watercolour ***Parton and Lowca 62 x 32 inches***, with a price tag of £100. There were also twenty five drawings, all West Cumberland, apart from two of St Monans in Scotland, two Brittany and two Cornwall with prices ranging from twelve guineas to thirty one pounds ten pence. There were also twelve lithographs from ten to fifteen guineas. The show was a huge success and PK appeared on local television looking nervously self assured talking about his work. His father Oscar came along to the opening and PK was pleased to see him scrutinising each painting very closely. He valued his opinion. Then he realised he was examining the mitres of the frames with a professional eye and ignoring the painting.

PK hated criticism. It had been a problem to him at college. In mounting a solo show and manning it himself he was bound to hear some comments from visitors. It was mostly euphoric praise but the locals found them too dark, too black, too depressive. PK was outraged at anyone daring to murmur anything deprecating. He felt exposed and vulnerable. It justified his retentiveness.

However, this début gave him the entrée to a wondrous social life. Miki's daughter Christine and her French husband, Jean Beaudrand, whose family owned a silk business in Lyon, lived in Roseneath, another grand house of the same period, just down the hill in Moresby. They were both designers and immediately loved and bought PKs work. Jean took him under his wing and gave him a lot of advice which was respected but rarely accepted. Lord Eccles, who had been arts minister in Harold Macmillan's cabinet was now Chairman of Sekers Silk. He and his family bought several works and began a lifelong friendship with PK at this show.

But more storm clouds were building. Percy still thought he could save his shaky marriage. He could now please Audrey as he was earning money and his college days were over. The days of the ageing student, liaisons with young women, talk of lecturers and examinations were now in the past. He was now earning praise and attention. He had been catapulted into high society. Although Audrey enjoyed the social occasions that followed she became jealous. She was invited into circles she could never have dreamed of. She sat at a dinner table with Princess Margaret and her then husband Anthony Armstrong Jones at Sir Nicholas Seker's house at Rosehill. She was invited to performances and after theatre dinners where she and Percy were in the company of royalty, politicians, actors and musicians. It was a rare and highly valued privilege to be part of the glittering circle of celebrity that Miki created around himself.

Above: **Glen Cottage, interior sketch** *mixed media*

Jean Beaudrand remembers what a handsome couple they made. Audrey had been a beautiful woman who dressed very well and enjoyed going out to these parties but she was self conscious and uncomfortable although she still felt her status was well above the Kelly family. She still speaks about this, her voice full of resentment and complaint. She was jealous because Percy had cruelly pointed out that she was only invited because she was his wife; true but better unspoken. Her resentment built and exploded just before Christmas 1968 when Percy's friend and patron Brookie Brooks Baker of Burke's Peerage sent a large Fortnum and Mason hamper stuffed with food, wine and spirits to Glen Cottage. PK wrote to Rosanna;

It arrived just before Christmas and what a surprise it was. I might have said Super Surprise but Audrey reacted in such a fashion that I wished at the time it hadn't come at all. The card inside the hamper said – TO PERCY - and Audrey was upset because her name wasn't included. She refused to partake of the contents so you can imagine my feelings. I sympathised with her but try as I might I could not heal the wound. I was left feeling so flat and depressed.

There was no way she could compete with Percy no matter how desperately she tried.

Even today, decades after her divorce and decades after Percy's death she is still full of anger and bitterness. A photograph of her father hangs on the wall of her room and she angrily points out the absence of her treasured photograph of her mother. Apparently Percy had to send a drawing to Canada about fifty years ago and he used it to stiffen the parcel. She can't forgive him. I suppose he was getting his own back at the way her mother had treated him.

Life became a hectic round of parties and dinners where PK held his own and others' attention. He was a good raconteur, he was charming and interesting. He had once again worked himself into a seemingly unattainable level of society for someone of his background. But art is a leveller. He was excused any social gaffes because he was an artist. They found him refreshingly relaxed and amusing. He was unfamiliar with the quirky customs and manners of the upper classes but he was a quick learner and got away with it. After all Sir Nicholas Sekers was also an outsider when he made the journey from Hungary. He had learned to adapt through talent and charisma.

Audrey was now insisting on having a make over of Glen Cottage to keep PK busy on anything other than art and to entertain their new friends. She was visiting fine houses and making comparisons. He just wanted a quiet mind to get on with his painting but he also wanted to please Audrey. So in his now familiar dysfunctional way he decided to begin with designing the printed fabrics for the kitchen and living room.

The view sitting in this chair looking through the glass partition and out through the front window is very stimulating. The lovely coloured bottles in the window, the delicate tracing of plant forms against the white woodwork – part white , part mustard; black,brown, viridian, green wallpaper and orange curtains makes it all exquisite – and the Chinese matting textured by the soft light.

He wrote to Rosanna in October 1966 - ***my mind is so cluttered it is difficult to evolve ideas. I have other things to make as well as laying down wood floors, a wall to knock down between the living room and front room, concrete to lay in the outbuilding where I keep the etching press. On the art front – The Stone Gallery, Newcastle are pursuing me about a show and Abbot Hall is waiting in the wings. No painting but I am pulling some beautiful prints.***

I met Jean B again yesterday (at Roseneath). ***It is almost certain that I shall have an exhibition in Sekers' London showrooms.*** (Sloane Street). ***It is a perfect setting for my drawings and paintings apparently. I think the dates will be left to me. It was lovely to sit in the large drawing room and look westwards over the fabulous landscape the light constantly changing as the sun sank towards the horizon.***

Left: **Trumpet Terrace, Cleator** *watercolour and ink*
Above top: **Over the top** *charcoal*
Above: **Whitehaven, looking south** *watercolour and ink*

In February 1967 he wrote

Things are going well art wise. I am busy getting things together for a London exhibition which is now definitely on. I am going to London in a fortnight to dine with an American millionaire and his Parisian wife. He is a delightful person who prefers Europe to the US. So many people are interested in my work I have no doubt that the exhibition will be a sell out, at least so it has been hinted.

Although he appeared to be relaxed and excited, he was in a turbulent nervous state. He was unable to cope with an exhibition and was well aware how important this was for him. This was the jumping off point for a brilliant career. He had at his disposal a team of people to help him. He had a wonderful sponsor in Sir Nicholas Sekers who had instructed his secretary to give Percy all the help she could. With the services of a top designer to oversee the hanging and his accommodation, invitations, framing, transport and guest list taken care of, everything was set to run smoothly and professionally.

The set up is going to be quite something. I will be meeting the press at a special evening do. Accommodation will be arranged in the centre as I shall be attending dinners etc for a period of two weeks. Princess Margaret and her husband will be one of the dates. The catalogue will be a super effort no expense spared. I shall do the cover design. This is good because it means that most of the presentation will be my effort.

But the contradictions within Percy's character came to the fore. He was frightened and things were moving forward too fast for him. A letter from Sekers' Sloane Square headquarters dated 2nd February 1968 dropped through the Glen Cottage letter box informing him of a request from the Arts Council's Craft centre for the loan of two of his paintings for a travelling exhibition starting at Goldsmiths Hall in the City of London and moving on to the Leeds City Art Gallery and the Laing Art Gallery Newcastle upon Tyne finishing at Glasgow School of Art mid September.

I am told the general aim is to draw the public attention to fine new work and also to show what distinguished art patrons industrial companies are becoming.

The criticism of his Rosehill exhibition which had upset him had been that it lacked colour. He had a lot of work in brilliant colour; not just Cumbrian landscapes, but Cornish harbours, bright flower studies and Brittany cornfields. He had jaunty red boats, yellow harvest fields, terraces of brightly coloured houses and bright green hillsides. as well as the gritty brown and ochre of the Cumbrian fells. One glimpse of these could cause a stampede of emotion. But he was going to hold on to these. His retentiveness was showing. He was finding feeble excuses. Depression was taking hold of him again. He wrote to Rosanna that he wishec he could show all the paintings but dismissed it as physically impossible without further explanation. He knew this attitude would lead to trouble and was almost inviting it.

I get furiously annoyed when people suggest using colour or flower paintings etc without any thought of the difficulties involved. It was said at Rosehill 'pity there wasn't more colour'. When the Sekers people learn the work will be all black and white they won't be pleased. Anyhow I am a sad person and I feel b/w but what exquisite blacks and whites. Pity people hadn't the perceptiveness to be aware of this.

Hard, harsh, incompatible, murky, frost melted rather than thawed by steely rain, a patchy covering of ragged dirty snow. Looking like great black giants badly whitewashed. Trees reduced by tempest to wintry bareness. Evergreen verdure, sombre, cast cold grim and rusty.

Coleridge 1839

These are beautiful lines and it is how I see the fells not in sunshine but in black and white.

To Rosanna

I woke up with such a dead and hopeless feeling. I went downstairs and looked at my paintings and they were empty and as dead as my feelings. Christine and Jean B came to dinner on Thursday and implored me to fill a room at Sloane Square with riotous colour expressed in flowers. Jean admires my colour but – all the work will be black and white drawings, black and white etchings and umber, ochre, brown and black dark paintings. This is what I visualise.

His depression deepened. Rosanna who was not in the best of spirits was the recipient of his anguish. Another letter said

I've tried all bloody day to get something going but have relegated most of it to the waste bin. One of these awful days I am like a cat on hot bricks. A walk in the gale force wind outside didn't help in fact I ran for the house. These days do happen but this one is real bad. I know why. When I lose touch with my work, life isn't worth living – no present , no tomorrow, I feel the same today. ... Although I criticise Audrey I wish she had married someone who might have given her a better life. She doesn't fit in with my ways - my ambition is too centred in my work...

I have a painting in front of me influenced by my wandering in Wensleydale. It is lovely and sad and in a different frame of mind I would say it is luscious colour and exciting – a few square inches are exquisite.

Please think of me

Percy

By Easter that year he not only had the two paintings travelling the country but the Beaudrands had taken others with them on a tour of South Africa promoting Sekers' fabrics. A cablegram arrived at Glen Cottage from them - *Paintings arrived safely – superb.*

As the exhibition drew closer Percy grew more panic stricken and depressed. His behaviour was becoming chaotic and he was struggling to make his own frames. Miki Sekers tried to help. He suggested that Percy send one of the home made frames to London for his framer to copy. PK packed the frame carefully using a Post Office Savings Bank display board

Left: **Ochre** *watercolour and ink*

Above: **Wensleydale** *watercolour and ink*

to strengthen it. The board was damaged so he repaired it, he just couldn't help these diversions and he couldn't leave the back of it blank. He playfully added three letters (two in capital letters and one in lower case). He painted these with carefully chosen colours. A few weeks later he had a telephone call from Miki's secretary.

'We have one of your beautiful paintings here,' she said. *'Shall I send it up to Whitehaven.'*

Percy was at a loss and asked her to describe it and realised it was the scrap board. He hadn't the heart to tell her. He picked it up a few days later at the Mill, crated and beautifully packed.

Looking at some of his lettering pieces it is easy to see how the mistake was made. A small rectangular piece of cardboard with the simple word OCHRE picked out in muted earth colours is beautiful in its simplicity.

He wrote to Rosanna

I have painted some lovely small watercolours recently – bits of Newlands – poetic ones with soft blue moons. I nurse a secret every day. I possess much more talent than most people realise – even you….. I think it will be appreciated when I depart this earth. The bits of drawings and painting will be little gems. My talent is often too much for me, hence the difficult time I am having -. Is there enough time?

Percy

Sunday

The weather report last night was poor but as often happens the day turned out to be a beauty. I went to Lorton and Buttermere returning via Loweswater, Lamplugh, Frizington and the back roads to Cockermouth. The vista Eastwards was so very beautiful. The bright sunshine filled the mountain slopes which were covered in virgin snow with blue and pale grey shadows. High above Fangs Brow, Grasmoor looked so impressive with with a plume of cloud trailing from its summit. The lakes were the deepest blue, the woods on the slopes of Blake Fell an indescribable black. Some of the walls were the most delicate black lines. It was wonderful.

But depression, self doubt and stress were once again taking a hold.

I know I cannot cope and need help. I am doubting my ability due to unconscious comments by people so I just don't know where to start. Perhaps the exhibition is the cause. Do you realise that there are 17 paintings and drawings hanging on the walls of these two rooms I have certainly transformed this place. On Saturday I am going to Sekers' silk mills to select curtains, chairs and a dress for Audrey…

14th August 1968… the time speeds by at an alarming rate so it won't be long before I am speeding south in fearful trepidation. I delivered the large work to Roseneath on Saturday – a relief I can tell you. Now all that remains is the etchings and lithos. Hope I can finish these by the weekend. On Saturday I had an interesting talk with Alan Sekers, Sir Nicholas' youngest son who went to art school but is now in films. Here I have a staunch ally and admirer. We enjoyed the large paintings propped up on end, much more interesting this way. He doesn't care for the etchings due I think to the small scale and the lack of complete involvement. Pity I have so few paintings but time is a cruel enemy. Ninety per cent have been done since February which seemed to amaze Alan. I was with Jean B when he said that in all the time we have known each other he has never seen me so fit and well. He thinks working under pressure to the September deadline is responsible.

Audrey ruins things with sarcastic asides. ' Yes you do look beautiful!' she said when I set off on Monday. But I don't mind now because there is such a happy accord with these friends of mine. After all is it so wrong to want to wear such bright clear colour. Of course I am told the feminine streak is so marked among artists – so what! I am aware of this but the masculine side of me always dominates. Jean is an ally because he was wearing lovely faded pink cord slacks on Saturday.

I sent Sofie – Jean Baudrand's wee girl, a small colour study of flowers and Jean thinks it is the loveliest piece of colour he has ever seen. He has asked me if I will do a painting from it 6 foot x 8 foot to cover the whole wall over the fireplace. These and others were done at such time that I feel I could paint a masterpiece. But I doubt if

Above top: **Cottage in Lorton** *mixed media*
Above: **Looking East to the Ennerdale Fells** *mixed media*

this painting will be done for I have lapsed into a world of black and white. Perhaps one day someone will take me by the hand and lead me to a world of flowers, birds and butterflies. A world of exquisite colour.

19th January 1968

....I started last night sorting through the remainder of the many drawings. Some of them reminded me how long many of these had lain dormant (1958/9 in fact). It occurred to me that it was time I realised my talents in £.s.d. It is interesting that I remember every sketch. Mary Burkett is pestering me to have a show in Kendal to coincide with the London one but I have refused.

It is a great pity I have few paintings but perhaps I shall make sufficient money to obtain larger premises so I may be more prolific in output.

This was a harsh comment when Miss Burkett had been trying so hard to help him. The exhibition in Sloane Square was a great success. It was once again mainly black and white. He could use colour with restraint and panache and his coloured washes were exemplary. His palate of ochre, browns and dirty greens worked well with his simple lines. He wasn't frightened of using colour but he was frightened of showing it. Was this because when people saw it they wished to buy it? Was this because, when he looked at his coloured paintings in private he wanted to keep them? He couldn't bear the thought of selling them, of their disappearing out of his grasp, his control. He loved admiration but not possession. It meant deprivation for him.

Rosanna was now living in Chelsea just round the corner from Sloane Square. She didn't attend. She can't remember getting an invitation. He probably forgot to send her one.

John Fitzmaurice Mills covered the exhibition in Art Forum. Below a charcoal drawing of a winding engine at St Helen's Pit Cumberland he wrote

Kelly, in pursuit of his art, has had no road of comfort; he has had many trials and setbacks to contend with. But he has contained within himself the generative spirit that is today finding fulfilment with his penetrating portrayal of the Cumberland scene. His landscape captures in tones of warm umber the harshness of the North West Coast.

When Kelly turns his attention to etching he draws out of the plate a coarse strength that hitches itself to the nature of his subject. He travels between the extremities of Cornwall and Cumberland searching for a cohesion between the two. As his work develops there is emerging a great sense of power and dramatic control.

Among a glittering array of celebrities Princess Diana's grandmother, Lady Fermoy was there. She had a gallery named after her, The Fermoy Gallery, in Kings Lynn in Norfolk. She approached PK for an exhibition and he readily agreed. So in 1969 at the age of fifty he arrived in Kings Lynn poised for success. He had work touring South Africa, had been mentioned in an article by Katharine Whitehorn in The Observer newspaper praising working class artists, had a letter of appreciation from the editor of The Daily Telegraph, and a letter from Lord Snowdon regarding a painting bought for Princess Margaret not to mention a huge deluge of letters from people who had been at the opening. Two big watercolours had also been commissioned for the maiden voyage of the QE2. So Percy Kelly had made a big impression in London. It had proved to be a marvellous spring board and the world was spread out before him encouraging him to make the leap. But it would be more than forty years before London saw his work again.

Monday April 8th 1969 Eastern Daily Press carried this upbeat story below a photograph of him.

Percy Kelly preparing for his opening tonight of his paintings, drawings, prints at the Fermoy Gallery has another preview on his mind – the eight day preview cruise of Cunard's super liner QE2. Two of his watercolours of Cumbrian seaside towns were bought for the liner.

PK should have been riding high but once again he was depressed. He and Audrey arrived in Kings Lynn on a Sunday evening in torrential rain. They were escorted to a place to stay in a nearby village which he found depressing. The next day was spent hanging the work. He had decided once again to show mainly etchings – all black and white. The centrepiece was a large painting of Whitehaven in browns and ochres but when the first people through the door asked to buy it he refused to sell. They were not happy. He wanted to sell only etchings but the guests wished to buy paintings. Result – impasse. He sold very little. This added to his dark mood.

He recalled this disastrous visit in a letter to Joan David. It is written on a painting of the cottage he stayed in;

This was the evening I dined with with the father of the Princess of Wales. What a jolly time we had. Extraordinary because his wife had left him that very day. His wife's mother, Lady Fermoy was another guest. When we went our separate ways Lady F gave me a jar of M&S marmalade.

This was not the happy successful time he had anticipated he thought as he walked out into the rain clutching the jar of marmalade. He had just wilfully thrown away another chance to become an artist of some standing, respect and renown. His work had been accepted outside Cumbria. London had admired it and now in the far reaches of East Anglia they loved his paintings and wanted to buy but he had denied them the chance. There were many others who also left that evening feeling disappointed.

After this disastrous show in Norfolk, things between Percy and Audrey reached crisis point. They had a big row and Rusty, Percy's dog died. He fell into deep depression. His eyes were troubling him again. He couldn't see. He was convinced he was going blind.

Above: **Moresby Church at night** *mixed media*

chapter 9

The Muse

Early in 1969 PK turned off the main road a few miles south of Cockermouth in his little 1932 MG Midget and stopped in the quiet leafy lane which led down to the village of Pardshaw. He got out his sketchbook and drew the scene before him. He was early for his appointment so he thought he might as well use the time. He frowned. His eyes were troubling him again. It hurt him to look at the white paper and then at the colour around him. This stopped him thinking and seeing. His stomach churned. The old familiar trouble was returning. Everything was turning black again. The optician had not been able to find anything wrong and had referred him to his GP. He had been to see his doctor several times but he had dismissed him impatiently.

'There is nothing wrong with your eyes,' he told him for the umpteenth time. He saw him as a nuisance to be quickly dealt with. Percy was upset. Did the doctor not realise how important his eyes were to him as an artist. His vision would suddenly become blurred, his eyes would hurt as light and colour shafted in and his heart would race so much he thought he would faint. These symptoms should not be cursorily dismissed. What would happen if he lost his sight? Panic overwhelmed him at the thought. The pencil in his hand shook uncontrollably.

He looked at his watch and started the car. He was going to see the top man privately. He could barely afford it but perhaps this man would appreciate his concern and his importance and help him. Audrey was in the business and for once she was in cooperative mood. She had asked

her boss at the hospital, Dr Ferguson, for a recommendation and he had suggested a choice between a Whitehaven and a Carlisle consultant. She chose Paul Griffith at Whitehaven. It was a random choice but a life changing decision.

The beautiful detached modern house on the edge of the Lake District National Park stands on the hillside at Pardshaw looking east to the Lorton Fells. Apprehensively Percy parked the car, walked up the neat path and rang the bell.

A handsome woman in her mid thirties greeted him at the door. Tall and slender she smiled at him as she led him through to the consulting room. The consultant made a very thorough examination but, like the others, could find nothing physically wrong. An hour later he found himself at the kitchen table drinking coffee with the consultant's wife. She was kind and sympathetic. He showed her his sketch book. She was entranced. She listened attentively to all his problems. He momentarily forgot about his eyes. They talked about art and life and it was love at first sight.

Christine Griffith had three young children, a lovely house, a successful, well respected and kind husband, and lots of friends in a similar position. She was the ideal doctor's wife. She adored her children. She met her best

Left: **Chris Griffith**
Above: **Lorton Fells from Pardshaw** *watercolour and ink*

friend and close neighbour, Wendy Rotarides in 1967 at a charity cocktail party at the GP Charles Aicheson's home above the surgery in South Street Cockermouth. Charles' wife Mavis, a speech therapist, along with Wendy and Chris joined an art class and later learned pottery together. They had children of a similar age. All seemed very well and normal in their sixties world. Three sensible educated mothers enjoying art and coffee mornings, children and animals; no financial worries in their professional middle class world. What more could a woman want?

Talking at the kitchen table with Percy that morning their eyes met and she was bewitched. Percy was fifty, tall and elegant. He was a good talker. He looked after his body and had a strong physique. He dressed well but eccentrically with taste and flair. He looked like an artist with flamboyant colours which showed off his deep tan. She was fascinated by his soft voice with just a trace of a local accent. He was unusual and he was passionate about art. He had a strong charisma and she was besotted with him.

He came to the house again and showed her some drawings. They went out sketching together. She introduced him proudly to her friends and they liked him too. Chris and Wendy were invited to Glen Cottage to see where he worked. Wendy remembers all the clutter everywhere but Chris was too visibly excited to be in his workshop to notice anything else. Wendy invited PK and Audrey for supper along with Paul and Chris. PK enchanted them with his stories but dominated the conversation. He dominated the room. Audrey was uncomfortable. She didn't like arty people. She had no idea what they were all talking about. She preferred high society now. He was stealing the attention again.

Soon after this she came home from work one winter evening to find a stranger in her house. She could see a woman sitting by the fire as she came through the front door of the tiny cottage. She was startled to see this stranger was wearing her grey Jaeger knitted dress. She was frightened. It was ghostly and unreal. It was even more unreal when the woman turned to face her and she realised it was her husband. He had make up on and held out a wand of mascara – her mascara – and asked her to show him how to apply it. His request for help and advice was delivered in an artificial high pitched voice. She was shocked, appalled and nauseated. She threw him out of the house.

'*Get your things tomorrow morning*,' she shouted after him ' *I'm getting the locks changed. And don't come back – ever. I never want to see you again*.' And she meant every word.

As he went she saw that he had on her high heeled shoes and he had cut the backs out so they 'fitted' his size eleven feet. He shuffled out into the night. Audrey shuddered.

'*I never want to set eyes on you again*' she shouted after him. '*You disgust me!*' and she slammed the door, locked and bolted it and stood with her back leaning against it trying to regain her equilibrium. She only saw him again once – in the divorce court. This was a pivotal moment in his life.

The cottage was stuffed with paintings, prints, art materials, a printing press and acid baths for the etching plates. There was no way he could take it all. He gathered up as much as he could next morning. Since leaving college he had shared a studio at Snow Hill near Caldbeck with his friend and fellow student Barry Dunglinson and he had recently been given a space in an old outhouse laundry at Roseneath by Jean and Christine Beaudrand. He had probably fled there the night before in the grey dress. The following afternoon his father Oscar came round at Audrey's bidding and changed the locks while she was at work. She didn't tell him why she had thrown his son out. She was too ashamed. Percy Kelly artist and genius was now alone. For the first time he had no woman to support him - but not for long.

Kim Griffith, Paul and Chris's eldest daughter was thirteen in 1970 when she was summoned to her parents' bedroom and was told that they were going to live apart and that she and her younger brother Andrew aged eight and sister Nicola aged six would be going with their mother to live with the artist Percy Kelly. Kim was deeply shocked at the news. She had no idea this was coming and she hardly knew Percy. As a teenager she was too caught up in her own friendships and adolescent concerns to notice adult visitors. Her world fell apart that day.

She was happily settled at Cockermouth School a few miles away. She had a good circle of friends of which she was always the mischievous leader and had a lively social life. This massive change was catastrophic. The two younger children were less troubled and more biddable. But they all wanted to know where they would live under this new unfamiliar regime.

The rented flat at Swallow Hill, Distington a few miles north of Whitehaven was very convenient for PK because it was close to his patrons and friends at Rosehill and it was cheap. But it was a dreadful contrast to the comfortable, stylish and modern home the Griffith's had left. Gossip was rife throughout the county. Friends, colleagues and acquaintances were shocked at this strange liaison. Why would Chris want to leave such a good man and secure background to live with a penniless artist they asked themselves – and each other.

Chris was accepted by the Sekers family and included in the rich social life at Rosehill but things were changing within the company. There were financial issues, divisions in management and a power struggle going on which would leave Miki Sekers on a limb. The focus changed. They had their own problems to sort out.

Chris's children had to start at new schools – Cockermouth was too far away for Kim to travel. Whitehaven School was close but she immediately fell in with a rough set of girls which became a problem. But her mother was oblivious.

'She was besotted with Percy' her closest friend Wendy records. 'She was overcome by a sort of madness. She saw herself as his muse.'

Reading PK's letters to Rosanna and his *(unsuccessful)* attempts to seduce her, one can see the tactics he may have used with Chris; promises

Left: **Yellow Farm** *watercolour and ink*
Above: **To the fells** *mixed media*

of adventure, of buying a lovely house with bigger studio space, of painting her and teaching her to paint, of undreamed of sexual pleasure, of travel to Cornwall and Brittany, of relocation and a new life. He was so convincing that she didn't realise he couldn't deliver most of this. She would have a new life for sure but it would be different from her romantic vision. However, she could deliver what Percy needed – a trained nurse, a woman to share his hopes and dreams, to give him unquestioning admiration, to give him security and attention. He would be the centre of her world. With her his eyes would improve, his stress would disappear and he would be able to concentrate full time on his art work. She knew his work was exceptional. She could help him to make his mark in the art world. She could be the wife of a famous artist. He would be her project and it would be thrilling.

Meanwhile Audrey filed for divorce. She regarded herself as the sacrificial lamb. She had to face her husband just one more time – in the divorce court. She was repulsed by him. She had no idea how long he had been trying her clothes on. Since she had thrown him out, despite his constant pleading and requests in writing, she had consistently refused to let him into the house or have any of his papers – even his driving licence and passport had been reduced to ashes in the smoke of revenge - he had to apply for replacements. She was vindictive and bitter and she was in a position of power. But there was only one thing that Percy wanted. She could have the house and everything else, he was not going to dispute that but he wanted the rest of his work. It meant everything to him. It was his life; his raison d'etre and his wife knew this. She stood firm. She didn't want it herself but she didn't want him to have it– it epitomised everything that had gone wrong with her marriage. Art had distracted him from her and her needs. She adamantly refused. to let him have it. Deadlock. The court was hushed. The judge turned to Percy who was visibly anguished. He had nothing more to offer but he had to have his precious work. He was a man in the dock awaiting the death sentence or reprieve. He looked across at Audrey and in a clear voice which rang round the court, he made an impassioned speech in which he offered her Chris' grand piano and Tasha her English Setter in exchange for his precious work. Whether Christine was complicit in this bizarre gesture isn't clear but Audrey certainly didn't want a dog or a piano and with a curl of the lip she said so which caused the court to break into laughter and disorder. Percy was awarded one penny and his work by the judge. The courtroom applauded.

Audrey afterwards said with some bravado that she could have stopped Chris running away with her husband.

'I only had to say one word,' she boasted.

'Then why didn't you say it Audrey?'

'I wanted her to find out for herself.'

And find out she did. But not for some time. Not until it was too late. Reader, she married him!

Above: **Yellow field near the Solway** *watercolour and ink*

chapter 10

Not just Talent but Genius

After less than a year at Swallow Hill, Distington, Christine and Percy were offered a cottage on the Levens Estate near Kendal in the South of the county. Miki Sekers had mentioned that they were looking for somewhere to live to Robin Bagot, the owner of Levens Hall, a very good amateur painter who liked PK's work. They were thrilled with the cottage and eagerly moved in. It was just what PK wanted. Chris's Cockermouth friend Mavis Aitcheson and her husband Charles had just moved to Kendal from Hawick. Percy knew and liked Kendal because of his good experiences when he he worked there in his first job so they felt very much at home immediately. Chris was adaptable. She welcomed the change. It was good to get away from all the gossip. They could start afresh. They explored the area round about and ventured further into the Yorkshire Dales. They had no money but they were very happy and PK did a lot of excellent work. The colours were bright. The future was bright. At last he had support and understanding. He had the freedom to paint all day long with no complaints and he had a woman who loved him to whom he could talk about art. His paintings of South Lakes villages, Dales villages and Kendal make a wonderful optimistic collection. They shout happiness and contentment.

For that first Christmas at Levens, Percy made their Christmas cards and Chris decked out the cottage. They were childlike in their anticipation of the festival. They kept in touch with Percy's friends from Rosehill and London. A card and letter from Michael MacLiammoir, a famous Irish actor, dramatist and writer who had studied art at The Slade, arrived in response.

Dated 17th December 1971 from Harcourt Terrace, Dublin he wrote

'This is merely to tell you dear Percy that one glance at the same incredible epistle with its really wonderful drawings disturbs me deeply for the drawings alone convince me finally that you have, not merely talent, but genius.

Thank you for sending me a great treasure. All fine and lovely things to you for Christmas and afterwards.

'I'd never met a genius before!' Mavis said when asked what she thought about Percy. 'He was unexpected, different. His clothes were from Oxfam but were stylish and original. He loved bright clothes He wasn't ill mannered or pushy He was a Gemini in every sense of that word. He was direct, endearingly childlike and seriously egotistic. There was a chemistry between him and Chris that you could feel in their company – a naked sexuality - although there was never any improper or embarrassing behaviour in public' she was quick to emphasise.

He and Chris were obviously infatuated with each other.

Percy now had the freedom to go where he chose and meet who he wanted with no questions asked, no nasty comments, no taunting. There was

Left: **Levens Park, Gamekeepers Cottage**
Above: **Village near Kendal** *watercolour and ink*

absolute trust. He renewed his friendship with the poet Norman Nicholson and letters and visits were exchanged. Percy did some magnificent paintings of the steel works at Hodbarrow near Millom where Norman and his wife Yvonne lived.

They made many new friends and contacts here with the help of Mary Burkett now Director of Abbott Hall. She again offered him an exhibition but was refused. Christine baked delicious cakes and held tea parties and soirées. Life was wonderful even if they had no money. They were in love. Percy made many drawings and sketches in the town which culminated in a marvellous large painting *(54 x 22 inches)* of Kendal for the Boardroom of Provincial Insurance for its Chairman Peter Scott who was the benefactor of Abbot Hall through the Scott Trust and who was to become important to them in their next move. This kept them afloat financially for a while. Every time they reached a financial crisis something turned up like magic. Christine had a Pollyana attitude to life. These were golden days. Her husband's work was beginning to attract the attention of other gallery owners. Chris encouraged this. Geoff Green of Tib Lane gallery came up from Manchester. He was overwhelmed by the quality of the work and offered to buy all his charcoal drawings. '*These knock Lowry for six*' he is reputed to have said. Percy was appalled at the thought of 'losing' them and fobbed him off with excuses. '*He really drooled over them - I had to pull them out of his hands.*' he wrote. He was pleased for people to come and see his work. He basked in their praise and blatantly encouraged them until it came to the selling point and then they were usually cursorily dismissed. Word reached Andreas Kalman owner of one of the best London galleries.

When Andreas Kalman was told about my work he came immediately and was so excited he went through the red lights where the road turns left for Barrow. He crashed into a car fortunately only receiving minor injuries. He found refuge in an hotel where he phoned to tell us the unfortunate news. I picked him up in George. He wanted to buy twenty drawings - all early ones 30 x 22 inches which I still possess They are so important to me I could never sell them. When they see the light of day they will diminish any drawings of this era.

But he too went away with just a damaged car and dented ego. Overtures from the mighty Agnews of Bond Street were ignored. Percy was turning down opportunities that most artists can only dream of. Christine was disappointed but not daunted by this attitude to galleries. She had a whimsical dream of them owning a little gallery and selling his work to lovely people over tea and home made scones on a summer's afternoon. They were both deluded. Percy was a master of procrastination. He would always find excuses not to sell any work but she hadn't yet realised what that would mean in reality. She was blinkered.

This honeymoon period was a marvellously productive time and they glowed with happiness and well being. This was what Percy *(or Bob as Chris now liked to call him)* always wanted. He had time, space, adoration, support and encouragement. Chris was a homemaker. She cooked and sewed. She adored her children and Bob was enjoying having them around as well. He loved taking them off fishing and playing games. He thought up expeditions. They were living on a country estate with a river close by. It was a glorious adventure playground. He did all the things he had never done with his own son Brian.

They were so caught up in all this and in each other that they failed to notice the disturbing behaviour of Kim, now thirteen. Although she liked Bob very much, he made her laugh and thought up exciting things to do, she was now very unhappy with all the change. It was a difficult situation for a pubescent teenager. She must have been aware of her mother's heightened

Left: **Yellow house, Wensleydale** *mixed media*
Above: **Levens Hall Kendal; Netta & Robin** *mixed media*

sexual excitement Mavis pointed out. She was fond of her new step father and likened him to Willy Wonka in Charlie and the Chocolate Factory which sounds like a good description from a child's point of view. But of course Willy Wonka had his dark side and she was well aware of this but at that age a teenager is more interested in friends than parents. And therein lay her problem. She was finding it hard to break into established friendships at school yet again. Teenage girls are cliquish and sometimes cruel. She was now at Kendal Grammar School- her third school in two years. She did some baby sitting for the Bagots, their landlords. She stole from them – significantly not for any gain, she buried the plunder in the garden - but to draw attention to her needs. It was a cry for help that went unnoticed.

It was a carefully planned escape. She left for school one spring morning with 'civvies' in her school bag ostensibly to get the school bus as she normally did but when she reached the stone arch bridge with the beautiful vista of the stately home of Levens Hall beyond, she impulsively and symbolically threw her Kendal Grammar School uniform into the fast flowing river, changed into her weekend clothes, stood on the verge of the A6 and hitched a lift in a lorry to London. When she was missed at the end of the day and her clothes were found floating downstream everyone thought the worst. A huge police hunt was mounted. The river was searched by divers. Her mother was hysterical, her father angry and demented. After some weeks she was found in London living rough having been raped.

Chris was alarmed at this turn of events. Her wonderful world had suddenly changed. She was riddled with guilt. Kim's father was furious and blamed her for her selfishness, for not noticing all the warning signs that things were going so badly wrong for Kim. He insisted that she be plucked out of the situation and sent to boarding school. He forbade her return to Levens. Chris was deflated and depressed. She genuinely loved her children and the thought of the family splitting up was deeply distressing.

Paul Griffith had a friend who taught at a quaker boarding school, Sibford, in Oxfordshire and he managed to get her accepted immediately. They tried to keep a tight rein on the pupils but failed miserably with Kim. She was out of the window at night meeting local village boys. Her childhood innocence had been taken away for ever.

Percy was also distressed by the situation. Anything that affected Chris impacted on him. He did the only thing he could do to help and he began to write to Kim; marvellous illustrated letters, recounting the adventures of the family. He was afraid she might feel excluded. Of his three step children Kim was the closest and remained so, maybe because she was a non conformist like him and also, as a friend suggested, she didn't have to live with him on a daily basis any more.

These magical letters were illustrated with dolls, jokes, sweets and toy trains. One was headed with a very realistic jar of humbugs; Have a humbug, he wrote underneath, Go on – take two. They made her laugh. She pinned them up in her room at school and was envied by her friends. They made her feel special. They were full of fun and nonsense and fantasy. She stayed with her real father in the holidays as did her siblings Andrew and Nicola but she was never allowed back to live with the others as a family again.

The dream was broken. Once all the fuss had settled down, Bob and Chris were faced with another serious problem. The Bagots had decided to charge a realistic rent for the cottage which had been left a bit vague. What was reasonable to people on a different income level was unmanageably expensive to them so they had to leave. This was a big turning point in their life together. Where would they go? The enforced move robbed Percy of years of work, thousands of paintings and it condemned Chris to ten years of hard manual labour in her struggle to survive and support Percy and her family.

Peter Scott, prompted by Miss Burkett, offered storage space for his work at Provincial Insurance offices and they went off to Cornwall to find somewhere to live. This was the first time hard reality kicked in for Chris. They had very little money and house prices were well above their means. A mortgage was out of the question because they had no income. Having found nothing they could afford, they began the return journey depressed and for some reason when they reached the Severn Bridge, Percy impulsively made one of his diversions, turned left into Wales and kept on going until they reached St Davids in Pembrokeshire. Neither of them had ever been to Wales. It was a long drive to the far west of the country but worth it because they discovered that property was cheap there. The landscape was exciting. It was by the sea. They thought they could settle there.

At last PK thought he had found happiness. He had not suffered any dark depressions since he had met Chris, he was painting like he had never painted before. He was now presented with a new and exciting terrain and the opportunity to break new ground. He had friends in high places who wanted to help. He was now on the path to success. At the age of fifty five he had the potential to make his mark.

Left: **Yellow bird letter to Kim** *mixed media*

Above: **Letter to Kim** *mixed media*

chapter 11

The Flight to St David's

March 1973

A lorry drew up outside a pair of derelict cottages in the centre of the tiny city of St David's Pembrokeshire. A woman and two children jumped out of the driver's cab. The driver walked round to the back and began to untie the cleats which secured the tarpaulin covering the open truck. Curtains twitched along the road – the Welsh are a curious lot. They had heard about the purchase of the two old tumbledown cottages that no one wanted in Gospel Lane. They heard that the couple were intending to do all the work themselves which seemed like insanity – but they were English which explained a lot. It was a condemned property unfit for human habitation. The roofs were falling in, there was no kitchen and no sanitation. Tension mounted as the driver worked his way around his truck finally pulling the tarpaulin off to reveal piles of old furniture and effects dominated by a rather battered home made sofa perched on top of it all. A man in a woolly hat was lying on the sofa. He sat up and surveyed the scene, blinking insouciantly at the light. The curtains were quivering now. It was the artist. It was never clear whether PK had travelled all the way from Cumbria

in this extraordinary way or whether he had only made the last few miles in style. Maybe he had followed in one of his veteran cars and it had broken down on the way as his self maintained cars inevitably did and he had hitched a lift on the lorry. We will never know the truth. It is too far in the past.

When Chris and Bob turned their fateful left a few months before and drove to the end of Wales they were still in romantic mode. They explored the back streets of St David's and found this undesirable property, 5 and 7 Gospel Lane, for sale. It had been on the market for a very long time – several years - and they decided there and then that it might be affordable and it might, with a lot of hard work, be suitable for them. This was a great leap of faith and imagination.

They bought it a few months later with the help of a two thousand pound loan from Peter Scott of Provincial Insurance in Kendal which he later increased by another £2000 and finally wrote it off as a gift. Chris chipped in with her divorce settlement and the proceeds of the sale of her jewellery

Left: **Gospel Lane, interior** *watercolour and ink*

Above: **5 & 7 Gospel Lane 1973; before building commenced**

Right: **Cottages near St David's** *watercolour and ink*

and Lord Eccles paid for a bathroom. Other friends contributed. Everyone who knew and cared about them was concerned. They could see the pitfalls ahead. This 'cheap' property was going to be very costly. It would cost them seven years of their lives and their physical and mental health. It was a mighty task to make this ruin habitable for themselves and two children. Bob had no building experience. He had made some alterations and installed a kitchen at Glen Cottage which was a mile away from the complete renovation of a property that was falling down. It cost a lot of paintings – the paintings that would have been done if PK had not been pushing barrow loads of cement about.

Bob and Chris spent seven years roofing this wreck; putting in doors, windows, floors and Heath Robinson type plumbing - there was no inside sanitation at all - building a lean to extension and turning a shed in the back lane into a workshop.

Chris had ambitions to turn the detached shed they had bought with the property across the garden and over the back lane into a small gallery where they could show and sell work but all hopes of that scheme receded as his retentiveness came to the fore. He always agreed in theory but found excuses not to sell any work. He now had the perfect excuse – no time because of the overwhelming task of making the cottages habitable.

Now that they were isolated, Bob needed to keep up the letter writing which was so much part of his life. In the evenings he wrote to Lord Eccles, his step daughter Kim and several friends and supporters back in Cumbria all of which have been carefully preserved because of the marvellously seductive illustrations. These letters when put together give us an account of their seven years in Pembrokeshire.

Bob's first letter to his friend Lord Eccles was a cheerful affair.

So here we are at St David's. I will celebrate my fifty sixth birthday soon – a long road to attain what I have always wanted – a place to work, warm, dry and with space.

I owe all to my wife a wonderful person of rare understanding because it was she who provided most of the money to purchase these two cottages and much more besides; trust and faith.

This was unbelievably blinkered optimism.

Lord Eccles was concerned about his welfare. Percy kept in touch and wrote to him to explain the move from Levens writing ***The Bagots felt we were not the kind of tenants they preferred so we had to move.*** Another romantic description of St David's arrived at their London home. Percy and Chris were obviously adjusting well, settling down and exploring their new environment. In the following letter to the Eccles dated 1973 this was confirmed. They sounded wonderfully happy which meant PK would paint well.

I love these sculptural high banked roads. They change so during the seasons; faded winter grasses change to fresh greens; snowdrops white, primroses and daffodils yellow, they grow in such decorative profusion.

Looking back towards the Preselli Hills we spied a rainbow lovely against the dark cloud ridden sky ... but our way led to the sun and clear skies.

We turned left down a road that followed a beck to the cathedral a few minutes away from the top of Snowdrop Hill and then home, two hundred yards. It is odd being so near to the cathedral and yet not able to see it except from the roof top and here only the tower can be seen.

Left: **Gospel Lane, interior** *watercolour and ink*

Above: **Cottages 5 & 7 Gospel Lane in a letter** *watercolour and ink*

The Eccles were reassured. When they eventually drove from London to see them expecting to find Bob painting they were deeply shocked at the reality which was far from romantic. The magnitude of the task they had taken on was clearly outfacing. Chris and Bob were living on site with no kitchen and bathroom with two growing children.

21st September 1974 brought a letter from Lord Eccles enclosing a sizeable cheque to help them with the renovation work. Percy replied immediately

When your letter arrived this morning I was busy contemplating two gaping holes in the wall of the cottage – I had taken out both windows the previous day. Your kindness overwhelmed us both – in fact it was some time before we could work we were so stunned. The letter seemed to be a good omen because people passing up and down the lane were so pleasant. A Miss Bailey who lives in a lovely pink washed cottage overlooking the cathedral stopped for a chat (the very first). She said she was on her way to her second home ; two cottages knocked into one set on the cliffs overlooking Ramsey Island. We were invited to go along any time. An hour later a neighbour to whom I have never spoken popped his head over the wall and asked if we would care to come and look at the views from his living room windows. I was loathe to break off work but we went along and the view was really beautiful. The window was on the third floor way above our humble abode. I was given permission to do a drawing of it when I have a spare hour.

Eighteen months later, that which everyone else had found obvious, that two derelict cottages could not be re-built by two inexperienced people in a theoretical 'allocated time' was proved true. Reality and disillusion were becoming apparent.

To David Eccles

15th September 1974

My world is rather mixed up. A building project that has gone on far beyond the time we had allocated so I cannot stop to do some serious painting. When we came here in March of last year we both weighed approximately eleven and a half stone – now our weights

are barely ten stone. Our building fund which at the beginning seemed adequate has dwindled at an alarming rate in spite of doing practically all the work ourselves.

20th September 1974

Dear Lord Eccles

I do not remember mentioning the cathedral at St David's in my letter. So often do I long for the Cumberland landscape. Pembrokeshire pales in comparison then I remember the wonderful church building and I am cheered and uplifted ... a masterpiece will unfold for I feel it was ordained that I should come here. Please forgive the quality of the sketch for my materials; paper and colours are all still locked away. I dare not bring them out otherwise our building will suffer so I use the children's colour box, pens and crayons. This card was made from a breakfast food carton

Percy Kelly

They loved it at first. Chris once again had her 'happy hat' on and was planning yet again to fulfil her dream of a little gallery where she would sell Percy's work and her own and live happily ever after - for she too was now developing her painting skills under her husband's influence and tuition. She still hadn't learned that life is never that simple. She always looked for the best in people. She was surprised and disappointed at the unfriendliness of the Welsh. The two younger children were unhappy at school. They had to learn Welsh and pass an exam in it. Nikki did well and passed, Andy wasn't so keen. They were picked on by teachers for being English. They happily settled for a while making friends with English ex patriots but they always felt alien there and so did Chris and Bob. Former friends were supportive turning up with gifts of food and buying paintings – ones which Percy would sell when desperate and then regret afterwards. He sometimes asked for them back. Peter Scott visited and took them all out for lavish meals. Lord and Lady Eccles came and offered practical advice. David Eccles persuaded the Chairman of the Welsh Arts Council to visit and he immediately offered to buy a suite of charcoal drawings for the National Collection raising a purchase grant to buy them and Percy summarily turned him down; the reason given was he 'needed space to work'. *(his quote!)* At the time Christine was knitting, making jam and cakes, growing vegetables – anything to earn money. A quote from a letter to Lord Eccles dated September 1974 is graphic and was accompanied by a large drawing of their 'sitting' room. Percy admits in the letter that he has 'tidied it up a bit' in the drawing. At the top of the letter there is a beautiful watercolour drawing of a six pack of matches that are so real you feel you could pick them up.

I intended to scribble on the large drawing but I failed to have sufficient space. This detail was observed sitting on a couch I once made and it is my domain; my corner. I have about twelve inches of space where I can sit midst drawings and books etc. My wife's area is the yellow chair hence the balls of knitting wool in an old basket. When we came to St David's this room was intended to be lived in for only a few months and little did we know that occupation would be more than eighteen months. It is not a pleasant room to live in for it is a little damp but we ought to have it all like new for Christmas.

Left: **Farm cottages near Wigton, 1974** *crayon on a cereal packet*
Above: **Near St Davids** *watercolour and ink*

Lord and Lady Webb visited them and tried to persuade them to move nearer London where they could be better helped but that was an unrealistic suggestion. There was no way they could afford to live nearer the capital. They couldn't even afford Cumbria or Cornwall. The property in which they had invested every penny was unsaleable and barely habitable. This far outreach of Wales was just affordable. Chris' dream of turning the detached shed the other side of the lane into a gallery was crumbling, and Percy's personality disorder was worsening making their position untenable in that closed Welsh society.

Letter to David Eccles

14 October 1974

Cottages in the country sound so romantic but behind the façade of the old stone wall weathered and lichen covered with roses around the door and bedecked spring and summer flowers lurks mildew and dampness.

The dream was fading fast but things were now getting even worse. Chris had realised soon after she married him that Bob was a cross dresser. She accepted this and found it quite amusing and at times titillating providing it was done in private – a secret between the two of them. But he was now feeling the need to demonstrate his love of dressing up in female

clothes in public. He wanted to be admired. He wanted to 'come out'. He recounted an incident to Joan David in a letter many years later about a delivery of coal that was made to their house in St David's. Chris was out – probably working – and Bob answered the door forgetting he was dressed as a woman. He proudly boasted that the man was very friendly and never suspected he wasn't a woman. He was deceiving himself. The small closed society was humming with the news. It was a bad place to do this. In 1976 anywhere was a bad place but the far outreaches of Wales was dire. The children were teased at school and their social life plummeted deeper.

With lack of money, lack of local friends and lack of a dry secure house surely things couldn't get any worse – but they did.

The house next door was bought by a solicitor and his wife and they began an access dispute which went on for years and caused Chris and PK much worry and stress. They proposed building a drive right across their garden to access a garage they were intending to build in their own garden thereby splitting the Kelly property in two leaving their workshop isolated at the other side of the drive. They produced legal arguments for doing this, accused the Kelly's of altering a wall and started proceedings against them. Their deeds seemed to be at variance with each other. So they were in conflict with their neighbours over this boundary dispute which took them to court. They were in conflict with the building inspector who condemned their first attempt at building foundations making them start again and Bob was in conflict with any of the trades he employed *(a rare event anyway)* because he knew how to do anything better than they did and always disputed the bill. He thought other people could and should live on next

Far left: **Near Strumble** *watercolour and ink*
Left: **Cottage at Strumble Head** *watercolour and ink*
Above: **Diary page** *watercolour and ink*

to nothing as well. He was in conflict with the puritanical Welsh community who were not tolerant of sexual deviation in this cathedral city of dozens of churches and chapels and only one pub.

The letter to the Aitchesons dated 20th October 1976 was a sad tale of woe. They were waiting for their planning permission to build a much needed extension, fighting the neighbours and Chris had stepped on a rusty nail which had gone septic. Bob coolly wrote;

But we had some blocking to do so quite heroically she began to mix mortar between showers. It was such a day sunshine washed out periodically with heavy showers. I managed to lay twenty six blocks by five o'clock

He then went into detail of obtaining building blocks with some doubtful arithmetic and economics.

We have to travel fifteen miles each way to obtain concrete blocks. They are extremely heavy so we are committed to carrying only twenty six per run. The cost is ten pence a block. A factor in St David's charges fourteen and a half pence a block – quite a difference. *(this was accompanied by a drawing of the trailer with the twenty six blocks neatly stacked.)* He justified it by continuing ***Happily the road to the village of Letterson where the blocks are made is one of the pleasantest in the whole area A few miles further on the Preselli Hills begin to rise. It was from here that our forbears*** (sic) ***created Stonehenge.***

He went on to write about the nosiness of the Welsh. They were visited by the local doctor who was interested in seeing PK's work. As soon as the doctor had gone neighbours made their way past hoping to find out the reason for the visit. Maybe some terrible affliction. When all seemed normal they lost interest.

... and so the Welsh village charcterises this particular Welsh quality. There is no particular pattern which one finds in an English village; no strength, no feeling of togetherness, no pattern, just a haphazard collection of poor building. No friendly morning greeting; merely suspicion.

I am qualified to say this because although in my work there is an absence of people I am conscious that they exist.

The people of St David's still remember him thirty years on as the artist who wore frocks. They are keen to talk about him at length viewing his eccentricities with a disapproving wonderment.

Bob did find some time to paint. He did several magnificent paintings and drawings of St David's Cathedral - the reason it can claim to be a city albeit the smallest in the country. He celebrated the coast line with a massive painting of Fishguard. Chris found a good gallery there and took some of her work in after she began painting. Percy dropped her off and drove to a high place and looking down on the harbour, worked up a beautiful piece of art on a long piece of lining paper *(again 54 x 22 inches)*. It is hard to work out how he physically managed with this length of fragile paper of an awkward size in a place with no space and few flat surfaces.

There were other massive paintings of Strumble Head and the Blue Pool. He wandered the alleyways, and surrounding villages of St David's drawing and painting. He painted high hedgerows, wild bogs and cliff tops as well as the Preselli Hills. The optimism of bright colours still remained despite the set backs. He had left behind the dark browns and ochres with Cumberland and the jaunty bright blues with Brittany. The light here was different. On the whole the work lacked the heaviness of the Cumberland work. It was becoming markedly softer and more feminine. His washes were more delicate. Since being with Chris he had lost the black and white in his life and work.

As a thank you gift he sent Lord Eccles a beautiful painting of a road near Caldbeck. He used a piece of mount board to strengthen the painting in the post. On the back of it was a bonus – a lovely painting of a farm in the village of Caerfaraefell Pembrokeshire dated 17th July 1977. The note inside said he found it difficult to send a blank sheet! He was homesick for Cumberland though. In November in a nostalgic letter to David Eccles he wrote wistfully ***Autumn till April is the best time of year for painting in Cumberland. I walked the fells before and after Christmas especially around Crummock. Loweswater and Lorton. I get homesick this time of year.***

Chris was sociable and made friends easily. She depended on them to retain some normality in her new life. She invited a young English couple

who lived nearby for supper. Percy wore a dress and they were embarrassed. This surprised Chris. She had thought better of them. She didn't think that in Cumbria or anywhere guests might find it unusual behaviour. Peter Scott came down to take them all out and found Bob in a yellow flowered dress and wrote him a stiff letter afterwards. He was shocked. He suggested he have some psychiatric treatment which Bob found preposterous and replied in outrage to this kind benefactor who had done so much to help, rejecting his advice very rudely, writing that there was nothing wrong with him. He did not need professional help. He described Scott's visit in a letter to David Eccles giving his own slant on the occasion. He made no mention of his mode of dress. He said they went out for dinner with Peter Scott who was displeased with him because he was unable to eat very much. Bob's excuse was that he had received news that his sister's husband had died. This was the first mention of his family since he left Audrey. He appeared to have made no attempt to contact any of them so it invalidates that story. Word got round back in Cumbria not about the transvestism but about their poverty and living conditions. This was much more shocking.

Chris did the garden. She grew all their vegetables as well as novelty items like sunflowers. She sold the surplus in the WI weekly sale in a tiny building near Gospel Lane. Every week since it started she had taken boxes of cookies, marmalade, toffee, fudge, gingerbread and gingerbread men decorated with raisins and peel all beautifully packed and top quality. Bob proudly stated to David Eccles that she only used butter and brown flour and sugar. The WI took 10% commission to cover their costs. He said that demand was fantastic and it contributed to what he referred to as their nest egg. Her speciality was Cumberland rum butter and as an afterthought

Left: **Fishguard** *watercolour and ink*
Above: **Near St Davids in blackberry juice and biro**

he mentioned that she also looked after his picture frames if they needed painting or touching up. He omitted to mention that she was also building, digging, heaving blocks and pushing heavy barrow loads of cement. He went on to casually mention the knitting machine which she had bought second hand. She was now producing a wide range of designer garments. This woman was a minor miracle and deserves massive admiration. She charged very little for these beautiful garments which were always quickly snapped up. PK was painting every day now as well. It was a battle for survival. Bob's comment after mentioning all this activity was ***'She loves being busy!'***

On Monday 26th October 1975 in a letter to David Eccles he wrote

I love to take a large piece of sympathetic paper and create spontaneous landscapes. Three recent ones are particularly beautiful most poetic.. I do wish we lived nearer London because I would appreciate your views on the marriage of these paintings and the strong dark drawing. The size is a constant 30 x 22 and in each case I have translated the very essence of the country in question. Normandy, Brittany, Cornwall, Cumberland, Westmorland, Mid Wales and Pembrokeshire.

In January 1976 David Eccles visited again and managed to persuade PK to sell him a Pembrokeshire painting. Percy wrote to him afterwards

It is my intention to do more painting in this vein in fact I have a great many sketches to work from. During the summer I did an exciting rough, 40 x 22 inches, which I intended to show you. There was a cardboard box containing a great many small bits and pieces which I forgot about too. One ink painting I must keep for you because I think it is quite delectable (9 x 3 inches) A very small winter landscape I love too, the colouring and suggestion of snow is unusual.

He mentioned the visit of Peter Trier and his wife who lived in Fishguard who had hotpot and stayed until midnight.

They were so excited about my paintings. On leaving Peter whispered to Christine – do you think Bob would sell me the large painting of St David's? We never learn what her answer was or whether he ever did.

As well as all the baking, knitting, building and gardening, Christine worked in a gift shop owned by an English couple Audrey and Jim Cartmel. PK told Lord Eccles with awe that Jimmy had given him ***a special type of table called a Black and Decker Workmate; the deluxe model – worth about £44.*** They had sold the shop and were moving away. They wanted to buy a painting from him. Audrey was often not well so to cheer her up he said he used to slip Good Morning sketches under the glass covered table in the shop. This sounds unlikely. He went on to say that usually when he took Christine a flask of tea in the late evening he'd do a few odd jobs because Jimmy was hopeless with his hands – he was an accountant. So Chris was working in the evenings as well! They were seriously skint and Christine was a saint. She was innocently, unbelievably resourceful and long suffering.

He mentioned gleefully that for his birthday Christine bought him a gadget for cutting the tops off bottles. He made storage jars with cork tops with it. He was thrilled with this – for a short time. He said, with no irony, that he made eleven and then went off picking blackberries and sloes. He then boiled them all in a pan and strained them through muslin and made some ink. It came out pink at first in writing and then changed colour to dark grey blue.

I intended to scribble on the large drawing but I failed to leave sufficient space. The detail was observed sitting on a couch I once made which is my domain, my corner. I have about twelve inches of space where I can sit midst drawings & books etc. My wife's area is the yellow chair hence the balls of knitting wool in an old basket. When we came to St Davids this room was intended to be lived in for a few months only and little did we know the occupation would be more than eighteen months!! It is not a pleasant room to live in for it is a little damp but we ought to have it all like new before Christmas. I managed to fill the hole shown on a previous page. A new frame and sill the a splendid home made concrete sill

My wife finished pointing the interior stonework 11pm tonight and it all looks jolly good.

Left: **Letter to Nikki** *mixed media*

Above: **Matchbox letter to Lord Eccles** *watercolour and ink*

Did you know Thomas Bewick made up ink from blackberries. His parents were very poor he wrote and then did a lovely grey blue painting near St David's using the newly cooked medium.

Chris kept in touch with her Cumbrian friends. Mavis Aitcheson kept her letters along with the illustrated ones Bob sent. There was never a complaint or a hint of regret for the life she left behind in Pardshaw. No hint of nostalgia for those exciting carefree first few years together at Levens. There was no anguished sharing of the problem of her husband's cross-dressing. She was stoical. She was putting on a brave face averring that she was enjoying all the hardships. She was positive. But surely this was a façade, a justification for the decisions she had taken which had changed all their lives. There was no going back so what was the point. She had burned her boats – she had to stick with it.

Then there came a glint of hope, a hint of commercialism. Chris was working on a plan to persuade Bob to sell some of his work to contribute to the household economy. Her long time dream of a gallery was going to be realised. She was desperate and would make it happen so the pressure on her would lessen.

Dear Lord Eccles Bob wrote in 1975

During the spring we decided to turn our front living room into a gallery primarily to show my wife's work; flowers and still life paintings.

He went on to say that they got permission from the National Park but her work dried up and so he agreed to show some of his. Maybe this was by design to force him to show and sell some of his work. Surely with a cottage stuffed with good, highly desirable work and no money in the bank he would overcome his scruples. There was no lack of eager buyers and he was seeing his wife exhausting herself with the efforts to earn enough to put a meal on the table.

But the former demons returned and he wrote ***I had hoped to show etchings and drawings of the cathedral but time ran out - having to turn the room into a gallery and frame up at least 28 items.***

It was always the same – he concentrated on the peripherals rather than the main task.

His exhibition eventually opened on September 1st - only six months late. He said it looked good but the response was depressingly poor. In three weeks they saw only a handful of visitors and very few sales. This too was possibly contrived. Gospel Lane is a narrow back lane with no footfall other than access. It would have required a lot of publicity and signage to make people aware of it. Did he send out invitations to friends who would have been eager to come and buy? Did he ask the Eccles, the Webbs and Peter Scott? Did he invite contacts who had bought his work less than a decade before at Rosehill? No of course not. He insisted on making his own printed cards for invitations. The envelopes were laboriously hand written. They probably never got made, finished or posted. He did all his own framing meticulously without proper equipment. He was distracted into side projects that were never completed. He probably sabotaged it because he didn't want it to succeed. Chris was upset. This was the first time we see a crack in her stoicism.

Mary Burkett of Abbot Hall in Kendal got in touch. She had been a regular correspondent ever since they moved from Kendal. Maybe Chris had contacted her this time in desperation. Miss Burkett had been pursuing him for an exhibition since his Allonby days and, like all the others, had failed but now they needed money urgently. They were engaged in a legal battle. The case eventually went to court and they won but it had cost them a lot in money, time, stress and morale. Bob reluctantly agreed this time under pressure.

Exhibitions threw him into a panic. He had masses of work sitting around completed but he never wanted to show or sell any of that. He would begin doing irrelevant things and get very stressed. He would do everything – simple things that other people could do more easily like framing. With a talent as phenomenal as his he could pay other people to frame his work, to paint his house, to service his car and work on the plumbing. But he wouldn't consider it. The whole dreadful cycle started again. He hadn't had an exhibition since 1969 in Kings Lynn and that had ended in disaster.

His two step-children were very helpful and loyal. They had the measure of him and his problems and saw how hard their mother was working to provide for them and they wanted to contribute. This family were living in poverty and deprivation worse than the Kelly family in Workington in the great Depression. They all worked hard and got behind their step father because they could see this was the way forward to a better standard of living and a happier mother. He introduced one of his negative non sequitors at this point. He had been working on a stag beetle painting and he wanted to finish it for the exhibition despite having stacks of completed work ready. He had done the original drawing at the V & A years ago and he now needed to check certain features. Chris was brightly encouraging. She suggested it would be good for the Kendal show. His step son Andrew went voluntarily to the library at Haverfordwest on Saturday morning on his bike or the bus and brought back the only illustration of a stag beetle he could unearth but Percy immediately argued that the legs were in the wrong position. Again he was annoyingly emphasising the negative. However he managed to work from it and said it was more painterly and glowing than the first one which was a rough guide for a three plate lithograph which was never completed.

He finished the painting but didn't put it in the exhibition. It is a double entendre of a work. On the surface it is a stag beetle but if looked at for a long time it becomes a lyrical golden Cumbrian landscape.

And so it went on from muddle to worse muddle with nothing being finished and excuses being made. Chris reported progress to David Eccles in January 1976 in a letter. Percy had taken over the living room which was strewn with work completed, work in progress and materials for mounts and frames.

It's a mess. Percy has been very prolific of late so our area is heaped up with drawings and ideas. What a mess we are in!

His frames were elaborate affairs involving newspaper backings *(which have since helped to date paintings – keeping in mind always that he may have backed them long after painting them or he may have stocked up the newspapers from former years)*, bits of wood for mouldings possibly salvaged from skips and an elaborate system of screwing the back board to the frame. The result was not particularly pleasing.

The other problem which always dogged him was his fascination with his own work. As soon as he began to sort out his boxes he would alight on some long forgotten piece and fall into a nostalgic reverie for some time before deciding he couldn't possibly let it go. And so the cycle would continue its tedious way.

Above: **Stag beetle landscape** *watercolour and ink*

David Eccles again leapt in with support. He reframed a painting that he had bought and brought it back to show to PK in the hope that he might see how he could be helped. He offered to get the others for the exhibition framed at his expense. Percy brushed this aside and complained about his lack of paper of the right quality. David sent him some paper samples he had sourced - imperial sheets as requested - which came from Robert Hall in Edinburgh. He asked him to let him know which he preferred and give him quantities and he would put an order in. PK replied ungraciously that they weren't big enough.

With the exhibition at Abbot Hall looming even closer, panic and reservations increased. He started to worry about pricing but this was not about pricing – it was about selling.

There will be a number with which I will be loth to part he wrote to David.

Disaster then struck yet again. They had managed in the midst of all this activity to start to build the much needed extension – again doing all the work themselves. The first set back was that the footings did not conform to regulations so the building inspector wouldn't pass them and demanded that weeks of effort be dismantled and a new start must be made. One can't help wondering why Bob couldn't see that concentrating on the exhibition and paying someone to build the extension would be sensible. He seemed paralysed by the fear of spending money. He wanted to do everything himself in the cheapest possible way. But he would have others believe *(and himself)* that everything was all-right.

On the domestic front things are going quite well. I have finished the kitchen except for some of the paintwork – we are waiting for the new plaster to dry out – and it looks good. he wrote to Lord Eccles

But a short while later, in December 1976, Percy wrote to David Eccles that Chris had cracked. Her spirit had gone. She had come into the new extension and sobbed. During the night, rain had got through the plastic sheeting on the roof and the new kitchen was awash. She was preparing for Christmas with no money trying to work out how they would manage. She was no doubt frantically making Christmas gifts and decorations for the children and friends. There would be no Christmas shopping for her – this was a luxury they could not afford. They had ordered a modest turkey for Christmas dinner and had to cancel the order which was humiliating. She was at her wits end and now this. Percy was surprised at her reaction. This was not a problem to him - he put another sheet on top of the old plastic with eyelets 'from stock!' as he quaintly put it. It got worse. A high wind and gale blew slates off the roof and it had to wait for the window of a spring day to repair it. And then they were cut off by snow on same roof.

How many times did Chris look back on the life she used to have in Cockermouth? How much longer could she go on pretending that everything was all right?

At last the exhibition dates they had worked towards for so long drew near and they set off for Kendal, the cars loaded with the paintings. It was the largest exhibition he had ever put together and again he had mixed feelings about it. There were finally fifty five framed paintings and drawings ranging from £40 to £210, thirteen etchings from £20 and four lithographs. Almost a quarter of the exhibition was marked as NFS - not for sale. The old pattern, the old mistakes, the old selling problem returned. Despite many exchanges of letters and hours of telephone conversations, he was still fretting about pricing right up to the last moment. He wasn't good at pricing his work possibly because that implied they were for sale or maybe because he was not comfortable with numbers. He kept on changing his mind. Once it was hung the exhibition looked very good but Percy was depressed and unhappy. He wrote that he was disappointed with sales and attendance at the opening. Miss Burkett had advised pricing them low he said but he both regretted that and in the same sentence wondered if they were still too high because some buyers had retracted after promises of purchase.

This was unfair. There was no pleasing him. He was in a position that made him uncomfortable and uneasy. He complained about the absence of any critics but there was a review of the exhibition in the Arts Guardian Wednesday August 18th written by Mereta Bates. It is notoriously difficult even now to get any art critic out of London and this was before the days of fast trains and cheap plentiful flights. He was exceedingly lucky to get a Guardian review.

Mereta Bates wrote

Above: **Diary page** *watercolour and ink*

Considering that the works stretch from the late 50s to today, the range is considerable. The dour, stark and explicit linear structure of studies of machinery or docks such as of a winding engine or Maryport Cumberland, satisfy in themselves yet also suggest the assured analysis behind other, apparently, spontaneous improvisations. There are for example two stunning sketches of Lowca and Millom. The slag heap at Lowca is a billowing wash of prussian that flows into the streets of terraces around obliterating all but a few on a hill beside the winding engine. at Millom, all is drenched in a golden bronze, the dark of a crater and chimneys set against the gleam of a pool and the smallest whitewashed shed.

Very occasionally Kelly breaks into thick black brush daubs with colour washes and textures as in the lurid pink, green and slate of Pit Tip Broughton or more convincingly, the autumnal hues of Near Muker, Yorkshire. But he seems aware of the dangers in bold, brash but easily empty gestures and, in his latest work concentrates hard on very subtle inter-relationships of shape and light. A series of Pembrokeshire landscapes focus upon a rift in the cloud, a dark silhouette of of rock with house lit by a stray beam of light, strange movement along an horizon above a bank of hedge or field. Studies such as these and also perhaps the bold foxgloves blooming pink and purple out of blue flagged leaves like a piece of stained glass, combine original perception with the skill and persistence to record it precisely. The effort so much more demanding than the mere topographical, breathes through every dab, sputter and wash of Kelly's brush. There is sincerity and drive but also at best the fire of inspiration.

Despite all the hard work on his behalf by Miss Burkett and staff, the result of the show at Abbot Hall was disappointing to Bob and Chris. It was an anti climax to all their months of frantic preparations. Bob complained that there were so many paintings left it would involve another journey. But one can sense he couldn't wait to be reunited with his work. To make matters worse Chris became ill – probably with the strain of it all. This woman was now desperate.

She had arranged an exhibition of her work at the gallery in Fishguard to take place soon after the Abbot Hall show. Oh yes, she was painting in watercolour now, dealing with her husband's endless advice and criticism. He insisted on doing all the framing for that as well. She did well. She wrote to her friend Mavis that she had sold thirteen at the opening with two more in the pipeline. Her knitting was selling in London as well. In a letter to David Eccles in January 1976 Percy wrote that

Chris discovered a wool shop with a closing down sale and bought £100 wool.

Mavis described a beautiful evening coat and dress she and Chris had designed and made which she sold immediately to a woman from London who had then commented that it would have cost her at least £200 there. Chris had charged her a fraction of that. Mavis thought she had seriously undersold herself. With Bob constantly talking himself up, Christine was losing confidence in herself.

Christine then discovered a painter called John Stopes who was opening a gallery in nearby Solva. PK had done quite a lot of work in that area drawing and sketching. She persuaded him to come and see Percy. Again PK was negative but in 1977 he did show ten paintings and etchings, again he was highly critical of the exhibition space and various other minor irritations in letters to David Eccles and Mavis Aitcheson.

Although by now her own work was good, Chris was doing everything she could think of to motivate Bob. She came up with another brilliant idea. Every evening he would sit with a board on his knees and write beautiful illustrated letters which he was posting out in all directions. He would start with a drawing or painting of something he'd seen, remembered or something that had happened that day. Maybe a clump of flowers, a bird he'd seen out of the window or a glimpse of the sea. He would leave a space for his beautiful writing to tell more. The recipients loved them. Chris suggested he make an illustrated diary – one page a day. He was enthusiastic about this and began straight away on January 1st 1978 with a bowl of snowdrops and a poetic piece of writing inserted skilfully on the page. He kept this up day after day.

An A4 sheet dated Sunday 5th February 1978 with a lettering heading VOGUE in pastel colours.

In a letter to Lord Eccles dated 20th February 1978 he stated that so far he had forty seven pages which meant he had almost kept up the one-a-day regime. But it began to become onerous. He was getting bored with it. He began diverting from the job in hand and following his habitual wandering from the main aim.

The diary which I told you about in my last letter has become very involved and as a consequence is taking up quite a lot of time. At the beginning I imagined I would do the odd drawing plus a modicum of writing. Instead the old grey matter was prodded into action and now I am engulfed in various books and note books with the aim of sparking off the odd inspired thought. To date I have forty five illustrated sheets.

Just after the holidays I made a wooden box to accommodate the finished sheets and pens and at the end of each day I simply pop each drawing inside. It will be interesting to take them all out in June say and look at them en masse. I am trying not to be too contrived which is not really difficult because I love to doodle and use any materials which are to hand and subjects. - the latter are very varied.

So, he spent time making the box they were to be put in. He was lyrical as usual about his efforts.

In May 1978 he wrote to David Eccles

Last night I checked the box and counted sixty seven illustrations which works out at almost a daily record. At the beginning the going was difficult but now I feel that I am much more involved. I have to be very wary because time goes by so rapidly one can quite easily lapse for a number of days. There are some very interesting drawings varied in context – a sort of personal doodling with no pretensions regarding technique and style. At the end of the year I think I will enjoy flipping through three hundred and sixty pages … perhaps a little more because to date I have introduced some large double pages.

These diary pages are exquisite but his output was not one a day. Once again his calculations were optimistically flawed. There are villages, flowers, cars, a sort of nature diary, notes on the weather and interiors of the cottage. Some are pages of poetry with lettering. Sadly the box never filled and there

Above: **Blue door** *mixed media*

were never 365 diary pages to look through. The last was May 20th 1978. It had lasted five months. He became very keen on this charming illustrated daily record so it was a pity he didn't continue it.

He sent some of the pages to Joan many years later as part of his correspondence with her. The other sheets were found in the cottage when he died – not in the custom made box but scattered randomly among all the other bits of paper. The box had now found a different purpose holding bottles of ink and pens.

His frequent obvious miscalculations are intriguing. His vocabulary, grammar and language skills were outstanding given his background and education but his numeracy was terrible. Was this a psychological block? Or was it a total blindness to numbers? Maybe this was the reason for his lack of interest in money and all things commercial. Together it adds up to a personality disorder.

One of the last pages of the diary is very beautiful - one of the villages near St David's - but the writing is a tirade against the Welsh.

Peter Scott saw some of these diary pages on a visit in March 1978 and suggested they should be made into a book. He offered to pay for the printing and publishing. Percy replied in his usual negative manner;

With regard to the diary I am not sure it will be suitable for publishing. Colour plates would be extremely costly.

After six hard years Chris and Bob were exhausted with their battle to survive. The house was still a mess and incomplete. Their cars were constantly breaking down. Their finances were worse than ever and they were ostracised in St David's as Bob's gender confusion became more overt. He now firmly believed he was actually turning into a woman. Chris was in a state of despair. It was seven years since she 'ran away' with Percy and she had shown exceptional loyalty, tolerance and endurance. But she was cracking up under the strain. She couldn't go on. She suddenly stood back and saw for the first time her own situation in its dreadful reality. The husband wife relationship was over. Her dream of selling his work in a gallery was over. She began to be more critical of his behaviour and he hated it. She began to question some of his decisions and he hated that too. As a former nurse she dismissed some of his health problems as psychosomatic. She became impatient with his constant complaints of headaches and colds using them as reasons not to do things. She stopped making allowances for him. She stopped balancing them against his phenomenal talent. Rather than exploding she became introspective. She became quiet and unresponsive. What was she to do? Her friends meant a lot to her but she still kept the sexual problems private. She was ashamed of all the mistakes she had made and found it hard to admit to them. After all she had sacrificed to be with Bob and then all they had gone through together, she couldn't see a way out. She couldn't just walk away from it. She had nowhere to walk to. They would have to move. They would have to make a new start somewhere completely different. The children were ready to move on. Her son Andrew would soon be leaving home anyway to do a two year A level course with a bias towards drama at Stratford Polytechnic and Nikki was back in Cumbria living in Pardshaw close to her father with Chris' friend Wendy who had a daughter the same age. But where could they go?

An army helicopter pilot had recently moved to St David's. He had inherited a scale model of a steam tractor. He lent it to PK who took it to the cottage to do some drawings which formed another page of the diary. They were invited round to his house and discovered he had moved to Wales from Norfolk. He told them property was cheaper there, the climate better and it was closer to London. *(so why had he moved?)*. They pounced on this as the solution to all their problems. Norfolk was a whim. Something to focus on; maybe a lifeline. They seemed to have overlooked the flatness

Right: **Pembrokeshire coast** *watercolour and ink*

Above: **Diary page** *watercolour and ink*

of the landscape. Chris swung straight back into her optimistic mode. They began to make plans. But then she began to vacillate. She was scared of making another big mistake. She went off on her own to see friends in Cumbria to discuss it with them. She was in turmoil. She was still keeping her biggest problem to herself. She just couldn't talk to anybody about what had now become Bob's obsession that he was becoming a woman. He was blissfully insensitive to all this. He couldn't see how it must be for her. He was becoming increasingly self obsessed.

He wrote to David Eccles

To add to my troubles, when Christine returned from her trip to Cumberland she did not want to set up home in Norfolk. oh dear the last few months have been awful. I never did even the merest sketch for weeks on end – the first barren period for almost twenty years. Happily things are now sorted out and we are going to Norfolk and I have begun my nightly drawing and painting routine once again. My illustrated diary came to a sad end in May after such an exciting beginning. The other day I placed about ten pages in a large frame; the image is very interesting.

She returned from Cumberland to find dissent at home. Bob childishly complained that Andy had behaved badly while she was away. He alleged he had been drinking and staying out late flouting all the rules – behaving in fact like teenagers do – testing the boundaries and growing up; getting ready to be independent. Bob was sanctimonious in tone – his strict religious childhood was coming to the fore. Teenagers are resistant to preaching and adult nagging and Chris was horrified. Her husband and her son had never really got on together. There had always been tension but this was now blowing up and Bob was behaving like a teenager himself. They had to get on with the move. They went off to Norfolk several times – a long hard cross country drive in an old uncomfortable unreliable car – but found nothing that fitted their criteria *(ie budget)* They stayed with friends, Sue and Tony Maufe, a young architect, in Sparham in the North of the Norfolk on the Lincolnshire border. They were looking for a house in that area, near the coast as Bob would miss the sea, with enough space to work and which was ready to move into. No more building work ever. That was the main thing.

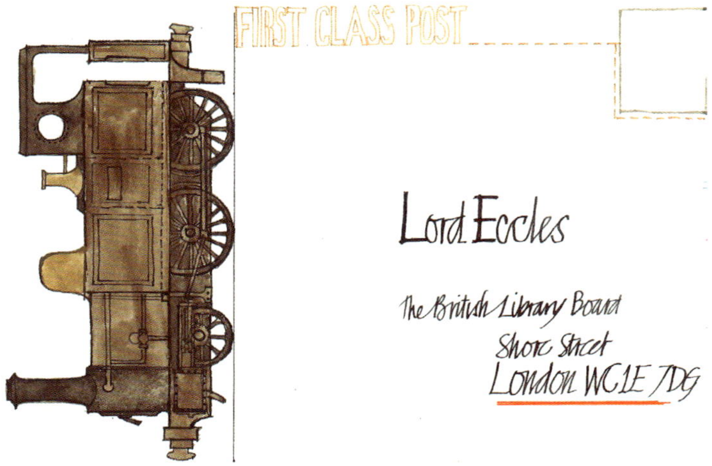

But they had no idea what they had to work with budget wise. After seven years hard work the cottages were still not finished. Would they sell?

As Bob put it in a letter to David Eccles

Trouble is the will to finish the cottages has gone and the other evening (Chris) suggested that we should sell them in their present unfinished state. I wasn't in favour of this because it would mean sacrificing a lot of much needed money. The kind of property we shall need in Norfolk will be expensive and I do not want to live in a small poky place and I want a ready made home. I have had enough of building. Changing tap washers and light bulbs will be my limit in future.

Their visits to Norfolk to find a house brought nothing and then Chris needed to go to Cumberland to hospital for an examination. Unsurprisingly she had health problems. Bob blithely dismissed it, and her moods, to the menopause. He had no concept that it could be related to his problems. He didn't think he had any problems although he was seeing his doctor regularly with a whole raft of symptoms. He was now sixty and things appeared to him to be getting better but he was deluded.

Our finances were in a bad state but out of the blue a friend called to see us one day just after my birthday and bought a large flower painting and a small landscape. A friend of this friend happened to see the paintings and promptly came to see me and purchased a smallish landscape.

The fact that virtually all the building work had been completed (just odd bits of painting still to do) appeared to spread around as if by magic - consequently there are more would-be patrons.

They found a house. It was in Norfolk but that was the only part of their criteria it fulfilled. It was not in the area they wanted near the friends who could help them. It was nowhere near the sea. It was old. It was too small. It needed work. It is frustrating to read this. Were their brains not engaged? Did they not stop to think about it a little more and go through their 'wish list'? These two intelligent people had made impulsive decisions ever since they met. They had behaved like children following any fancy which presented itself. They had played house, played with cars and played at building. They had played with children's lives and they had paid the penalty. Their options had been too wide, their budget too small and they had the wrong priorities. They had decided to live in Wales by simply turning left at a junction and now they were to move to Norfolk on a chance meeting with a pilot. Worst of all they had decided to buy a house which did not tick any of the boxes on their 'must have' list. Did they ever make a list? Bob describes this wonderful place they had found in a letter to David enthusiastically extolling its beauty.

Sunday 15th June 1980

Dear David

I am glad to tell you that we have finally found a new home in Norfolk. Pear Tree Cottage, Magpie Lane, Rockland all Saints near Attleborough.

Attleborough is a small county town south of Norwich and on the main line Kings Lynn to London railway line.

The cottage is very old, small but quite delightful with lots of open beams. Christine fell in love with the place after the initial shock had worn off. We spent a frustrating three days looking over so many properties and the poor girl was rather jaded.

We then rushed back to Wales to get our own cottages on the market.

Left: **Envelope to David Eccles** *watercolour and ink*

Above: **Letter to David Eccles - page eight** *watercolour and ink*

The price asked for Pear Tree was £26,500 and our property has been valued at £40,000 but we advertised it at £38,000. If we can get this figure the profit will help to develop Pear Tree Cottage; a new kitchen and bedroom extension project has been granted by the District Council and the plans will be handed over with the deeds.

The day after arriving back here I had a surprise visit in the form of the Director of the Welsh Arts Council, Aneurin Thomas. We had an interesting conversation but I had a vague notion that I was being interviewed. I learned from a friend who called very late that evening that Mr Thomas was very impressed with my work especially the prints.- I've never seen finer prints was his remark.

I gather my name was mentioned in connection with the Civil List. Can you tell me what this entails David? Whatever it is I cannot see how I can possibly be considered living as I do in such obscurity.

The Welsh are an odd lot. Shortly after Mr Thomas' departure the news spread like wildfire so now I am something of a celebrity.

If all goes well we could be on our way to Norfolk soon so I shall keep you informed. The prospect of an early meeting is very exciting. Christine is anxious that you should try a glass of her quite excellent blackberry wine.

Love from us both

Bob

It was the name that sold it to them. Chris loved the resonance of names; Swallow Hill, Levens Park Cottage. She had loved Gospel Lane when they found it. All their cars had been given names and now she found Pear Tree Cottage, Magpie Lane irresistible. Chris was again thinking romantically of the garden feeding them. She liked the tiny village strung out down the road. It was completely different from anywhere they had lived - and it was habitable. Well – more habitable than the Welsh property had been when they found it. It was too small but had planning permission for an extension. Oh dear. Did he not remember his drawing of 5 and 7 Gospel Lane showing what it was like before building work began in 1973 with a little drawing of the proposed extension at the bottom and the words

I reckon it was seven wasted years upgrading this property. But we are only made wiser by hindsight. Tragedy is - wasted years cannot be reclaimed.

There seems to be no learning curve whatsoever for either of them. They were older but sadly no wiser.

They came home, 'finished' the building work and found buyers for Gospel Lane - The Eagers. This was a propitious name. So they immediately and impulsively paid a deposit on Pear Tree Cottage in July 1980 of £2650. The balance of £23850 had to be paid by 8th August. Friends were worried and Laura Webb gave them a loan cheque for £2500.

Then as so often happens, it looked as though the sale of Gospel Lane was going to fail. The Eagers were hesitating. Their eagerness to buy was waning. Chris worried about this and started to make Blackberry wine.

Bob made a drawing of the living room full of bottles, pipes and pipettes in a letter to David Eccles. In the midst of all their troubles she had found and bought the equipment cheaply and gone out picking pounds and pounds of blackberries. Their small sitting room was like an alchemists den. If the sale fell through it would not be good for prospective buyers when viewing and if it went through it would be difficult to transport gallons of blackberry wine to Norfolk. Whatever was she thinking of?

Meanwhile Bob was worried about the extension that would have to be built on to Pear Tree – wait a minute – he was never going to do any more building work?

Finally after months of worry and upset, the sale to the Eagers and the purchase of Pear Tree went through. At last they were on the move to a supposedly better life.

I never want to hear another word of Welsh said Bob as they said goodbye to St David's. And Chris agreed with him.

Left: **Towards the Presellis** *watercolour and ink*

Above: **Letter to David Eccles - page six** *watercolour and ink*

chapter 12

A Troubled Genius

Though not as dramatic as their arrival seven years before, the departure from St David's was not without its drama. They had a removal van this time but took the cheapest quote and the smallest van. They left a lot of things in the shed – the one that had been designated as a gallery in those early heady days. They decided to retain that - which proved to be the wisest decision of the whole saga.

They followed the van in convoy with Bob driving Hugo their Fiat van followed by Chris in Marco their Morris Traveller towing a trailer. *(They had already deposited the old MG with their friends the Maufes)* There was not a spare inch of space anywhere. Both cars had been road tested and Marco had failed involving Bob in a lot of last minute mechanical work to make it roadworthy. However the convoy soon fell apart and the two Kelly vehicles were left behind. The journey was a nightmare. It is not an easy route from the furthest West to the furthest East – England/Wales at its widest, criss-crossing major north south trunk roads all the way. It was not without incident.

Friday 19th September 1980 Percy described this epic journey to David Eccles

Dear David

At last we are back in England and how good it feels. The move was a very hectic affair ... first my rear lights failed just as we were about to move off at 9 am. They had been checked earlier and functioned perfectly. The problem was sorted out so off we sailed; Chris driving the Morris Traveller plus trailer and I leading the way in the Fiat van.

After a stop in Cardigan the Fiat's starter motor gave up the ghost. This meant pushing to start the engine. Beyond Shrewsbury the Morris' battery began to act queer after a halt for tea. The engine would not turn over so I had to give Christine a tow and thankfully the engine fired. Pushing and towing after stops was the order of the day so it was a relief to turn into Magpie Lane after being on the road for fourteen hours.

The few days we have been here have been hectic ones and we are still feeling the effects of packing, travelling, unloading and trying to sort things out. We shall have to dispose of much furniture because Pear Tree is very small. The garage which measures 16' x 20' is packed to the doors so it is going to be quite a job making room to manoeuvre.

Chris had spent ten years pushing vehicles and being towed but she still hadn't got used to it. It is not clear why they hadn't thought about which furniture they would need and leave the rest behind behind because it wouldn't fit. Why haul a lot of unnecessary stuff across the country? Of course PK was reluctant to leave anything behind so all sorts of spare parts for the car, his printing press and scrap metal, building materials and odd bits of anything that may come in handy were lugged across. The removal van arrived in Norfolk hours before they did on account of all the towing and pushing so when they eventually pulled into the driveway in the dark in the

Right: **Norfolk house** *watercolour and ink*

PK

middle of the night, all the contents of the van had been unloaded, the house filled solid and the surplus put into the garage. Were they expecting the furniture van to be waiting for them? They were horrified. Every square inch of the garage had been filled. All the art materials and paintings had been loaded last for safe keeping so they were unloaded first into the garage with all the other junk piled up behind them so it was impossible to get at them for some months Everything was packed in so tight the doors would not shut. Some of the work when he finally reached it was spoiled with damp.

Still, Bob wrote to David in glowing terms about how happy they were in their new environment.

The main thing is although there are certain shortcomings we love the cottage.

Already we have made friends and the neighbours opposite came over to see if all was well on move-in day. They gave us a bag of coal, milk, tomatoes, vegetables, dessert apples and a mine of local information. These neighbours Bernard and Mary Rose were born in the village and have lived in the lane for forty four years. Bernard is very cheery and Mary shy.

Already due to the kindness of the ironmongers in Attleborough four miles away we have stacked away a large quantity of timber. Everywhere we go we meet friendly people even the bank officials were a revelation. Christine cannot believe it is all happening such is the change from life in Wales. On Friday the library in Attleborough is open till eight o'clock. The other day a charming young lady called selling Battle of Britain flags. We had a long and interesting conversation and she turned out to be the local vet's wife. She and her husband live in a cottage similar to Pear Tree in Rectory Lane. Children on cycles shout a cheery hello.

The cottage is tinder dry, the water is untreated and the vista from the kitchen window and the view up the lane reminds me of Pissaro; apple trees backed by a white wall and red pantiles.

Love from us both

Bob and Christine

Christine is so very happy which is wonderful.

This was born out by her letter to her friend Mavis enclosed with a Christmas card.

December 18th 1980 Pear Tree

Dear Mavis

.... We find life very different here from that in St David's. For a start we have wonderful neighbours who actually speak to us – nay not only speak but come bearing gifts of vegetables etc. On one side a dear old 81 year old spinster, a gentle but very active lady with a delicious sense of humour. We are in a group of five cottages and bungalows about half a mile from the village proper and the Spar grocery and Post Office. I have purchased the most beautiful bicycle at our weekly local auction – it is a pre war sit up and beg 'all steel' Raleigh. I got it for £6.50 and nearly died with delight when it was knocked down to me. I upped and rode it round the auction yard in triumph much to the amusement of all the old farmers. It is in

marvellous condition and I feel very queenly as I sail down the lanes peering over all the hedges. Everyone, including all the children are very friendly and always wave and shout a greeting whether they know you or not. We have one or two hills (63 feet!) at the back of us and the landscape is very English with lovely trees and fields of winter barley and sugar beet; the architecture is varied and interesting. The farming is mainly arable but pigs, goats, ducks, geese, hens and turkeys abound I feel ever so sorry for poultry at this time of year.

Our cottage is very small – one room down stairs and two bedrooms up with a lean to kitchen tacked on one side and a front lobby tacked on the other and about a quarter acre garden with apple, plum and three lovely holly trees, honeysuckle, forsythia, japonica and roses, roses all the way, the whole area bounded by a seven foot hedge. The cottage dates from the early seventeenth century is wood framed and clay lump – heavily beamed and wood on the walls also,

The outside has been clad in brick at a later date and there is a pantiled roof. Inside we have restored an original fireplace in the sitting end and the other end has an ancient Rayburn which after a struggle and some plumbing we have now persuaded to function. It is actually fantastic and keeps the whole place cosy, constant hot water and cooking too. What more could anyone want?

Bob got very low mentally and physically at the time of the move which needless to say was very traumatic and he is still a bit under the weather and feeling very restricted as he has nowhere to work until we build a lean to at the gable end in the early spring. Anglia TV want to do a programme but we are hoping they won't want to film until into the New Year.

We are both so pleased to be in England again and I feel very happy here. It is very 'country' gumboots and wellies.

Anglia Television came and filmed him in November 1981. It was a delightful programme. He started a painting of Caston church, showed a few more paintings and letters. talked about them in his 'studio' and drove his little MG. He wore his habitual woolly hat and plus fours with red socks. His shoulder length grey curly hair flowed down on to his shoulders. The

Top left: **Named cars** *watercolour and ink*
Left: **The studio at Pear Tree**
Above: **Magpie Lane** *watercolour and ink*

woolly hat had become a regular item of clothing. It never came off. I suspect he went to bed in it. He wore it in hospital and he died in it. He was even more convinced he was becoming female. He thought it was happening of its own accord like a pupating caterpillar inevitably emerging from its chrysalis and opening up into a colourful butterfly.

They made their own Christmas cards December 1981 – their second Christmas at Pear Tree. This had become a ritual. Chris had been writing regularly to Mavis in Kendal who had also been to visit them twice. Once again Mavis had shown concern for their life style and Bob's health problems but Bob didn't cross dress during her visit so she was unaware of the biggest problem.

On January 25th 1982 Chris wrote a reassuring letter to her friend saying she had great faith in Bob's etchings and lino cuts and to a lesser extent her own ability to earn hard cash.

If we ever do get really stuck I shall end up in the onion pickling factory in the next village. Phew.

... just returned from a trip to Norwich on the bus – we have no cars on the road at the moment. Always a treat – beautiful and stimulating city. Smiths clearing out paint and brushes at ridiculous prices. Oil paint 13p a tube, watercolours at 16p brushes and varnishes at less than half, so filled tatty Hessian bag with a lovely squirrel like feeling. Bob was thrilled when I got home with the booty. (also bought pair of badly needed shoes).

She also bought several kilos of carrots to make carrot whisky. She was going to need it!

Bob wasn't so happy though. He needed somewhere to work. He bought a second hand wooden chalet that was advertised in the small ads in the local paper to use as a print workshop. After a lot of 'negotiation' recorded in words and pictures in letters to friends, he persuaded the vendor to erect it as part of the deal. The vendor, who must have been desperate to get rid of it, bitterly regretted this as soon as he began. Maybe he had invested so much time loading it in a hired van or on his roof rack that he felt cornered and committed – beyond the point of no return. He had forgotten to add the clause – buyer collects and more importantly – buyer erects! When it was eventually erected Bob discovered that it was too hot in there to do anything. The paper was too dry to print and became curled and brittle as a crisp. He began to get depressed and ill again – the old recurring pattern. Meanwhile Chris had her own agenda. She had quietly planned an escape route if things got bad – and they did. His health problems had been ongoing for some time but they now worsened. He had tinnitus and dizziness, a hernia and masses of unrelated ailments real and imagined. This began to get tedious because he complained and moaned all the time. The cars were off the road and he didn't repair them because he never wanted to go anywhere because he was too ill. If she did tempt him to come out he became dizzy and sick and had to come home.

Things came to a head on Chris's birthday June 1982. Friends who lived in Norwich had invited her to a jazz concert as a birthday present. They asked Bob as well but he declined on health grounds. Chris had been looking forward to it for weeks. As her departure time drew nearer he complained of stomach pains. She ignored this but they got worse. She got ready to go but when she came downstairs he was writhing on the floor begging her not to go. She had had enough. She marched out of the door and got into the car. It wouldn't start. PK had removed something mechanically crucial. She marched back into the house, stepped over him moaning on the floor, walked to the telephone and rang her friends. They came out and picked her up. There was still time.

On top of that the building work began again. He was too ill to do anything so Chris knuckled down and got on with it. Her heart must have dropped to be mixing cement and pushing a wheelbarrow - again.

In a letter to David Eccles dated Tuesday 19th October 1982 Bob wrote that Christine was a treasure and she undoubtedly was. That woman deserved a medal. In July she had dug out the foundations for the extension to Pear Tree single handed because of his hernia. He minimised her effort though by pointing out in a letter to David Eccles that the soil was light and she borrowed a cement mixer. They then employed a bricklayer who laid the brick walls and when he reached the required height the 'old firm' took over as he puts it.

The 'old firm' was dismayed to be doing heavy manual work again. He didn't notice. He was totally absorbed in his own problems.

Above: **Pear Tree Cottage** *ink*

On November 8th Christine wrote to Mavis that a 'moonlighting' brickie had put the footings in *(850 bricks)* in three and a half hours. She was astonished at how quickly a professional had done it. It was just beginning to dawn on her how quickly and efficiently their seven years hard labour in Wales could have been achieved with professionals. Percy had been boasting about laying twenty five blocks a day. She innocently wrote ***Yours truly who was labourer had to be standing to attention by 0730. It nearly killed me but it was well worth it. We are planning to have an exhibition in June emptying out the cottage ground floor and using the considerable wall space in the extension for hanging – just open for the weekend and I expect I shall do some sort of refreshment also.***

Melvyn Bragg is coming to spend the day with us on the 19th and Bob is looking forward to it enormously – I am too but I think it is more of a responsibility when one has food to think about. Bob has been working hard on the building recently but no painting so perhaps Melvyn's visit will perk him up.

Bragg came as arranged and saw they were seriously hard up. He looked at a few carefully selected paintings and discussed prices. At the beginning of the conversation things looked hopeful but as soon as it came close to doing a deal PK changed and began to make excuses for not selling; this wasn't signed, that wasn't finished, the other was not for sale and another needed framing. Having driven from London, Melvyn Bragg wasn't too happy to be leaving empty handed. He did return a few months later after being promised that this time he would be allowed to buy but by then things were even more confusing. It was to be more than a decade in the future *(1994)* a year after the PK's death before he managed to buy the two big charcoal drawings he wanted.

Bob began to get jealous of Chris. This was very silly. It was a sort of female rivalry. By now he was helping himself to her HRT and boasting at the miracle of his developing breasts. Chris was still generous in her support of him and his talent. That was what had attracted her in the first place. She was still stoically making allowances and excuses. But he became paranoid if anyone paid her any attention. She was increasingly disturbed by this and suggested he see a psychiatrist as did their new GP. It was obvious there was something very wrong. Bob sent off for a horoscope *(possibly found in the small ads)* and when the analysis of character and future prospects arrived he read it out to her and asked for comment. It was much later he revealed he had given her date of birth not his. He was indignant and turned it round very neatly to her. She was beginning to doubt her own sanity.

Percy got a letter from a gallery in Yorkshire who'd heard about his work – they wanted to come and view. A date was arranged. His own skewed version of events as related to Joan David a few months later goes like this;

On this particular day I was working on a large West Cumberland townscape in the hut when I decided to pop over for a cup of tea. The cottage appeared deserted and then I heard voices in Christine's bedroom which doubles as a workroom. Turned out to be the gallery owner and when they came downstairs a collection of Christine's work was parcelled up and in the conversation that followed there was no mention of MY work.

In the summer John Leal who has a gallery in Fishguard invited Christine to send some work (flowers). All this stimulated Christine so much that I decided to drop any idea of flower paintings myself. Her work is very good indeed especially the drawings and I advise and encourage her all the while.

In the fifties I had a flower drawing in the crypt of St Martins in the Field for some months by invitation and was told that Epstein had been very impressed by it. At my best I achieve lovely colour and poetic overtones. It would be dreadful if comparisons might be made if Christine and I were to show together. Of course some people MIGHT prefer Christine's but that would not trouble me. I have painted lots of flowers and fruit, drawn lots of churches and cottages so I am far from being inactive in fact I am surrounded with drawings that heap up around me. I try to keep going even if I feel unwell. I also refer to old studies and try to improve them. At the moment I am experimenting with lino cuts - a pleasant occupation on a cold winter night by the warm stove. At times my hands are rather shaky but happily for only a couple of days' duration. My chief problem is that I miss my native Cumberland more than I have

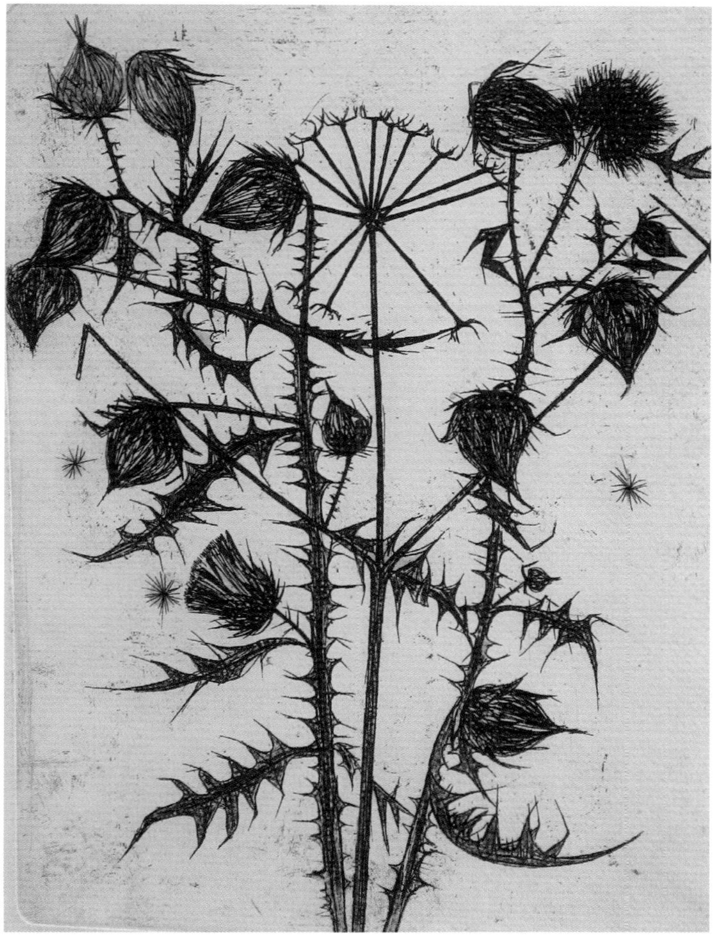

ever done, Perhaps this is due to the flat and uninteresting Norfolk landscape. I love the native domestic architecture and the large fund of beautiful churches.

Since I had a nervous breakdown in '58 my life has been very much up and down. The symptoms recur from time to time but I can cope by concentrating on creative thought and painting. For twenty years the creative thread remained unbroken even in spite of building work in Wales. I could readily switch especially in the evenings. But life soured somewhat in 1978 which caused the thread to break for a while. Since moving here I have only created one good painting and on reflection the last two years have been the unhappiest in my whole life. I have never known such sadness. My state of health was poor when we moved into Pear Tree but this was partly caused by the awful trauma of buying and selling. We made a good profit and this created a problem. I expected a large proportion would go into my bank account being self employed. However Christine took charge of the total amount – very impractical for my accountant and the tax people.

His letter to their friend Mavis on 10th March 1983 was not his usual beautiful handwriting but small cramped writing. The news was not good.

My dear Mavis

Last Thursday we nailed the first layer of felt on the extension roof. The following day Chris went to Brighton to stay with Andy. In a telephone conversation she found it all fascinating but on the Sunday, instead of giving me the time to meet her in Attleborough she briefly said 'I am not coming back.'

I tried to converse in a bewildered fashion but she would not listen. 'I'll get in touch' and that was that.

So I am left with the cottage the extension unfinished, a wheel-less traveller we were to dump etc etc. The cottage gives me the creeps and an ache in my heart will not go neither will the tears.

Above: **Teazles** *etching*

chapter 13

Desolate Shores

Percy Kelly's personality disorder; possibly avoidant, dependent or narcissistic had been accelerating for some time. He had always been self-centred, egotistical and a perfectionist. He had always behaved and talked in a contradictory way. He had always suffered from bouts of black depression if he had a non painting period. He had always been difficult to live with. He had always needed someone to lean on. But looking back objectively over his life so far, he had fitted in with all levels of society. He had impressed so many people with his art, his wit and conversation. He had fitted in at college with people much younger than himself – they had looked up to him. He had been sought out for dinner parties and been a brilliant raconteur. He had been invited to stay with people of influence.

So what had caused this decline? What had effected the transformation of a gifted, popular man into a paranoid hypochondriac? It wasn't just ageing – it was more serious than that. He was impossible to live with and clearly in need of professional help. He had had problems from time to time all through his adult life; mood swings, erratic behaviour, paranoia, illogical thoughts and depression. This points to a form of autism which explains his exceptional proficiency in the narrow field of art and sport and his inability to calculate. His overriding egotism and inability to see anything from another point of view, his lack of empathy with others to perceive their distress and his lack of judgement to prioritise tasks combined with an unnatural retentiveness over anything he had made or collected points to an autistic disorder. He felt himself isolated - in exile from his beloved Cumberland. He needed the familiar fells and landscape of his first fifty years. At the age of fifty he had been torn from everything that was familiar into an alien land and a life which was beset with problems. These problems interfered with his over-riding need to paint and draw. He had been catapulted into a life with much more responsibility for others – a thing he had avoided with his own son and family. He was no longer in a secure place.

The main thing was his inabilityto cope with criticism. All his life he had endeavoured not to put himself in a situation where he might be criticised. Hence his avoidance of exhibitions. Yet he craved attention. He was proud of his looks, his physique, his sporting prowess, his intelligence and his artistic ability. He was used to the admiration it brought him. He wanted unconditional admiration. Wearing bright colours, unusual clothes, eccentric behaviour gave him a sense of identity. Although he was a dominant twin, maybe he needed the constant reassurance of that.

There may also have been a physical cause which contributed to this increasing personality disorder. In the Sixties, at the time when he began etching, there were no health and safety restrictions on the process. He worked for long hours in the print room at college – longer than any of the other students by far. Then subsequently at home on etching plates, dipping them into nitric acid baths with no protective face masks or clothing, waiting sometimes for several hours until he got the right depth of bite - removing them periodically and testing before replacing them in the acid. The strong vapours from nitric acid could have slowly attacked his central nervous system. There is evidence from industry that this has sometimes been the case. In his letters to Rosanna in the sixties he mentions feeling strange and

Above: **Brown farm** *mixed media*

dizzy after working on etching plates for hours in a confined space. Genius and insanity are closely related. He had suffered from depression all his adult life which had never been diagnosed or treated professionally. So now he was alone for the first time in his life; nobody to lean on; feeling rejected. He was convinced Chris would return to him. He rang her continually. She had gone to stay with Audrey Cartmel - a friend in Worcestershire. She refused to speak with him on the telephone and ignored his letters. She never saw or spoke to him again.

She asked Audrey Cartmel to collect her things from Pear Tree. When Audrey arrived, Bob was upset and indignant. He wrote to Mavis Aitcheson in great indignation.

Audrey is a friend of mine and I have phoned her constantly for support. She came today in her car to pick up Chris' clothes, sewing machine, knitting machine, paintings and paint which was a kind of finality. Chris has always insisted in holding on to our money so my bank balance has remained at £10. She did leave £30 and an open cheque before leaving for Brighton which appeared at the time slightly ominous but a few days earlier she said how much she loved me and would never leave me. I think she ought to see a psychiatrist because she has had three weird and frightening bouts of memory doubt when she felt she was losing her head. We have had a traumatic period... It would have been bad enough if I had been younger and fitter but at sixty five with a stupid blaring in my ear, crashing noises at bedtime, a painful spine condition and a hernia it is too much. I have only been able to go to Norwich recently for the first time because I cannot walk far without feeling unsteady and ill. On the last visit to Norwich all my strength went and I fell to the pavement. A man kindly helped me up and got me on a seat by an ancient monument. I felt so awful it seemed ages before Chris arrived having been in a shop. Irritably she said 'You are supposed to look after me!' helping me along to the car park.

So I am stuck in the cottage trying hard to retain my sanity and my life. It is lonely. Worst of all I love Chris so very much I can't get rid of the awful ache in my heart. Initially I telephoned a few friends but I have only had one call in the past three days. This one

was a friend – a Samaritan. God was he comforting? He told me he had a friend in a mental hospital who is so well cared for they are so good nowadays. I told him to stop – imagine me in a mental home. This made me even more suicidal.

I think Chris is not in her right mind because Audrey Cartmel is in cahoots for when I said the cottage would have to be sold she got on her high horse. 'Well Chris has left you the cottage so you can work in peace and she can work in the workshops in St David's.' But Chris won't speak to me and doesn't intend to so the estate must be wound up. This place is doing me no good – there are too many memories. I think I am upsetting some hidden plan.

She then said 'You have nowhere to go?' Whereupon I said 'Yes that's right; nowhere because my life is at an end.' So she and Chris had assumed all was well. I showed Audrey around to show her the awful state this place is in. We were supposed to do the exterior woodwork this summer. It would seem Chris has taken the easy way out. There is money in Chris' bank but not too much. It appears she is splitting it down the middle but it was earmarked for building and there is a whacking bill to pay on a standing account. A decent person would have talked all this over before leaving.

There is masses of wool; four huge bags, blankets etc; a complete house....

I really despair. I have had a nervous breakdown; battered into a coma by my first wife; and rescued by Chris and her friend Wendy who called because they were worried about me. In Wales I had a period of hysteria and depression. I came here on the verge of breakdown which was horrible. So I am not the ideal type to undergo this sort of treatment.

Above: **Yellow Car** *watercolour and ink*

Right: **Teazles and poppy heads** *lithograph*

I rang my doctor the following morning and he said he'd pop round to see me. He lives a hundred yards away. Of course he hasn't called. The nights are frightening, the days a nightmare. I thought the daytime might be bearable. I have printed a large sign

I AM PERCY KELLY PLEASE TELEPHONE MRS CHRISTINE KELLY 01496 2376

On Sunday I thought I would motor to Cumberland and call on you with the painting because of the money. I packed the car up and after five miles had to turn back; the old head was rather queer - a common occurrence.

Klaus Trier said if I got my mind on something positive it would help so I tried again to motor to Wales to collect a lot of lithographs and paintings from the workshop where Chris hopes to live. But I had to give up.

20th April 1983

Dear Mavis,

I have written you three letters but they were so gloomy and depressive I felt you deserved something better. I am glad to say that during the past week I have felt so much better.....

I am planning changes in the cottage and have pulled off the paper in the hall because there is damp along the skirting board. Blossom in the hedgerows never looked lovelier in fact the whole world has changed. If I had been fit and well how different it would all have been.

It is a long justifying letter

Mavis must have replied with soothing words. In reply he says bitterly that he knows Chris is now with happy people! He says he knows who they are – they are drinking and womanising. All his resentments now come tippling out like a dam with the sluice gates open. He says he is a better cook than Chris – people keep asking for his recipes. French people too. Judy Preston 'brought' one of his recipes with her and cooked a good lunch but not as good as his.

'Anything I tackle I have to do to the highest standard. I never throw things in a pan and never keep vegetables till the next day. Chris was slapdash which is why she will never be a painter.'

He went on to say that his solicitor was well aware that Chris had thrown aside a large fortune – presumably in the value of his paintings! Well, that was theoretical.

He was now intent on taking out a loan to get the cottage finished then sell it. He was also making a new will. Then he contradicted himself yet again.

Of course I shan't leave her the cottage. I shall have to be dragged out. One shouldn't tamper with creative types – I would rather put a match to it and it isn't insured so she wouldn't get a penny.

I have 'given' my work to Abbot Hall – a safety measure and I gather that one room will display a permanent collection. I am sorting through my boxes and there is so much good work I am at a loss how to cope. There are up to three hundred 30 x 22 drawings and paintings alone. Thousands of small efforts; etchings, lithography etc. But I am not finished - perhaps the best is yet to come.

Miki (Sekers) said my work in time will be more important than Lowry, Herman Millar or Sutherland. Even in the 50s my work was hung with Picasso, Roualt, Vlamink and Duffy and were very happy in such company. *

He turned to women as always to help him. He had made a friend of the vet's wife Heather Jackson who lived round the corner. He frequently called on her and talked for hours. He also wrote extensively to all his other friends especially Mavis Aitcheson in Kendal who was originally Chris' friend and Mary Burkett. Significantly he didn't write to Lord Eccles, Peter Scott or the Webbs again. He focussed on and identified with women now.

He became introspective and paranoid.

It isn't right doing things this way. I am trapped I cannot go far and have only spoken to two people in the last eight days The neighbours turn their backs on me. Hardly a car goes by and not one footstep and Chris' knitting is still on the chair.

The car has thrown a gasket and the neighbours next door will get me a new one from Norwich. You would have thought they would ask me in for a cup of tea. I cannot eat just digestives until they are finished and lots of tea. I did try and make some slippery elm but all the jars are empty. Mary (Burkett) told me that Peter Scott will pay to have the extension finished and David Ralli is bringing two men to help. If I have company such as Chris or a visitor my ears are not so bad but alone it is not good. I see the weeks stretch on and all the work packed up with despair. But I try to look beyond the hour. It will be awful when this place is sold because I will have nowhere to go. I suppose I relied on Chris as a person to help. If she changed back to Chris, everyone knows she would come, but this other side which appears from time to time took over.

He means changed back to the sympathetic person she once was. He mentions her headaches, tantrums, period, menopause? These are his theories of the reason for her leaving him; anything but himself and his behaviour!

Actually there were other factors to consider because I know this place was getting on her nerves. After the New Year we were planing to go to Cumberland house hunting. She badly wanted to get back to the fells. After 1st February when I spoke about Cumberland she would not answer. She painted a lot but I could see she was sloppy in other things. Watercolour painting is very demanding and creates enormous tension.

Then of course we have few friends and few visitors. Chris often commented on this. She exploded in the kitchen recently 'I am just a bloody skivvy round here.'

She complains about not having achieved anything and ten minutes later says she is going to apply for a job as a bread delivery van driver.

She hated Wales and wanted to die in England and now she is going back there to paint.

Not long ago she hurt me unnecessarily and she commented 'Your trouble is you are too sensitive.' I am paying for this sensitivity; without it I would be unable to paint as I do.

* *These works referred to were in Seker's office alongside PK's.*

Above: **Interior; Pear Tree Cottage** *watercolour and ink*

chapter 14

Return to St David's

May 5th 1983

Christine Kelly was sitting on a single bed in a small cheerless room in the staff quarters of the Warpool Court Hotel St David's. She was looking tired but good. It had been very strange returning to St David's. The house on which she and Bob had expended so much energy was now occupied by the Easies. Everywhere was redolent with memories. She had come to this place ten years ago full of love, hope and joy and left three years ago disillusioned, depressed and desperate. She was now light-headed at the unaccustomed freedom she had. She was no stranger to hard work and long hours. Her life had changed from menial domestic to menial commercial.

She was writing to her friend Mavis in Kendal.

Yes, I'm fine and I have said I'll stay at the hotel until September. I have sold six paintings so far and a lady rang up last week to see if I'd have an exhibition in her gallery at Solva which she is opening this year above her craft shop. So I said yes as it is a good opportunity for starters as it's not too high powered.

I am finding painting difficult due to lack of space and a rather warm room as it has a large window facing south and the paint dries so quickly But I manage and do lots of drawing....

I am saving all my earnings and hopefully may be able to afford something with wheels by the winter and hope to have my first holiday in twelve years and tour round the country painting and visiting my one or two dear old friends, you included if you will have me. I have applied for Outline Planning Permission for the workshop and land here which we own jointly and also for permission for a temporary caravan. I haven't told Bob yet, only our mutual solicitor, as I know he doesn't want me to have it but as he has decided to stay in the cottage and has all the cars etc so I feel it is the least he can do.

If I am not successful with this project I don't know what I shall do for a home of my own but I expect something will turn up. Difficult when one doesn't have financial security but I feel surprisingly optimistic – things seem to be falling into place so well. I think Bob is OK but very deranged and paranoid about himself and everything else. He seems to have several people calling on him and in touch and Mary Burkett is in constant contact. I rang her up not long ago as she hadn't replied to my two letters to see how Bob was. She was very weird and among other things said 'Well I can't worry about both of you.' So I said 'OK – you just worry about Bob then. I'll look after myself' and put the phone down. I haven't heard anything since so I guess that's the end of a beautiful friendship. But people have been generally very kind and understanding I have been quite overwhelmed.

I am just about to go over and do lunches – we were quite quiet this morning so I was able to sneak extra time to write to you. Time seems so precious and with starting at 7.30 am I have to get to bed early. My hours are 7.30 – 3.00 and Tuesdays off. Sundays I clean and make beds 9 – 1 pm. It's actually hard work but not unpleasant

Above: **Cathedral, St Davids** *watercolour and ink*

though I wouldn't like to have to do it for ever. I am learning quite a lot and meeting some nice people who come to the hotel and the girls are very patient and kind to me so I feel really lucky. My freedom is worth all the other losses and I look ahead not behind and am determined to make a good future for myself.

Kind and understanding Mavis was at the receiving end of dramatic letters from both parties. Her patience, tact and neutral stance were admirable and helped both of them.

Meanwhile back in Norfolk, Bob was in a desperate state. He was sorry for himself. He had hurt his toe trying to mow the lawn before visitors arrived from Cumbria. He moaned that he didn't know when he'd see Cumberland again. He intended to enclose a painting for Mavis but it wasn't ready. Surprisingly he did send it later.

10/6/83

Dear Mavis

The ill informed seem to think that a person with my talent and in this unique situation can just pick up a brush and create masterpieces. I can cope with physical problems but I have to be in the right state of mind which can be triggered by some exciting impulse. There have been stirrings but invariably I am pushed back to rock bottom. Illustrated letters from Chris - so normal as though she is on a painting holiday and biased letters from my solicitor have the worst effect. I have put an end to them because I want to put her out of my mind completely.

On 15th August 1983 he sent a drawing of his feet and injured toe to Mavis and Charles complete with blue stitching and a graphic account of stitch removal and dealing himself with the one overlooked by the district nurse. I'm sure they really appreciated this. He was totally self absorbed.

I made a new friend in the form of a three week old budgie he went on *whom I named Pepi. I bought him 25th June... the loneliness is not so absolute because I can talk to him. He is quite comical and has started to chatter so delightfully. He gets very excited when I talk and whistle to him. It is very touching at night when I say goodnight He looks so tiny.*

The Aitchesons sent him a sizeable cheque. They were being careful not to take sides and supported Chris as well. These people were real friends.

Meanwhile back at Pear Tree, Bob was still in the land of dreams.

On 15/8/83 he wrote to Mavis and Charles

When I get the extension finished sufficiently to work in I intend to mount a lot of small work in order to earn some money. Beginning of September through to October I shall have some hectic bills to pay. Once this collection is finished and despatched I intend to send you a small collection of interesting bits and pieces. I want NO money and I won't take no for an answer. I want the boys to have something of mine which they can call their own. It will take time but this is a promise.

When you sent the cheque, words cannot describe what it meant to me. I shall never forget your kindness and concern. I expect I will tell you over and over again. But a kindness such as this never disappears. I have told all my friends and my sister Sally Kelly. Poor Sal who does not enjoy good health is a casualty of the separation.

It isn't clear why his eldest sister was a casualty of the separation. This was only Bob's second mention of his family since leaving West Cumberland

Above: **White barn** *mixed media*

in 1970. He never mentioned Audrey, Brian or his siblings apart from using Sally as an excuse for his behaviour to Peter Scott in Wales. But we do know that, fearful of losing some of his work as he did in his first divorce, he sent off several consignments of his work to different people for safe keeping. One of these consignments went to Sally, another to Abbot Hall and others in different directions some possibly still undiscovered. It was rather random but his mindset was totally illogical and his actions dysfunctional. The small collection referred to never got to the Aitchesons. Some significant collections lay forgotten and have come to light since – including the shoe box containing fifty beautiful 'little gems' in 2010. It had lain on top of a wardrobe for nearly thirty years like sleeping beauty. It was pulled down in the hope that it might contain photographs of PK for this biography. When it was opened it was not promising. On top there was a recipe for marmalade written on the back of an envelope, several shopping lists, a few scraps of paper with contact numbers on and a few notes to himself – aides memoirs – but below that there was treasure. In a house clearance it would have surely been thrown out. For someone so retentive about their work, it is surprising to find he was so forgetful and negligent about its future. Maybe he thought that if he disguised the box with rubbish it would keep it safe from prying eyes and predators. Sadly this appears to have worked. The box that went to Sally has never been found. She died in an old people's home in Workington in 1993 a few months before her brother so it probably ended up as ash or landfill when her house was cleared.

His letter to Mavis finished on an upbeat note. He gave her the good news that he had found the woman he so desperately needed to help him and to lean on.

This all came to mind because a hitherto complete stranger has been so very supportive and kind to me. I doubt if I would have survived without her caring and trusting nature. She is destined to go to heaven. Her name is Mrs Joan David.

Above: **Diary page poppies** *watercolour and ink*

chapter 15

The Saviour

Writing letters is like painting a picture. With a painting you do the initial framework maybe in pencil and then add colour. Writing can start in the same way – any old blather and then like a painting the mind begins to expand and remember. There are bound to be negative patches just like in painting but a painting can be altered – not a letter. Of course the overriding factor is enthusiasm for the subject in painting, the person in writing. One day my letters will be seen as the most unique ever written.

In 1983, on a cold January day, Joan David sat in front of a roaring fire in the sitting room of her small cottage and wrote her first letter to Percy Kelly. She had seen her first Kelly painting a few days before at the Windermere home of Miss Mary Burkett. She couldn't take her eyes away from it. It had exerted its usual magnetic pull and made an enormous impact on her. She wanted to know more. She wanted to buy one. How many times has that happened? Thousands. There is a seductive quality about his work which makes it irresistible. It induces people to sleep walk their way into owning it.

Joan was a scientist and discriminating collector who had retired to Cumbria a few years earlier in 1971 aged 51. She had many links with the county and remembered all the happy times she and her family had spent on holiday in the lakes. She had studied for her MSc at the Freshwater Biological Association's laboratories at Wray Castle during the war. Now in her early sixties and living alone, she had settled down in a charming small cottage in Troutbeck near Ambleside surrounding herself with beautiful but modest furniture and works of art. She had a wide circle of friends and an insatiable curiosity about everything. She went on courses, attended openings at galleries, travelled to national exhibitions and read widely. She was unusual appearing to be much younger than her years, dressing in bright unconventional clothes, interesting hats and shoes. Her budget was not lavish but her taste was impeccable. She bought at auctions and galleries, was quick to spot a bargain and had an eye for the gem in an exhibition. She found artists, tracked them down and commissioned work. Like Helen Sutherland she was passionate in her desire to support artists.

The picture that had captured her attention at Miss Burkett's house was a large charcoal drawing of a road in West Cumbria. It was love at first sight. Miss Burkett had kept in touch with Percy from his days in Cumbria, given him encouragement and moral support and she happily wrote down his address for her. Joan was surprised to discover

Top left: **Joan at Troutbeck reading a letter from Percy Kelly** *1983*

Left: **Joan and Percy at Pear Tree** *1990*

Above: **Pear Tree Cottage** *watercolour and ink*

he was living in the backwaters of Norfolk, at Pear Tree Cottage, with his second wife Christine. They had recently moved there from St David's in Pembrokeshire. Miss Burkett had recently received a hand printed Christmas card from them. She reached up and took it down from the mantelpiece and showed it to Joan. It was exquisite, signed Christine and Bob. Joan was so envious. She would love to have a card like that. If it was hers she would frame it and treasure it. She didn't yet know that she would receive one next year, and the year after and.... but we are jumping into the future too fast.

Miss Burkett handed over his address saying she hoped it would result in a sale because they needed the money. So, here was Joan in early January 1983, after the flurry of Christmas was over and done with writing to Percy at Pear Tree Cottage telling him how much she admired his work and how much she would like to buy a painting if he could spare one. The fells were covered with a dusting of snow and frost crackled under her pink booted feet as she walked down the lane to the post box not realising as it dropped into the red box that this would be the beginning of ten years of intense correspondence. That it would change her life. That it would bring her both joy and some measure of anguish. They would only meet five times in those ten years but he was going to dominate her life and thoughts.

A few days later, an exciting letter dated 24th January 1983 dropped through her letter box. The envelope presaged its contents. It had a painting of those snow dusted fells she could see from her tiny window and a small blue and white cottage not unlike hers. In beautiful lettering the address was laid out

Joan E David, Strands, Thickholme, Troutbeck, Windermere, Cumbria

She carefully slit it open not wanting to spoil such a lovely watercolour and took out a painting of Pear Tree Cottage in Magpie Lane, Rockland St Peter, Attleborough. She was enchanted. Her heart sang. From that moment she was lost.

Dear Miss David

she read from the writing, skilfully superimposed on the painting

Thank you so much for your letter which arrived today. Your very kind and appreciative words about my work really touched me. It is so rare to hear such compliments and since I am experiencing the darkest period of my life I got quite a lift.

I would be more than pleased to do you a painting and as regards price simply pay me what you can afford. I am staging a weekend exhibition here at Pear Tree in June, however if my health will allow I hope to visit Cumberland around April time. I could bring one or two things to your home because I hope to stay a week or so. I will however give you good warning.

I am at the moment endeavouring to complete a new extension to the cottage where the aforementioned exhibition will take place. It will be a private show and I hope to get friends etc to pay a call. Here in Norfolk I am an alien in a foreign land. The Northern Landscape is not readily appreciated.

I included the sketch because it does to some extent illustrate the local scene. Warm brick, red and orange pantiles, white and coloured barge boards, clay outbuildings and barns painted black and white and often in the less settled villages a nice untidiness which the butterflies appreciate. In our garden we have a weed patch and a magnificent clump of nettles hidden behind the garage. The local inhabitants hereabouts are native born so there are few outsiders which is good because much of Norfolk and I dare say Suffolk has been ruined by modern building.

I will keep in touch regarding my visit to Cumberland and I must thank you again for writing to me

Sincerely and kindly

Bob Kelly

Incidentally Fen Street is only a mile away. There is a letter box which we often use strapped to a short pole and covered in Ivy. It is quite a charming way to post ones letters.

Joan was trembling with excitement. So this rather convoluted answer must be a yes but whatever else happened she had two paintings by this wonderful man in her hand already in the form of an envelope and a letter with the promise of another painting as well.

Above: **Letter to Joan David** *watercolour and ink*

Joan David was one of the kindest, most generous people on earth. She always believed the best in people and she judged people by her own standards. She always meant what she said; she always kept promises and she was truthful and trustworthy. She did not even begin to suspect that Percy was unrealistic in his promises. She had never met him. She didn't know the number of times he had planned to have an exhibition and then retracted. She didn't know how many years it had taken him to build an extension in Wales and how many years it would take him to create any extra space at Pear Tree. She didn't know that the gallery planned in Wales had never happened nor any of the exhibitions he was going to have there. She didn't know that the drive to Cumberland was getting increasingly difficult both for him and his fleet of patched up self maintained vehicles that constantly let him down. She didn't know that he would only visit Cumberland once more and it would be at her behest. She didn't know that his wife would walk out on him for ever just a few weeks ahead.

Euphoric, she sat down and replied immediately and enclosed a book of stamps and a poppy postcard in the hope that it would cheer him up and encourage him to write again. It worked. By return of post a large A4 envelope arrived decorated with a painting of poppies and a cornfield echoing her postcard. The letter inside, again beginning Dear Miss David, was written on a watercolour painting of the back road from Lorton to Buttermere and it was signed Percy Kelly. It told her the proposed trip north had been cancelled due to his ill health - so he was already backing off from his stated unachievable plans. It was a long letter full of little personal anecdotes; memories of the past. For only a second letter ever to a person he'd never met it was packed full of irrelevant detail but fascinating to the recipient. Joan read it many times. She just loved to look at it. She proudly showed it off to envious friends. She saved every single one of his letters and envelopes. and there were thousands. She realised their importance. Nobody knows what happened to Joan's letters to him. After his death they were never found. Maybe he didn't keep them or maybe they were burned when the cottage was cleared. He almost lost all the paintings in this way. He was within a mouse's whisker of losing them all when he failed to make a proper Will and his estranged son inherited everything and initially dismissed his father's life's work as a pile of tatty worthless paper.

Letters then flew back and forth between Troutbeck and Pear Tree and by 20th February when Chris was once again digging foundations and mixing cement, Percy made a subtle confession possibly to test her reaction.

I have a feminine side to my character which has been and still is a curse. Today my days and nights are a perpetual nightmare. No doubt if I had been normal I might not have possessed the same creative spirit.

This was signed Bob Kelly and must have puzzled his innocent friend.

He posed another clue in his letter of 28th February with a painting of a yellow vintage car, a model boat with a red sail *(a Kelly trade mark)* and a doodle of the name Roberta in the margin surrounded by stars but again signed Bob Kelly.

With that the letters stopped. Joan was worried that he was ill. Maybe he had given up writing to her for a while. She felt disappointed. She now found herself lurking by the window, watching out for the postman every day with anticipation and anxiety. Had she upset him? Would she never again get these marvellous letters from him? She didn't like to telephone because all their communication had been the written word and he had never put his telephone number on the letters so she rang Mary Burkett and discovered that Christine had left him and he was devastated and suicidal. She sent a sympathetic card immediately and this opened a floodgate of letters. This was just what he needed – someone who admired him, loved his work and who didn't know his treacherous wife. He told her he hadn't seen the break-up coming. He was amazed and hurt by his wife's leaving as he didn't think there was anything wrong with their relationship. He was lonely and penniless. Strangely he saw no connection between his current problems and the reason for her going. His constant real or imagined ill health which prevented them going anywhere, their impoverished state which ground her down and his sexual confusion which dominated his life and ostracised them in this small community. It was not common to meet a cross dresser on the rural lanes, mending a puncture in a dress or shopping in the village post office in a wig and make up or patronising the nearly new shop in

nearby Watton for extra large female shoes and interesting colourful clothes.

On 17th March she received a letter in which, feeling very sorry for himself, he touched on these problems and set out his predicament. She was still Dear Miss David and he still signed it Bob Kelly.

The past two weeks have been a nightmare. I cried for help to several people but to no avail. Few people understand the creative mind and I have given so much to people in pain or who needed help.

He went on to mention his constant Tinnitus, the pain in his back and his former nervous breakdown which all his current supporters were aware of ad nauseum. He then carried on in despair; - he didn't mention all the people who were concerned about him including Chris who wanted to be sure he was all right. He had a new, fresh, receptive audience who didn't know the back story.

I cannot carry on here Miss David so the cottage will have to be sold. We own some workshops in St David's Pembrokeshire which will need to be sold too. I have always disliked this cottage because it is claustrophobic. It is very dark inside too. ... At the moment my priority is to survive and endure a feeling of devastating loneliness.

Sincerely

Bob Kelly

The letters then came shuttering through her letterbox almost on a daily basis. They were full of his troubles; neatly written but not illustrated. Joan became very concerned about him. She was also curious to meet her correspondent. She and Mary Burkett decided to go down to Norfolk and appraise the situation. They booked into a Bed and Breakfast in a village nearby for the end of May. Percy was excited at the prospect of meeting her and sent a painting of his living room at Pear Tree which looked interesting and whetted her appetite to see it for real. It accompanied a short letter dated 27th May 1983 with a Post Script ***I have never looked forward***

Left: **Roberta**

Above: **Envelope to Joan** *watercolour and ink*

to meeting anyone so much before. I feel like a girl going to her first party.

That set the tone. His letters now began ***My Dear Joan*** and were signed off ***Roberta***. In one written just a few days before the impending visit he wrote

I have been racking my brains what I should wear. Should I be ultra feminine or dress with a certain restraint? Mauve and blues; black and browns; red and black; a mixture of browns, tartan and grey; pinks, cerise and oranges. I am even particular about my underwear – of course my toe creates a certain restriction.

I will take you to our special letter box and some lovely places.

Fortunately she was spared the painting of his toe bestowed on the Aitchesons.

This black and white photograph of the first visit was taken by Mary Burkett. Joan is pushing an old heavy hand mowing machine with difficulty through some long grass with Percy at her side in a long skirt and neat blouse protected by a white apron. His wig is long and curly and I suspect that, as he was in his early sixties, his hair was thinning on top and the hats, wigs and scarves disguised the fact. He was very vain about his appearance and physical attributes. He always had been.

Joan and Mary had arrived at the Bed and Breakfast the evening before and set off for Pear Tree the next morning. He greeted them dressed in plus twos, a sweater and a his habitual woolly hat. He must have changed into Roberta at some stage of the day. The chaos was far worse than Joan had imagined both inside and out. She learned about his frantic attempt to cut the lawn the day previously when he had chopped his toe and his neighbour Sheila who hated the sight of blood and whom Percy always criticised for being uncaring and withdrawn, drove him to hospital for treatment. The District nurse had already been round that day to change the dressing. The grass was far too long and the mower far too blunt and decrepit *(another find from a skip!)* that Joan managed to finish the job with some difficulty. The photograph is mercifully cut off above the feet.

The painting he had sent of his living room was somewhat idealistic. He said he had tidied it up but it was still a mess. He had tidied it up in his head – a common Kelly trick – hence the painting. He probably really believed he had done it. The kitchen and bathroom were very dirty. The extension he had referred to in his first letter to Joan in January was far from finished. The one where he hoped to mount an exhibition in the spring – yes that one! It opened out from the sitting room with a dividing curtain. Joan remembered it as a jumble of pictures in various states of completion - and non completion. It was so full and disorganised that they could hardly move. He showed them a few paintings – just enough to tantalise - which he drew out of the piles strewn around. She was not allowed to touch. He allowed her to buy one of St Monance harbour. He gave her two more out of his sketchbook and a little watercolour of a hamlet in Cumberland with his trademark orange sun. He was in generous mood and never stopped talking. At 3 o'clock he put the kettle on and produced, in what seemed like an eternity Joan records, a cup of cold tea and a digestive biscuit. An antiquated Rayburn can take forever to boil a kettle when you are really thirsty and it takes nearly as long to not boil it. Although Joan had thoughtfully taken a hamper of food and presented it to him for their lunch he appeared to have put it to one side and forgotten all about it. He thanked her for it in his next letter.

Left: **Joan mowing at Pear Tree watched by Roberta**

Above: **Paintbox letter** *watercolour and ink*

He presented Joan with an old paint rag which he had cleverly transformed into a painting and he entrusted a large stack of charcoal drawings to Miss B for Abbot Hall's permanent collection. These are the ones that he asked Joan to bring back to Norfolk for him a few months later. He had changed his mind – once again.

Joan drove back to Cumbria in her Polo, exhilarated; the letters continued and she sometimes struggled to keep up with them. He kept throwing his problems her way. Of course once thrown and caught he could forget about them. Joan had to deal with them.

His biggest problem was money. There had been very little in their joint bank account when Chris left but he now alleged she had left him with nothing. He said he had no pension. He had opted out of the state system years ago. First Joan went down that well trodden and obvious route and tried to encourage him to sell some work. There were enough galleries eager to show him. But he was insistent that it was out of the question for various reasons mainly involving tax and death duties which was illogical. He was now approaching sixty five. He had written to Joan in April before her visit

It is odd that I have talents which could have brought me lots of money and here I am stuck with one of the least lucrative occupations. Do you know that if I had stayed in the postal service I would have been retiring in four months on an enormous pension?

There was some muddled thinking here. The ever patient Joan encouraged him to apply to Social Security for Supplementary Benefit. He did but when they replied he flew into a panic and this time it wasn't the usual what to wear dilemma. He was terrified that the official would see all his paintings and value them and consider him too rich to have a pension.

Before he comes he wrote to Joan ***I shall have to get rid of the paintings. I am sure I shall be OK because of my disability and change of gender. Of course selling work creates a problem. I shall have to be paid in cash and hide it under the bed or a hole in the wall. What a cheat I am.***

The officer came, assessed his situation and calmly granted him a supplementary pension providing his savings never exceeded £2500. She told him he could sell some paintings and not affect his pension. He was ecstatic after she'd gone. The weekly amount was ridiculously low but it seemed like a fortune to this man who continually looked for bargains, who would drive six miles to save ten pence, who maintained his cars and did all the building work himself, scrounging materials where he could. His clothes were all second hand from the Nearly New shop in Watton and he even recycled his calendar each year by sticking an overlay with new dates on it over the old. If he had added up all the time spent on these money saving schemes he could have painted countless masterpieces, sold them and paid professionals to build him a studio and service his car. - and the rest!

He wrote to Charles and Mavis Aitcheson on Wednesday 16th November 1983 a few days after his sixty fifth birthday

Just a few words to tell you I am now an old age pensioner from the third of this month. I was always under the impression that I was not eligible because I claimed exemption from paying the usual contributions.

The wonderful letters to Joan continued. She ignored his personality disorder – who wouldn't when they were receiving letters like these. He sent her a painting of the red GR post box set in an ivy covered wall just round the corner in Fen street where he posted all his letters to her, a beautiful red poppy, an early watercolour paint box all signed Roberta.

On the 24th February 1984 he wrote a Wordsworth poem – ***Not yet frail flower*** – on a painting of a stark white farmhouse and two days later she received another version of the cottage at Loweswater all in February browns this time and no yellow door.

Joan made her next visit alone in March 1984 – a year after Chris had left him. She was worried about his mental state. Even though his letters were as beautiful as ever, the contents were turgid. She was filled with disquiet that all was not well. She now was well aware that what he wrote, what he drew and what was really happening were wildly at odds. She needed to see for herself at first hand. She booked into the same Bed and Breakfast as previously and this time she wisely took a hamper for herself as well as one for Percy and secreted it in the wardrobe. There was a bottle of gin and some tonics to keep her going. She was also returning all the charcoal drawings he had 'given' to Abbot Hall on her previous visit. He had changed his mind. He wanted them back.

He made a small attempt to feed her this time though all that was available were lethal warm stews which had been on the decrepit Rayburn for days. She cautiously picked at her food and was glad of the tuck box when she got back to the B & B. The cottage was as chaotic as ever – worse than her first visit. Being a neat and tidy person who liked order she was probably tempted to try to tidy up but she realised it was an impossible task. He would have intervened at every turn. Like his attempts to write his biography, he would get distracted and similarly when he tried to tidy up he only got to the first thing and was led sideways into a new project which he never finished. Once again he was full of plans in the run up to the visit suggesting things they should do and wonderful things he would show her but again none of it happened. He had promised to go out with her to paint but he talked incessantly and got side tracked and then it was too late to do anything. They did go to a village nearby to shop at the health food shop but as soon as they got out of the car Percy became light headed and sick and had to grab hold of Joan and be helped across the road. Joan suddenly had one of those out of body moment seeing the absurdity of the situation and then she started looking at everyone else who was out and about wondering if they too were men dressed up as women. He was dressed in a long skirt and blouse in bright attractive colours with a colourful scarf round his head. They looked like two old women helping each other along. Joan had great trouble suppressing her fit of the giggles.

When they got back to Pear Tree they discussed this ever present problem of the divorce and giving Chris half the assets. He was terrified he would lose the cottage and be destitute. He showed her a letter from Chris' solicitor saying a valuer was coming on the 6th June. He realised he would have to make a settlement. He was in danger of losing the cottage. He would have nowhere to go. It wouldn't fetch much but he would have to share the proceeds with her. He wouldn't have enough to buy anything else. This of course was over dramatic – Chris was not going to make him

Above: **Little Farm** *watercolour and ink*

homeless. She had emphasised this many times and, unlike him, she would keep her word. But she had worked hard for ten years to keep both of them. It was her savings and jewellery which had bought the property in Gospel Lane and she now needed somewhere to live. She wanted the workshops primarily but she also needed a bit more money to make them habitable. She couldn't stay in staff quarters of an hotel for the rest of her life.

Percy turned to Joan for the solution and she again advised him that he would have to sell some work to raise the money. He wouldn't accept that. She told him he had no alternative. She offered to put on a three day exhibition in Troutbeck in the home of friends. After a long discussion he reluctantly agreed. She quickly clinched the deal and fixed a date. The date would be early in October – six months ahead. He promised to pack up some work and send it to her before the valuer's visit. He refused to sort anything out for her to take back which would have made sense – but when did sense come into any of it? Joan could see trouble ahead. And nothing at all happened except lots of letters full of good intentions and regrets that he had to sell anything. Three months went by. Joan was nervous. He wrote to her on the very day of the valuer's visit telling her he had hidden some special paintings and things in the coal bunker. He had made a lining out of corrugated sheeting and the coal man had carefully topped it up with coal.

But he still hadn't sent anything to Joan for the exhibition. He was even more paranoid and retentive but the reality of the valuer's visit and subsequent letters from Chris's solicitor forced him to face up to it.

He wrote to Mavis a few weeks later, mentioning the pending exhibition

Many of the items are treasured and I did want to keep them together. In April a valuer came. Detestable individual. Would come back to take photographs of Pear Tree to put it on the market.

He fell into depression – again. His favourite source of clothes, the swap shop in Caston, staffed by sympathetic volunteers was closing down, Joan was pressing him to send her work for the exhibition and he went to pieces at the thought. Joan was worried about his failing resolve and organising the framing She was regretting her offer to mount the exhibition already.

Dear friend he wrote on 6th June before the valuers' proposed next visit in a letter which must have relieved her anxieties a little.

I shall parcel up as much work as I can and post it off to you. I shall list the ones for framing. I must try and dispose of the box of work you brought down in March. I would go quite mad if some alien handled them.....and in the meantime I have removed all the important paintings from the extension to the bedroom. I shall put them between the bed mattresses temporarily. This leaves the Abbot Hall box you brought back but I will seal it up and put it in the trailer ready for off! Isn't it awful because I had some of my best work out on the bench for inspiration. I love having things around me when I work.

Left: **Envelope sent to Joan David** *1986 when she moved to Kendal*

Above: **Ashness Bridge letter** *watercolour and ink*

chapter 16

The Last Exhibition

I still posses ALL my early work and probably the BEST drawings and paintings. Fame was never an ambition of mine and I always felt reluctant to sell anything – far better to give to appreciative friends.

Letter to Doreen* 13th June 1987

Cringlemere is a beautiful house set in its own grounds high above Lake Windermere on the Troutbeck road. The owners, Rosemary and David Mustoe, were Joan's close friends and neighbours and had shared her excitement in the correspondence with Percy from the beginning. She had shown them lots of her letters and little paintngs. They loved his work and were eager to offer their help. They agreed to clear the downstairs rooms of everything on the walls and any clutter and watched progress with interest as the months went by. To begin with there wasn't any which was disconcerting. Eventually, after the valuers visit to Pear Tree, parcels of work began to trickle through.

Writing to Mavis Aitcheson on the third of September 1984 PK told her how he had gathered up work and hidden it away from prying eyes in the coal bunker. and continued to tell her how the coalman delivered his coal and buried it. One can't help wondering if it was ever retrieved. He parcelled up a lot of 'not for sale' work as well and posted it to Joan for safe keeping because he trusted her implicity now. He had promised her a list of works for sale with measurements and prices but this kept fluctuating all the time according to his mood. It was a repeat of his concerns about

his exhibition at Abbot Hall eight years before. Joan was becoming more and more confused about what to frame, what was for sale and what was merely to be stored. This would be just his fifth exhibition in his sixty six years. His first was at Rosehill Theatre near Whitehaven in 1967, another at Sekers' showroom in Sloane Square, London in 1968, the third at The Fermoy Gallery, Kings Lynn in 1969 and the last one at Abbot Hall Kendal in 1976. This was not a promising record. All of them had been fraught with difficulties. His earlier letters and diaries tell a sad tale of his inability to get an exhibition together; his indecisiveness and reluctance to sell anything. He cancelled one programmed exhibition at Abbot Hall at the last minute which caused a lot of trouble for the organisers. Of course Joan was unaware of all this. She was about to find out what she had enthusiastically taken on.

The problems increased as time went on. She had a good framer, Fenwick Patterson, near Ambleside but Percy had always botched together

Left: **Winter** *oil on board*
Above: **Red house** *oil on canvas*

his own frames. She wasn't sure he would approve of her choice. He began to waver over pricing his work as usual. First he was afraid of not making enough money and then he was frightened of making too much. He thought they should be priced a little bit more than his 1976 show in Kendal but then worried that very little sold there. He got into a panic about income tax and benefits. Joan was fearful that this was the crunch point. Was he about to back out?

Time galloped forward to the date of the opening and as beautiful framed paintings were delivered from Fenwick Patterson, Joan began to feel happier and more confident. But it was short lived. The invitations were printed and plans had been made for the opening when Joan realised that he was unable to drive up to Cumbria. He had too many complaints real and imaginery. So she found a direct train that would bring him from nearby Attleborough which was on the main line as far as Manchester. She would buy him the ticket and then arrange for a car to meet him at the station and bring him the rest of the way. He immediately protested he couldn't do it – it would make him ill. At this point she had so much to do she was greatly tempted to run the show without him because he was being so awkward but David Musto generously offered to drive to Norfolk and bring him up to Troutbeck. He had diverted a journey north a few times in the last few months to pick up work from Pear Tree so he was familiar with its location and he had met Percy. Joan was relieved at this solution but was pretty certain that David was not familiar with the Roberta problem. He would undoubtably have mentioned it to her if he had. Percy had probably worn unisex slacks and sweater *(and woolly hat)* when David had called. She had had interminable correspondence with Percy about what he should wear and had told him very firmly that he should come as Percy. She hadn't told anyone about Roberta. She worried about the impact it might have on David and the exhibition. This was thirty years before Grayson Perry appeared as his alter ego Claire and it was still regarded in most circles as rather shameful and sensational. She was pleased when Percy agreed but alarmed again when he then said he would travel as Roberta and change according to circumstances for the opening. She was quite sure that David Musto would not be comfortable with this arrangement.

On 12th September he wrote this worrying letter complete with a self portrait – full length – of how he would look.

I always used to be quite formal at Private Views – tweed jacket and slacks but in October I shall wear more artistic attire. I have a lovely cotton top. It is Indian and has a super neck. It is paired with a medium long skirt. I think the top would pass – not the skirt because it is very full. Shoes are the main problem because the top is ideal with sandals but I haven't got a suitable pair. ... The only male garment I posess is a windcheater! .... As Percy I would have to wear a hat to keep my hair up in place and more importantly to keep my head warm.

The hat affair was laughable. Percy always wore a hat or a scarf whether he was Percy or Roberta. It was usually his khaki woollen hat which he was wearing when he died. It would look bizarre with his indian skirt outfit. Oh dear, what tricky problems for her to cope with. If she tried to discourage him he could well renege on everything. The correspondence continued.

In the meantime Mavis Aitcheson had received an invitation to the exhibition from Percy and she immediately got in touch with Joan. On the third of September they met for the first time for coffee and Joan was relieved to have someone to whom she could talk openly about the problems she was facing. They got on well.

Meanwhile PK was still vaccilating over which paintings he might sell. He wrote to Joan;

The majority of the paintings are small - some very small. This was a deliberate exercise because apart from the cost of large paintings few people have the wall space. Actually it is a sale of paintings not an exhibition in the truest sense and the aim is to make sufficient money so that Chris can, in her words, have her pound of flesh and allow me to live in and I hope own Pear Tree. I haven't been able to do what I wanted to do, a new collection of medium sized landscapes. I am a bundle of nerves. And I am having to sell some things which I treasured. I could never survive if I was bundled out of Pear Tree and this is the greatest worry of all.

As the big day drew nearer his apprehension rose. Joan was nervous about his fragile frame of mind because they had now passed the point of no return. She had put so much effort both physical and emotional into this that a cancellation was unthinkable - she was losing sleep. She was such a placid, peaceful person who hated confrontation. She was well aware that it was three years since he had last travelled north and that had ended in disaster.

Top left: **Engine and tender** *watercolour and ink*
Left: **Windy day** *oil on board*
Above: **Percy Kelly at the Troutbeck exhibition**
Right: **Red sun** *oil on floorboard*

On that occasion his tinnitus had become so bad he and Chris had to return home after only a few days and she had castigated him for spoiling the trip.

So, having been obsessed by worry about the journey, now overcome, he had moved on to the worry of what to wear, not yet resolved, and now it was health on which he focussed.

The Private view is my greatest worry because there will be lots of people talking he wrote later in September. That was very true if things went according to plan.

Joan was apprehensive when David Mustoe set off on the long drive to collect him a week before the opening of the show. PK wanted to be present for the hanging. He was going to stay in Strands, Joan's lovely cottage further up the hill. David Mustoe drew up in Magpie Lane outside Pear Tree Cottage in his beautiful sleek black car and was shocked at what he found. Percy wasn't ready of course and had a plethora of tatty cardboard boxes and bags which were overflowing with indeterminate stuff. These took an age to load into the immaculate car. He kept changing his mind and cramming more in and taking things out. Hours later it seemed to David that the whole of the contents of Pear Tree Cottage was in his car. But no, Percy disappeared inside once again and the last thing to be loaded was his budgie, Pepi, in his cage. David couldn't believe it. Whatever was Joan going to say. At last, after hours of indecision and hanging about, everything was loaded and then to his horror Percy began to barricade the doors and board up the windows with scavenged wood, hammer and nails and wouldn't leave until it was all done to his satisfaction. He was afraid there might be a raid while he was away. As all his valuables were in those cardboard boxes in his car this was a bit futile. He stowed away the tools on top of one of the boxes and they finally set off. David was feeling a little hungry by now with all the time spent hanging about. He hadn't been offered even a cup of tea and wasn't allowed to speed things up by helping to load. It was now mid afternoon so he offered to stop and get something to eat for them both but Percy said he wasn't hungry and insisted they carry on. He had no thought for anyone else's needs but his own.

Joan was at Strands to greet them when they arrived. Her mood of blissful excitement was short lived. It was replaced by horror when she saw the awful state of the lovely car. She was so embarrassed. Percy got out dressed in Plus twos and a red sweater which must have been a relief. He did look slightly normal apart from his yellow stockings and his ubiquitous woolly hat.

Top left: **Caldbeck Mill** *mixed media*
Left: **Winters day, Cumberland** *watercolour and ink*
Above: **The oval pond** *mixed media*

Joan recorded her feelings some time later; - ***PK descended from that beautiful car with an incredible amount of luggage of all shapes and sizes – cardboard boxes etc – general chaotic muddle. The last item to be handed out was a cage containing a budgerigar, Pepi, who was also to be my guest though I hadn't known it until that minute!***

She cringed as all this was carried up to her dainty pink and white guest bedroom. What had she let herself in for? When they left the cottage later, PK insisted they leave Radio Three on in the house while they were away to keep Pepi company. This was a very cultured bird! Joan had carefully made lots of casseroles in advance because she knew PK liked them but he rejected them all and mainly ate baked beans out of a tin supplemented with Complan and Sanatogen. She drove him around to many of his favourite places and he made drawings near Caldbeck and Loweswater. These were his last Cumbrian drawings. This was the pleasureable part; she loved watching him working on a drawing. All his problems disappeared when he had a pencil in his hand. He focussed on a subject and drew with a deftness that was uplifting to watch. She couldn't believe how easy he made it appear. Cottages, bridges, roads and trees came alive under his hand and he got everything right first time. There were no corrections, no rubbing out. But he was very difficult at all other times. He kept strange hours and Joan was awakened in the middle of one night by the noise of hammering. She was furious when she discovered PK had removed one of Fenwick Patterson's beautiful gold frames and was replacing it with one of his bodged up efforts which he had brought with him along with his tools.

The Mustoe's gardener did most of the hanging with directions and advice from Percy and soon they had a marvellous exhibition which transformed the house. It was now a gallery. Joan had sent invitations to everyone she knew. She encouraged Percy to invite members of his family who mainly lived in Workington and assumed he had. He had invited his twin brother John but only in a vague manner indicating he didn't really want him there and was vague about the venue and contact details. Ever faithful John was determined to find it and arrived late with his wife and disabled son. Percy was annoyed they'd come and largely ignored them as he had for the last forty years. Again Joan was surprised and cross with him for being so rude. However the exhibition was a great success and achieved its purpose; enough money had been realised to buy Chris out and give him a tenuous security in the future.

At the end of the exhibition Joan and the Mustoes were absolutely exhausted. Once again Joan suggested PK should go home on the train. She offered to hire and pay for a car to take him to Manchester where he could get the through train. He became pitiful again saying he would be sick. Joan realised that he couldn't go on the train anyway because he had so much luggage – far more than he could handle. David Mustoe gallantly offered to drive him back. There was no alternative unless he stayed on in Troutbeck and Joan had had enough. She wanted her lovely orderly house back. Before the show PK agreed that Joan's family and those who had helped with the hanging and framing should have a small discount on purchases. He conveniently 'forgot' about this and insisted on full payment even from the Mustoes who had done so much and the Mustoe's gardener who had bought one. Joan was disgusted. He had barely thanked the people who had helped him. She came the closest to giving up on him. She could see why Chris had left him. She wondered how she had managed to live with him for ten years.

As soon as he got back home, PK wrote a beautiful illustrated letter to Joan in appreciation of all she had done. This softened her up a bit. She gently chastened him about his behaviour. He said he would send illustrated letters to all the buyers - and he did – and they were really appreciated. He had exonerated himself in the nick of time. He had come dangerously close to rejection from the only person he had left to help him. His letter on the 8th October was fulsome in its praise.

The past week seems like a dream especially the heavenly day we spent in Carlisle, surely a day to remember for all time. You are a good companion with a sweetness of disposition which is all too rare. I am glad you dress so beautifully and with such good taste. This factor was the special delight of my visit......

Sat here confronted by such a devastating muddle of heaps of drawings, mounts and frames, I remember your lovely cottage with much envy mingled with pleasure....

I departed with a deepened sense of friendship. When you think, since our friendship began, we have spent so little time together...
I feel like Cinderella after the ball.

They had corresponded for only eighteen months at this point and only met twice before the exhibition. To Joan it seemed a lot longer! Years later she confessed to me that if they had less than 300 miles between them she couldn't have continued. His demands would have been too great.

PK now thought that he could make a new start. He had a new optimism and a new resolve. He could now settle his debt to Chris, enjoy full ownership of Pear Tree Cottage with no worries, finish the work on the cottage and find another place with more space to work. He wanted to paint on a bigger scale.

Of course, as with everything else, he never got round to it.

* *We don't know who Doreen was. It wasn't Brian's Wife - she never met her father-in-law.*

Left: **Road near Caldbeck** *charcoal*
Above: **Three arch bridge** *watercolour and ink*

chapter 17

Roberta

September 6th 1985

Eleven o'clock on the morning of September 6th 1985 found Percy in the home of Penelope Morris, a sympathetic solicitor. This was the moment that he became Roberta Penelope Kelly. He changed his name by deed poll cleverly keeping his initials the same as before. He had been alone for eighteen months and was finding it hard. It was the first time in his sixty six years that he had lived alone. Being born a twin in a large family he had to seek solitude when he could and welcomed his time in lodgings with a family in Kendal when he joined the postal service but he had never lived alone. The army and marriage came next with a seamless transition from one marriage to the next. But now he was truly on his own. He had few friends in his own right. Chris was attractive and gregarious. She had been the home maker and cook. She loved entertaining. She made new friends easily because she was interested in them. He was only interested in himself. His social life was built on the back of hers.

He had now endured two miserable solitary Christmas periods. He realised that his cross dressing had alienated people in St David's so he tried to curb the urge to walk out dressed. When he said dressed he thought in terms of a skirt or dress. If he wore jeans or trousers as most women did he didn't feel feminine. He often wore breeches with long socks and of course, always something on his head – usually the woolly hat. He often changed into a skirt in the evenings and felt he was then Roberta but over Christmas he had forced himself to remain as Bob all the time just in case anyone called but sadly they didn't. On 16th January 1984 after his first Christmas alone he wrote to Joan

My situation is hopeless because I cannot make friends openly as you know. It would be lovely to make friends and mix with women. Imagine since the 23rd December I have spent 2 hours with sweet Heather and 5 minutes with Richard. I have had 10 silent days since the New Year. This is not good enough.

Someone had helpfully suggested he take a male lodger at the beginning of his life alone which enraged him. He complained to Joan writing ***I cannot stand the male species – I find them quite pitiful. They have brought me so much misery during the past twelve years.*** It isn't clear what he meant by this because he mainly sought female company. Maybe he felt rejected by men. Maybe when he went out in Wales as Roberta it was men who were repulsed by him. He often said he feared two things – the disappearance of his creative urge and rejection. It is ironic that it was the emergence of Roberta which caused both the things he feared.

In a sixteen page letter to Joan's neighbour Sami * dated 26th October 1983, just six months after Chris had left him, he sent her a map of the area of the village of Rockland where he lived with the houses shaded red or blue.

The red coloured dwellings denote the friendly ones, blue the enemy. The blues ignore me completely.

Bernie and Mary Rose opposite are blue as well as Evelyn his 82 year old next door neighbour.

The cottage next door is white with green woodwork and a red pantiled roof. In the evening the sun sets behind it. The occupant is

Above: **Blue landscape** *mixed media*

a very odd elderly woman (81). When we first came here Chris went to introduce herself and was invited in for tea so a friendly feeling developed. When my wife departed I went over to tell Evelyn the news and she reacted in the oddest way. She backed away from me and went indoors banging the door and I heard the sound of a bolt being pushed home. Since that day she has avoided me.

He continued

Due to circumstances I cannot live entirely in the female gender, however mentally I do. ... being a professional artist and known as Percy Kelly presents problems.... I am too old to consider the sex change operation because it can have fatal results at my age.

...In male or female dress I never change – I am just myself. I am fortunate in that I have a good figure (size 16 - 39.29.38) and do not resort to artificial packing. My eyebrows are naturally fine and it appears I can get away with wearing colour which I LOVE. The skirt in the photograph is silk and a beautiful gold colour.

I remember last summer when Chris was away for a week I took off in George my ancient MG. I wore a lovely flowered lemon dress, pale stockings and rather nice white sandals. I stopped in a village and was admiring the scene when I noticed a police car coming slowly towards me. It stopped by the side of George and the two officers stared intently.... George's driving seat is as restricted as a Spitfire cockpit so I tried to get out with a degree of elegance. Of course quite a bit of leg had to be exposed but I am fortunate in having very shapely legs. As I got out so did the police officers. They actually touched their hats and said 'You have a beautiful car ma'm' and then moved off. But this is the crunch Sami - George was neither road tested or licenced – this is what really bothered me.

Dear kind Joan was still desperately trying to help him. She researched an organisation called The Beaumont Society which was formed to help and advise people with gender problems. Percy joined and learned much more about how to change gender. This scared him. He had always been proud of his body. He decided the operation was for younger people and he was changing into a woman naturally anyway particularly since he had changed his name officially. He was working hard on it - his voice was lightening, his walk was more womanly and he was developing breasts. He was sexually confused.

I have become aware that I have lost the rather nervous state when people call. When the nurse came I left a bra and slip drying over the stove and I never thought crumbs what will she think of Roberta. I am quite natural now. I haven't to remind myself that I AM a woman and today when I am occasionally Bob I now feel I am a woman first and not the other way round. He wrote to Sami.

That was good enough for him – no operation neccessary. Of course the HRT was helping but he wouldn't admit it. After his death his recycled calendar with HRT days marked was pinned to the bedroom wall.

He thought that this day – the day he changed his name – would be a new start and it would solve all his problems and allay all his fears. Of course he was wrong yet again. It just added to his problems. He left Penny Morris with renewed hope, a dozen eggs and a pint of milk. As he left she reminded him that it was customary for anyone who had changed their name in this way to see a psychiatrist. He nodded and ignored this. He had had enough of them. When he got home he looked in the mirror and imaginatively observed that as Bob he had looked old and drawn but now as Roberta he was young and feminine. He wrote to Joan in celebration ***I just love being a woman. I smile a lot and enjoy lovely spells of fantasy.***

His life was now a fantasy of self delusion. He tried hard not to offend his neighbours and always appeared as Bob - except when he forgot. He thought they were not aware of his other persona. Of course they were. He would go to the nearly new shop in Caston as Roberta for his clothes where the volunteer staff were very sympathetic. He shopped in Watton as Roberta and in Attleborough as Bob except when he got muddled and forgot which was which. He didn't like driving as Roberta though in case he broke down which was very likely. He couldn't visualise getting out and under the car as he so often had to do in a skirt. The concept of women wearing trousers had passed him by.

But now he felt much more confident. He could be Roberta because he truly was. He wouldn't have to be constantly worrying about changing

Above: **Roberta in a green coat** *mixed media*
Right: **Roberta** *watercolour and pencil*

his clothes. He enjoyed having people looking at him and smiling at him. At the supermarket check out one day he looked at the girl at the till and thought how careless she was about her appearance. Her hair was untidy and her nails were shoddy. He smugly thought to himself how much better he looked; how much more feminine. ***I am constantly aware that lots of people look at me these days but I prefer to think that it is because I make a nice picture. I must admit I do feel superior to most women for I have yet to see one hereabouts attractively dressed.*** He did dress quite normally as Roberta. He loved bright colours but they were carefully chosen and matched. His clothes were in keeping with his age and demeanour. He was careful with make up. He was not a figure of fun. He was definitely not a pantomime dame figure or a Danny la Rue comedy spectacle but people did look twice and realise there was something strange about him. They weren't quite sure what he was.

1984 in a letter to Sami he wrote

I have a dark cotton shirt which is beautifully styled and a perfect fit so I wore it today and a light blue wraparound denim skirt with pockets. I decided to go bare legged because they are brown. I tied a blue cotton square with a pretty white design around my neck which went perfectly with a dark blue white-spotted headscarf. My sandals were blue so apart from my pinkish specs I was an apparition in blue. Why – even my shopping bag was faded blue denim. I am constantly aware that lots of people look at me but nowadays I prefer to think perhaps I make a nice picture. I even wore a blue slip and a blue bra!!

Shortly after this Sami asked Joan to stop him writing to her because her health was deteriorating and his letters were exhausting her. Joan immediately did but was astonished to find he never again asked after her health or took the slightest interest. If people rejected him they no longer existed.

Now that Pear Tree belonged to him he recommenced the building work with new resolve.

My whole life has been strewn with broken promises' 'The extension is just as it was in February. I can overcome most problems by a sort of Heath Robinson set up but my hernia restricts me. All I

want is another pair of hands. There are 5 rolls of felt I want up on the roof ... but they are too heavy and fragile. I am strangled in the cottage but not to worry. I will find a way once my foot improves.'

A few days later he sent a lovely drawing of an ingenious contraption he had rigged up to get tiles up on to the roof, complaining that if he went up the ladder his shoes got caught up in his skirt. He marvelled at how women manage with these problems. Once he recounted how, when he had run out of cement, he had gone to the builders' merchant as Roberta in the hope of getting a bag cheaper – and it appeared to work. He said the men were much more friendly and smiled a lot and found him a broken bag which they loaded in his van for him and waved him off without making a charge. He thought he would do it again as women obviously got a better deal.

The change of name was a kind of liberation. It authorised Roberta. He had wrestled with her for many years. She began when he went to college. For the first time he could dress in bright colours and unconventional clothes and get away with it without comment. He could indulge his colour sense. He was vain. He spent a lot of time getting a tan in summer and boasting about it. He did body building and yoga. He was conscious of his age at college. A fellow student remembers a cross-dresser in their year but this has not been verified. If it is true and was a little sensational, it may have appealed to PK as a means of attracting attention. For the college prize giving in 1966 he wore denims including a denim Bob Dylan hat. He was 48. His letters to Rosanna were certainly testosterone fuelled. He was sexually attracted to her. He got on well with women and they were certainly attracted to him. Jean Beaudrand remembers that at all the social occasions at Rosehill and Roseneath, PK was surrounded by admiring women. These parties were full of artistic theatrical guests, musicians, actors, artists many of them gay but PK took little interest in men. He was certainly not homosexual at that time – he loved women, he loved their clothes and he loved to dress up. The mirror was his best friend. In 1970, he and Chris turned up for a New Year Party at Roseneath and PK decided to dress up as a Frenchman – it was not a fancy dress party. Jean answered the door and was confronted by Chris smartly and casually dressed as she always was at that time accompanied by a man with a false moustache and a string of onions. 'Bonsoir Jean,' he said.

'Hello Percy,' came the weary reply. 'You'd better come in. Please leave the onions outside.'

He was photographed for Tatler. There was a similar photograph of him in Queen magazine dated 9th October 1968 in a suit and tie (dark shirt, light tie and striped jacket with seriously thinning hair – the only photograph we have over the age of forty without his woolly hat). He was among celebrities, Right Honorables and titles alongside Sir Nicholas Sekers and Christine Beaudrand, Sir Nicholas' daughter. He said afterwards that she told him he looked old in it – older than when she had seen him a few weeks before. 'Roberta was stirring' he wrote retrospectively.

This was probably the beginning of the woolly hat habit. Within a few years he would be bald on top which would not be good for his vanity or his female persona. He was not prepared to admit it. In the way some men in the same situation have 'comb overs', he decided to grow his hair long and stick a hat on top.

We know that he had been experimenting with Audrey's clothes and make up for some time but that was behind closed doors. Roberta made her first tentative public appearance in Wales. Percy referred to it as The Swing - something that happened from time to time that was out of his control. It worried him. He talked about her in the third person but conversely, when she was dominant he referred to Percy in the third person.

In Wales his work began to change. The strong dark lines became lighter and finer. He began to paint flowers. Everything became more delicate. Sexual sterotyping in art or any other field is to be avoided but this change was so pronounced it cannot be ignored. When the full body of his work spanning more than fifty years came from Norfolk after his death it was easy to spot Roberta's work. In Norfolk he began to sign letters and a few of his flower paintings as Roberta.

He dated only about a quarter of his finished works. This became very confusing when he moved to Norfolk. Drawings and paintings he did in the first eighteen months at Pear Tree before Chris left him were definitely

Left: **Percy Kelly;** *Queen magazine, 9th October 1968*

Above: **Newlands valley** *ink*

Roberta works – thatched cottages, pretty gardens and churches, but they were followed by a series of strong, dark paintings of Cumbria dated 1984. These were massive townscapes of Maryport, Whitehaven and Parton featuring pit heaps and industrial buildings. There were harbours and mountain paintings, dark and strong. It was logical to conclude that in his loneliness and anguish he had returned to his Cumberland sketch books and worked up paintings from that time reverting to his PK style. The final paragraph in the chapter about Roberta in The Painted Letters* about the correspondence between Joan and Roberta reads that his name change marked ***a frenzy of painting. He embarked on two large Cumbrian townscapes and began to finish and rework many others. It is unclear whether this was because he had at last, after years of fluctuation, resolved and accepted the gender problem. Had he become comfortable with himself and found peace?***

The answer to that is definitely no. Joan David died in 2000 just before her eightieth birthday. Two years later when his letters to her were being catalogued, a letter he had written to her during his divorce from Chris revealed that he had deliberately changed the dates on some of his best and most powerful pieces of work. His large 1964 works had been changed easily to 1984. He did this out of fear that Chris would claim half the value unless they had been painted after she left. How easily a biographer can be misled.

His creative life now was directed solely to becoming Roberta and writing his beautiful letters daily. These grew longer and more elaborate. They were lavishly illustrated. They were mainly to Joan but a few other lucky people got them as well – but he always expected a return-of-post reply. If he didn't get this he didn't write any more. Silmilarly with his Christmas cards. He began to think about them in September, tried out a few ideas and was in a panic by December to get them done in time. He made a careful list of those who would be lucky enough to receive one and ticked off those who responded with an appreciative card or letter. Any who didn't thank him were struck off. He made this clear to Joan at the very beginning of their correspondence which was a kind of warning to her.

His world had suddenly become very small. Since the move to Norfolk he only drove short distances – within a ten mile radius of the cottage. He still did building work and scavenged skips for firewood and materials. He shopped almost every day for just a few things and he made jam and marmalade in huge quantities. He found it therapeutic and also gave lots of it away. It was an entree to friendship. When Ena the mole catcher came the first time (he had moles!) he gave her a jar and then often went to see her taking more as a gift. He had a friend called Gladys who lived close by in a bungalow but he talked non stop for hours, outstaying his welcome and although Gladys still speaks fondly of him, her husband became annoyed. He also used to call on two women artists and made plans, with their persistent encouragement, for exhibiting work in local exhibitions - but he always missed the deadlines and that friendship faded away. He discovered the wonders of the photocopier which he regarded as a minor miracle in a Hockney-ish way. He could do clever things with his work with it. He made friends with the secretary at a local printers who operated it for him in the shop at the front of the print works. He spent hours there talking to her until her boss noticed and moved the photocopier into the back where he could keep an eye on it. Roberta was upset about this – not seeing the connection. The owners of a small gallery in Attleborough became very interested in his work and encouraged him to call if he had anything for them.

Above: **Norfolk Cottage** *watercolour and ink*
Right: **Harebells in Norfolk** *watercolour and ink*

Above: **Poppies** *gouache*

He called on a Sunday lunchtime when they had guests just sitting down to eat. He had taken along, not his own work which they coveted, but an old Pears Soap advertisment board titled Bubbles on which he wanted them to make him an offer. When he was politely sent away he was furious. He thought he should have at least been invited in. He appeared to have lost all his social skills so beautifully demonstrated in sixties high society.

He also began to meet people with gender problems through the small ads in magazines. He loved small ads and always scoured the local paper for bargains. He had found several cars this way also the chalet he hoped to use for printing, tools and often useless 'bargains' which just added to the heap of debris which surrounded him. So it seemed natural to find friendship the same way.

This was when the quiet village of Rockland began to take notice. Magpie Lane was well away from any main road. There was little traffic and few strangers. A stranger would be picked up on the local radar straight away. Bernie Rose, his neighbour in the bungalow opposite Pear Tree remembers the procession of strange visitors who came to see Bob - as he knew him. He was disgusted and disapproving but was eager to talk about it. His disabled wife Mary was alive then and he used to put her wheelchair by the large window which had a prime view and she was entertained all day. She was particularly amused by a regular visitor from London who did lots of jobs. 'She' always wore a short skirt and long boots and climbed a ladder to clip the hedge which made Mary laugh.

On the whole this method of finding friends was not successful. They were appalled at the state of the cottage and garden. Like everyone else, they found 'Roberta' difficult. He was highly critical of them. He described some of them to Joan and was quite scathing about their appearance and lack of any credibility as women. He dressed quietly and tastefully having observed women closely for many years. He felt he managed it much better than these people of course and made disparaging comparisons.

He wrote indignantly about one such visitor. In his version, he greeted her and found her somewhere to sit (with difficulty I would imagine) and offered her a cup of tea. He put the kettle on the malfunctioning Rayburn and sat down to chat but she hardly looked at the paintings on the wall which annoyed him. She seemed restless. Then she said she'd left her car on the road and she ought to move it. Roberta suggested she could put it in the car port and she agreed and went off and was never seen again. He was furious. He wrote that probably his paintings and conversation were above her – too intellectual – which was why she so rudely left.

The only lasting liaison was with Jayne, an ex policeman from London, over six feet in height and broad shouldered. Roberta was again disdainful about him but went on to say he had a better car than his, drove him about, was very strong and did lots of outstanding jobs. He was the mini skirted hedge trimmer. This redeemed 'her' in his eyes. It was worth putting up with her.

In August 1989 he wrote ***In spite of the possibility of a drive to Southwold and help with concreting. I am not really keen having a guest this weekend.*** In a letter to Joan dated 15th June 1990 he said Jayne has been for a visit but he wanted her to leave because her conversation was tedious – the same stories over and over again and she watched television all the time at full volume.

Tomorrow is Jayne's last day, she departs early on Sunday morning. I am sure it will feel unbearable as she disappears up the lane. Although she makes out she looks very young I found her generally much older and not so feminine as she was on the last but one visit. At that time she was receiving voice therapy but now this has gone by the board so she sounds awfully masculine and not pleasant on the ear especially when driving together. Her endless booming chatter gives me a headache. My voice tends to be soft so most of the time I have to repeat myself because of her deafness. Of course the television has to be turned up to deafening proportions but thankfully I have cut the programmes down to an absolute minimum. I just had to put my foot down on this visit....

Jane did some hedging in the garden but how she talks ... poor Jane she always appears to back losers. She told me on this visit that the electrolosis on her face – perhaps about a third – cost £1350 and the area treated is now worse than before.

... Jayne has a mind like a sieve. I asked her to get me two Gossard wonderbras but in spite of a reminder I am still waiting.

This appears to have been Jayne's last visit to Pear Tree Cottage which is not surprising.

Then on ***Friday 30th October 1992*** he wrote

I received a birthday card from Jayne, the first for three years. I think she is endeavouring to re kindle our friendship which I severed during the summer. She must be beginning to miss my interesting letters. Actually she began to fade a year ago. We exchanged gifts up to Christmas 1990 but last Xmas I sent one and a special card but she did not reciprocate and letters took months before a reply came; also she stopped telephoning so I thought it was time to call a halt. It is now more than 2 years since she last came to stay and quite frankly my state of mind was such I could just not have her come here sleeping in a chair and being a kind of servant and nursemaid. However I enjoyed the trip we made to the seaside and around the countryside. I used to fill up a Fortnum and Mason hamper with goodies and flasks of tea .. but my health is such I could not do it today.

This was Jayne's last visit *(1990)* and the Birthday card she sent was her last communication with Roberta though she probably didn't realise it was. Nobody told her of Roberta's death *(she was six years younger)*. Nobody knew her address.

Left: **Dotty Fish** *watercolour and ink*

Above: **The white house** *watercolour and ink*

chapter 18

Beauty and Truth

June 1995

I would dearly love to be transported to the shores of Loweswater. But now I am alone could I bear the beauty of the place?

Buttermere, Crummockwater and Loweswater form a necklace of stream strung lakes which join forces to form the River Cocker and dance their way down into Cockermouth where they join their big sister, the River Derwent and continue together to Workington and the sea. Percy's last request was to have his ashes scattered on the shore of Loweswater.

After the funeral at Norwich Crematorium in July 1993, Percy's son Brian was given his ashes in an urn to be brought back to Cumbria. Joan David and I were keen to be present when they were finally scattered. Neither of us had been at the funeral and we wished to pay our last respects in a place so close to his heart and life and work. We urged Brian to set a date and time. PK's twin brother John also wanted to be there and he regularly urged Brian to take some action. It didn't occur to any of us that Brian might not know where Loweswater was. The first anniversary of his death had passed unmarked and we felt, as the second anniversary approached, it was now or never. John rang Brian and was astonished when he said he had already done it. He had gone alone. He blurted this out defiantly.

John asked him when he had gone. '*Oh a bit ago.*' he said vaguely.

He asked him where the ashes had been scattered and he said '*Under a tree.*'

'*Which tree?*' persisted John.

'*A tree near the car park.*'

'*Which car park?*'

'*I walked along by a river and up a hill and I dug a hole and buried a pot of his marmalade and his budgie. Then I scattered the ashes.*' came the mysterious answer.

John was understandably upset. Joan was furious and I was disbelieving particularly because I knew Pepi his budgie had died long before PK and almost two years had passed since PK's death. Unless Pepi had been embalmed there would be nothing left of him. This cast doubt on the whole sad tale.

There were four exhibitions at Castlegate House of the work that Brian had inherited and he died in the last one – August 2000 aged 54. The wealth his father had brought him was a poisoned chalice. He was unable to handle it. He had a drink problem which had already got him into trouble and resulted in a driving ban. He then got into more serious trouble driving while disqualified and over the limit. The large cheques from his father's work funded his journey from beer to spirits to amphetamines to hard drugs. Doreen had divorced him and the house was in a worse state than his father's had been at the end of his life. His body was not discovered for some time. There was no bed in the house – he was found in a sleeping bag in the bath – a sad end to a sad life.

Left: **Above Loweswater** *watercolour and ink*
Above: **Melbreak, Loweswater** *watercolour and ink*

chapter 19

Peace in Eternity

July 3rd 1995

I long to walk down Fangs along gentle Loweswater, Low Park and Crummock quite alone – almost a pilgrimage.

On July 3rd 1995 two years after PK's death Joan and I made our own pilgrimage to his favourite places – the area Chris referred to as Percy's happy hunting ground. Driving down the Lorton Valley from Cockermouth to Buttermere, the first view of Crummock Water reveals itself at Lanthwaite Gate. What a view. We walked through Holme Wood down to the lake to the sound of the rhythmic hollow knocking of woodpeckers in the oaks and a curlew crying above. We took the lane to Scale Hill through ferns and pines down to the lakeside and crossed the bridge over the river to walk to the other little beach overshadowed by the steeply rising Melbreak; a fell that always appears black against the sky regardless of weather or time of day or year. We felt the presence of PK very strongly as we silently crossed the fields to Low Park, an old farmhouse and barn complex which PK loved to paint. The owner, a retired claergyman, was mowing the lawn and gave us a friendly wave. As we made our way up to Loweswater Church we crossed the old stone bridge we had seen so many times in his work.

Yet another bridge he wrote. ***I love these places where one can sit and muse – just watch the world go by. Bridges, lonely roads that seem to go on and on; down hill up hill through lonely woods, over lonely moors and on – and on.***

Life isn't really like this but for a time one finds peace in eternity.

We found the place where he must have often sat to make his many

sketches of the church and graveyard. Joan got out one of her letters dated ***8th March 1984***, titled in red along the side ***Loweswater Church and Crummock Fells C'land*** in his perfect script. I left her in the Kirkstyle Inn looking across the river straight up the Melbreak scree while I retrieved the car for the last leg of our journey. We drove the tarmac road to the lakeside at Loweswater and walked the flat path over Maggie's Bridge, past Watergate Farm and through the woods to the old bothy on the edge of the lake. We sat down on a fallen tree. This was where the young PK had camped with the scouts, where he had boiled up eggs they had found which then exploded messily. From her bag Joan produced another beautiful letter of deep dark woods and a distant glowing light from a farm cottage.

Friday 4th July 1990,

When I was small I often walked long distances so it was not unusual to walk back home for miles in the dark. I was terrified I can tell you. When I passed a lonely farm or cottage the lighted windows gave me much courage. Perhaps when I did this sketch the days of my childhood beckoned some latent instinct. Perhaps the many roads I depict with farm, cottage or even barn were seated in childhood or perhaps they are symbolic of life.

Left: **Loweswater Church** *charcoal*
Above: **Low Park** *watercolour and ink*

We were close friends Joan and I and we were sharing the same thoughts. What if Percy and Audrey hadn't married? What if Audrey hadn't minded the smell of oil paint so much. What if he had gone to Carlisle hospital to see the eye specialist instead of Paul Griffith. What if he and Chris had not turned left at the Severn Bridge on their return journey from Cornwall. What if they had found a little house in West Cumbria or Cornwall rather than taking on seven years hard labour in Wales. What if he had accepted the offers of an exhibition from great galleries like Agnews of Bond Street, Tib Lane in Manchester and Crane Kalman in Kensington in the early seventies when he was at his peak. What if he had sold his suite of charcoals to the Arts Council and rented a big studio where he could produce more.

It was unbearable to go on. We were both thinking of this deeply disturbed, lonely old man called Roberta living cold and hungry in a chaotic mess in lonely exile in the flattest part of Britain. We thought of the genius, the promise, the legacy of marvellous compelling work. We thought of all the people who had helped him along the way driven by the quality of that work. We returned to the car and drove over Fangs Brow down to Mockerkin as he must have done hundreds of times with his home town Workington and the Irish Sea beyond spread out before us.

His work is his memorial and it will live on for ever in his paintings, drawings and in his letters and also in the books and catalogues and articles that have been and will be written about him.

Fame was never his ambition during his lifetime. It exposed him. After his death it was a different matter. He wanted admiration, recognition and immortality through his work. Between us Joan and I had got the collection back to his beloved county. Between us we had made a record of every piece. Between us we had seen a very successful exhibition the year after his death. He was now on the road to immortality. We resolved that between us we would make his wish come true; his wish to achieve his rightful place in the world of 20th Century British Art. We would let the world see the beauty and truth which he had portrayed.

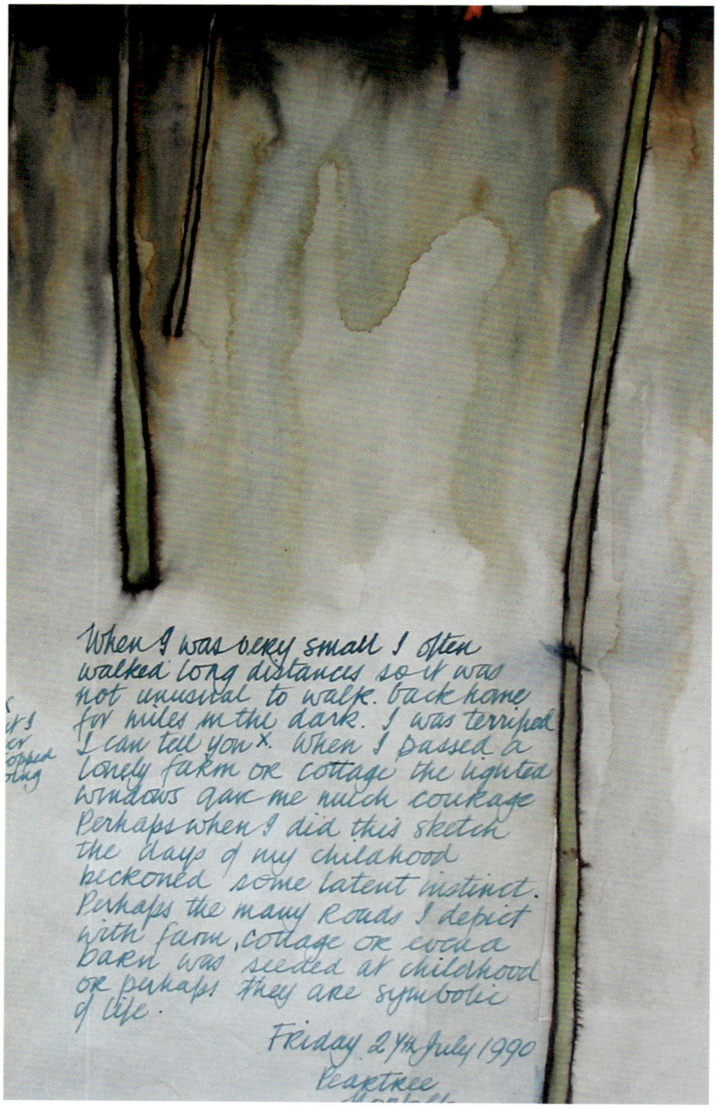

Far left: **Red barn** *oil on board*

Left: **Letter to Joan,** *1990*

Above: **Near Ennerdale, Cumberland** *watercolour and ink*

Epilogue

I cannot paint for monetary gain. I would rather starve than sell one piece of my work.– but when I depart this world people will stop and wonder at the beauty and truth that I have endeavoured to portray.

Letter from Percy Kelly to me, Chris Wadsworth, September 1987

September 1993

Sitting among a sea of paintings, drawings, etchings and sketchbooks in the large studio which spans almost all of the second floor of Castlegate House, I was conscious of the responsibility that had been passed on to me. After a lifetime of poverty and obscurity, it was now down to me to make sure Percy Kelly achieved the recognition he deserved I was the last in the long line of women to help Percy. I was the only woman in that line who never met him. I was the only one not to have succumbed to his personal charisma. I fell under the spell of his paintings, of his outstanding ability to draw. I fell under the spell of his unerring eye. I fell under the spell of what Andrew Lambirth, Art Critic of The Spectator, years later referred to as Earthbound Magic in his appreciation of Kelly's work in 2011 after his second exhibition at Messums in London's Cork Street.

I turned over sheet after sheet of rough paper. The collection was of a quality I had suspected but was never sure existed. Every piece of paper held a seductive element that was hard to resist. I disappeared for hours up to the studio. Search parties were sent to drag me back downstairs.

I started on the stack of open topped wooden bread trays overflowing with paintings and drawings. They were carefully labelled on the short side of the box in PK's beautiful lettering; ETCHINGS, BOATS, CUMBERLAND, LITHOS. EXPORT went the legends and they were legends. There was no order within. Each tray was a chiaroscuro of work in all manner of media and on a variety of materials ranging from art board, hand made paper, sheets of A4 copy paper, bits of sketch books, old envelopes, cereal packets and shopping lists. This consignment of work had arrived the evening before in a van from Norfolk. The driver had set out from London that morning with a tapestry from the V and A and several paintings from The Tate bound for Glasgow and Edinburgh. He had been instructed to pick up an important collection of an artist's work in Norfolk and all he'd had was a nightmare day and a van full of rubbish he grumbled as soon as he arrived in the dark, hours late. His instructions were to bring everything in the studio but the studio appeared to have spread everywhere. The whole house and carport was a studio. I was fearful at that moment that he might be right especially when he opened up the back of the van and gave me a challenging stare. I was confronted with old paint pots and brushes, rusty bits of metal, dirty cardboard boxes splitting their sides releasing rollers and printing inks.

'It's like I said – it's just a load o' rubbish,' the driver said watching my reaction nervously. *'And it's tekken me all day to load. I'm an art carrier not house clearance.'*

I hastily climbing up onto the back and could immediately see that it was everything I had imagined – and much more. As I feverishly flipped through the top pile on the top box I could see the unmistakeable Kelly style. The first item I withdrew was a painting of Loweswater and Melbreak in mellow greens, ochres and browns signed Percy Kelly 1968 in his beautiful handwriting. It was backed with The Cumberland News dated 1969. My heart sang. I was speechless with emotion and burst into tears. The driver

Above: **Melbreak** *mixed media*

sympathised with me. He kind of knew I would be upset he said as he laid a friendly hand on my shoulder.

It was hard won. There had been times in the early days after PK's death when I thought I might lose the collection - or at worst it might be destroyed. Brian found it hard to make decisions. Distrust stood silently between us at our first meeting at the gallery soon after his father's funeral. He had never been in a gallery before and was uncomfortable with the art world and suspiciou of me. He looked sceptical when I emphasised the importance of his father's work and looked blank when I pleaded the case for its return to Cumbria for proper cataloguing and evaluation. I was not sanguine it was going to happen.

I was astonished when he returned to the gallery a few weeks later and told me the work would be coming up to Cumbria. He was proposing to bring it up from Norfolk in his mini and keep it under the bed at his home. I managed to persuade him to let me send an art carrier to bring it all to Castlegate House. It was months before I found out what had caused this change of attitude.

But now I was triumphant, happy and painfully aware of the responsibility that was now mine. I did not want to squander this unrivalled opportunity to handle the work of a genius and make his name – get him to his rightful place in the art world. This was an unseen collection that gallery owners can only dream of. I took my time savouring every moment of discovery. I employed an assistant who had to virtually sign up to my Unofficial Secrets Act to help catalogue everything – even the corn flakes packets and shopping lists – with drawings and paintings on the plain side. I employed two professional photographers to record every single piece of work. I wanted Brian, and posterity, to have a full record of his father's work.

Every day was a day of excitement and discovery. I was handling works that had been made in the Fifties and Sixties that nobody else had ever seen or touched. There were early pre-war watercolours and drawings and some small early fifties conventional watercolours signed PERCY KELLY and large charcoal drawings with a copperplate script signature with sometimes his full name and date, sometimes just P Kelly or PK with or without a date. There appeared to be no consistency. Where had he learned to draw like this? His sense of perspective was unerring. He had a natural sense of balance and composition. The tonality and use of charcoal was nothing short of genius.

And then there were the paintings; all sizes from tiny watercolours to massive townscapes made on rolls of wallpaper lining paper. Bridges, cottages, long roads, a haunting red house, a yellow door were common themes, some with an abstract quality. Then there were the prints; screenprints, etchings, lino cuts, lithographs.

Those few months alone with Percy in the studio were astonishing – heart stopping at times. I fingered each piece as I placed it carefully in its acid free sleeve. I tried to conjure up the man who made the marks.

When everything had been catalogued I could keep it to myself no longer. My sojourns alone in the studio looking at and enjoying everything were coming to an end. Decisions had to be made. I called Brian in. I was fearful that he would take it away - after all it did belong to him. I had no right to stand in his way. He could do whatever he wanted with it.

We went up to the studio and sat down. I handed him several large slide boxes with each slide numbered. I had an identical box. I was nervous.

'*The whole of your father's life and work is in this room. It is recorded in those boxes,*' I said solemnly. '*What do you want to do about it?*'

There was silence. I could hear my heart pounding.

I again emphasised the importance of the collection and I offered him some alternatives. I said I thought a permanent collection should be put together and kept for exhibition where many people could enjoy it. Maybe a gallery space could be found in West Cumbria to show it. The rest could be sold at Castlegate House. I could make him an offer for it all or sell it on commission for him. Or there could be a compromise; I could buy one or two of the bread trays and their contents to give him some instant capital and sell the rest on commission. There were too many options for him to take in.

He spent time thinking about it. The silence was oppressive.

'*Sell it.*' he said baldly.

I was shocked. '*What, all of it?*'

'*Yes, I hate my job in the factory. I want to retire.*' he said.

He was forty six. He worked in a factory making car seat covers. I explained that the chances of it giving him an income which, even wisely invested

Above: **Letter to Lord Eccles** *watercolour and ink*

would keep him to retirement age, were small. I tried to help him see that there would have to be a series of exhibitions. The whole collection could not be thrust on to a new market straight away. Surprisingly he meekly accepted that and I offered him a series of four exhibitions with about eighteen months to two yearly intervals in between. The first would be in six months – the following spring. Brian showed no interest in the carefully protected, numbered and labelled drawers of work. They filled my double chart chest; all ten large drawers.

'Brian,' I said as he stood to leave clutching the boxes of slides. *'Is there a painting here that you'd like to hang on your wall. I'll get it framed nicely for you. What do you think? Come on – it's your Dad's work.'*

'Happen there'll be summat left.' he said and went.

May 1994

Excitement was swelling to a crescendo by the time I hung the first exhibition of a hundred works. It looked magnificent. The glossy catalogues had long been posted. The front cover showed an inset painting of a simple white cottage in a yellow landscape. When it landed on people's doormats it caused a stir. We were inundated with calls enquiring about this new artist. Everyone wanted to buy one.

Percy Kelly's work has a fatal attraction for many people. It has a simplicity and universal appeal. I watch people fall in love with a piece and sleepwalk into possessing it. It is a compulsion. People have camped outside on the doorstep all night, have queued in inclement weather and travelled long distances in order to possess one. They have come from Europe, America, Australia and even north of the Arctic Circle to acquire a piece. People who never queued for anything in their lives before have fought off opposition to gain a special piece. Almost a year after his death, the floodgates were open and people were eager to buy. I can only compare it with the first day of Harrod's sale.

That evening after the opening I dined at The Trout with Jacquie Ralli. She and her husband David had organised PK's funeral and had provided a holiday cottage for his family to use as a base while sorting things out at Pear Tree. She told me how Percy had relied on them when he was worried or upset. Despite being frantically busy people, they had responded with kindness. They had also helped Brian to sort out his father's affairs. It was then that I discovered what it was that had caused the sea change in Brian's attitude to his father's work. I realised only then how indebted I was to the Rallis.

Brian had come down to Norfolk for the weekend soon after his negative and worryingly inconclusive visit to the gallery. David asked him what he intended to do about the cottage and its contents. The Rallis were also unaware of Percy's status as an artist. They had seen little of it. Brian muttered to David that somebody had told him the art was important – but he said it without conviction. Now this was something David could do. He was a practical man with contacts. He had a school chum with a weekend cottage a few miles away who worked for one of the big London Auction houses. Perhaps he was there this weekend. He picked up the phone and explained the situation. The friend agreed to look at one or two. He said they should bring a few – no more than five paintings – as he had very little time. They grabbed a few randomly and set off. Brian stayed outside in the car and waited, still unconvinced. David took the paintings in and explained about his neighbour Percy the artist.. The friend took one look and asked who the owner was.

'I thought you were bringing me a Sunday painter,' he said, 'but this is astounding. It's good. Where is the son?' he asked. *'Ask him to come in!'*
Brian slunk in reluctantly looking uncomfortable.

'Where was your father from?' he asked. 'Where are the places in these paintings?'

'Cumberland sir.'

'These paintings are important. They could be very valuable one day. David tells me he had no gallery, he didn't have exhibitions. He tells me there are a lot of them and they belong to you now.'

'Yes, sir.'

'Right, well my advice is this. You must begin in Cumberland and see where it goes from there. It will take time. There is a very good gallery up there. It's in a place called Cockermouth. Is that near you? I think it's called Castlegate House. The woman there will be able to help you. I can't remember her name.'

For the first time Brian stood up straight, pulled his shoulders back and said

'I've been there. I went last week. I saw the woman - she 's called Chris.'

And that is how the collection of the works of Percy Kelly came to Castlegate House.

Since then other collections have been discovered; his stepchildren, his first wife, Joan David's letters, many of the small collections that he sent off to friends in 1984 during his second divorce. It adds up to a phenomenal output.

In 2001 three pieces were purchased for the government collection. Baroness Hilton, Chairman of the selection committee sent the curator up to see them and choose. He was transfixed when he saw them. When David Messum ventured North in the autumn of 2009 in search of Northern artists, he couldn't take his eyes away from the Kelly pieces I showed him. Percy made his London debut in Cork Street the following January to wide acclaim.

So now, as the Kelly magic weaves its web drawing more and more people into its thrall, it is time to tell the story of his extraordinary life.

Earth's Last Picture

And no one shall work for money, and no one shall work for fame,
But each for the joy of the working, and each, in his separate star,
Shall draw the Thing as he sees It for the God of Things as They are!

Rudyard Kipling

Left: **Moon Flowers** *mixed media*
Above: **Newlands round** *lithograph*

Chronology

1918
Robert Percy Kelly was born at 113 Corporation Road, Workington, Cumberland. He had four brothers - one, John, his twin and two sisters. His father Oscar was a Manxman carpenter and his mother Martha was a Scot.

1924
Attended Victoria Road Junior School, Workington.

1928
Family moved to Salterbeck and he attended Central School for Boys.

1932
Left school to become a telegraph boy messenger

1934
Passed exams and became Postal and Telegraph Officer, Kendal.

1939
Joined the 6th Boarder Regiment.

1940
Transferred to the Royal Signals and was used to draw maps and diagrams.
Sold his first watercolour for £3.

1940 – 1946
Served in the war in Repton, Wentworth GHQ Whitehall and in France.

1942
Married Audrey James.

1946
His only son, Brian born.

1946
Resumed civilian duties at PO Workington.

1951
Became a member of the Lake Artists.

1952
Became sub-postmaster at Great Broughton.
Submitted watercolours to Royal Academy, Royal Glasgow Institute and Royal Scottish Academy – all the work was accepted.
Played for Workington AFC under the management of Bill Shankly.

1955
Met the Cumbrian Poet Norman Nicholson.

1958
Had a breakdown. Resigned from the Post Office.
Moved to Glen Cottage, Allonby.
Met Sheila Fell and L S Lowry.

1959
Taught part time at Derwent School, Cockermouth.
Saw an Exhibition of French Contemporary etchings at the Settlement, Maryport.
Met Helen Sutherland.
Purchased an etching press from Sydney Buckley for £20.
Made enquiries at Carlisle College of Art re printmaking courses and discovered there were no tutorial classes.

1960
Applied for four year NDD course at Carlisle College of Art but refused a grant on account of age.
Taught part time at Nelso Tomlinson School, Wigton and night nursing at Dovenby hospital to raise funds to do the course.

1961 – 1965
Having raised £500 he attended the college for a dregree course in lithography and printed textiles.

1963
Considered to be doing so well that he was awarded a grant.

1964
Awarded a travelling scholarship to Brittany.

1965
Left college with distinctions in drawing and lithography.
Sir Nicholas Sekers commissioned a series of paintings of the interior of the Silk Mills at Hensingham, Whitehaven. He bought 15.

1966
Sir Nicholas Sekers gave him an exhibition at Rosehill Theatre Whitehaven and invited many influential friends who bought work.

1968
Exhibition at Sekers' new Sloane Street showroom in London.

1969
Exhibition at the Fermoy gallery in Kings Lynn. After this his depression returned.

1970
Divorced Audrey and went to live in Distington.

1971
Remarried. His second wife was Christine Griffiths. They lived in a cottage on the Levens estate by courtesy of Robin Bagot.

1973
Bought, with the help of a loan from Peter Scott of the Provincial Insurance Company Kendal, 5 & 7 Gospel Lane in St David's, Pembrokeshire.

1976
Exhibition of more than 70 paintings at Abbot Hall, Kendal.

1980
Moved to Norfolk, hoping for a better climate and a fresh start, to Peartree Cottage near Attleborough.

1983
Miss Mary Burkett introduced him to her friend Joan David and their correspondence began.
Christine, his second wife left him and he was desolate.
Miss Burkett and Joan went down to Peartree to see him.

1984
Joan David made her second visit in March.
In October he had an exhibition at Cringlemere, a private house near Troutbeck belonging to David and Rosemary Mustoe.
This was his last visit to Cumbria and his final exhibition.

1985
Changed his name by deed poll to Roberta Penelope Kelly.

1992
Went into hospital suffering from malnutrition and exhaustion.
Joan David and her son Robert made a final visit to Peartree Cottage.
Changed his name back to Robert Percy Kelly.

1993
January – became ill.
March admitted to hospital in Norwich.
Transferred to a convalescent home in Holt.
June – taken back to the Norwich hospital where he had a private room.
Visited by his son Brian and twin brother John.
Died in hospital July 3rd.

Fells at sunset *mixed media*

Sunday
4th December
1983
PAPER.
Japanese.
EXPORT